W9-AEX-629

THE SOVIET SECONDARY SCHOOL

The Soviet secondary school is an important topic for comparative educationalists and also for political scientists interested in how the Soviet education system shapes the outlook of Soviet children. This book charts developments in the Soviet secondary school, beginning in the pre- revolutionary period and coming right up to the present. It shows how the system was radically changed at several different points. The author, who emigrated to Israel from the Kharkov district in 1977, has considerable personal experience of the system as school-girl, teacher, director of studies and headmistress and this experience naturally colours and enriches her analysis.

Dora Shturman, Soviet and East European Research Centre, Hebrew University of Jerusalem

THE SOVIET SECONDARY SCHOOL

DORA SHTURMAN

Translated by Philippa Shimrat

ROUTLEDGE
London and New York

Published in association with the Marjorie Mayrock Center for Soviet and East European Research at the Hebrew University, Jerusalem.

First published in 1988 by
Routledge
a division of Routledge, Chapman and Hall
11 New Fetter Lane, London EC4P 4EE

Published in the USA by
Routledge
a division of Routledge, Chapman and Hall, Inc.
29 West 35th Street, New York NY 10001

Printed and bound in Great Britain by Mackays of Chatham PLC, Kent

British Library Cataloguing in Publication Data

Shturman, Dora
The Soviet secondary school.
1. Education, Secondary — Soviet Union — History
I. Title
373.47 LA835

ISBN 0-415-00575-2

Library of Congress Cataloging-in-Publication Data

0-415-00575-2

Contents

Acknowledgements

I would like to express my sincere thanks to all those who helped me in the preparation of this book.

I have received financial aid from a few sources. First I would like to thank the Ministry of Immigrant Absorption Fund to Aid Immigrant Scientists, Writers and Artists from the Soviet Union, financed through the estate of the late Eva Minsker de Villar, which provided generous help. Second, the Leah Goldberg Special Fund in Russian Studies at the Hebrew University supported this work, as it has other projects of mine. Furthermore, a very kind grant came from the British Friends of the Hebrew University.

The work on this book was carried out at the Marjorie Mayrock Center for Soviet and East European Research at the Hebrew University in Jerusalem. I am deeply grateful to Dr. Edith Rogovin Frankel and Dr. Theodore H. Friedgut for their advice and guidance. Dr. Frankel was instrumental in seeing this book through to publication. Without both of them it could not have seen the light of day.

I would like to thank Philippa Shimrat for her wonderful translation. Shulamith Tsur of the Mayrock Center solved the innumerable technical problems which arose during the period in which this book was being prepared.

Last but not least, I owe an enormous amount to my husband, Dr. Sergei Tiktin, for his constant and invaluable help in everything connected with my work.

Dora Shturman/Tiktina
Jerusalem, 1987

Glossary

kolkhoz	collective farm
kolkhoznik	member of collective farm
krai	administrative subdivision of republic of USSR
oblast	administrative subdivision of republic of USSR (larger than krai)
obshchina	the Russian peasant community which in many areas involved the periodic repartition and equalization of land holdings
okrug	district - territorial division of USSR for administrative, legal, military, etc. purposes
samizdat	unofficial literature which is reproduced and circulated illegally in the USSR
sovkhoz	State farm
subbotnik	voluntary unpaid work on free days
tamizdat	samizdat which is smuggled out of the USSR and published abroad
volost	small rural district
vseobuch	vseobshchee ob"iazatel'noe obuchenie - universal compulsory schooling
zemstvo	elective district council in Russia 1864-1917
Znanie Society	The Society for the Dissemination of Political and Scientific Knowledge, an official public organization

Introduction

This work was originally intended to give the reader an idea of the period in the life of the Soviet secondary school which is usually referred to as that of the 'thaw', of the post-Stalin reforms and of the Khrushchev administration (1954-64). This indeed is the topic of the main bulk of the book which examines the process and results of the school reforms of that period. However, this topic could not be approached without first making at least a brief and cursory examination of the previous history of schools in the 1950s and 1960s. Schools, more than any other social institution, reflect the nature of their time, their country, their people and their state. Soviet schools did not arise out of a vacuum: Russian schools had existed for centuries before them. I therefore considered it essential to give a brief outline of the development of and main trends in Russian schools from the 1860s until the Revolution.

After October 1917 Soviet schools passed through two successive periods which were completely different from both the pre-Soviet tradition of Russian schools and their development in the decades prior to the Revolution. I am referring to the periods 1917-31, which for the sake of convenience I shall call the schools of the 1920s, and 1931-53, the schools of the Stalin period. I considered it impossible to pass from pre-Soviet Russian schools to Khrushchev's educational reforms without giving at least a brief description of school education in the previous two decades. I could then survey the schools of the 1950s and 1960s in detail and conclude with a brief description of the schools of the 1970s.

During the 'thaw' the periodical press was literally flooded with the subject of education. This work devotes much space to analysing the public opinion of teachers and writers connected with schools as presented in the press of those years. I also considered it essential to include a study on the situation in Soviet schools today (the first half of the 1980s) which, judging from articles in the Soviet pedagogical press, are on the threshold of another reform.

It is only natural that this work also reflects my personal experience as a pupil, schoolteacher, deputy director and director of a school. In recent years my personal experience has been enriched by knowledge of the everyday life and problems of the Israeli school which, despite its indisputably unique features, is an organic part of the free Western education system. The confrontation between my Soviet school experience and my impressions of the West engendered the concluding part of this book.

To sum up: my intended study of the Soviet secondary school in the 1950s and 1960s turned into a survey of all its periods, incuding a brief excursion into its pre-October past. I hope that the reader who is concerned with problems of secondary schools, both Soviet and Western, will find something of interest in my experience and the documents I have researched.

Chapter One

THE RUSSIAN SCHOOL BEFORE THE REVOLUTION

Liberal researchers into the pre-Revolutionary Russian school considered its history to begin in the 1860s, not because there were no schools in Russia before then, but because those were the years when 'the initiative and leadership in this matter gradually began to pass from the hands of the state and government to the hands of society itself'.[1] Such a transfer was quite inconceivable a hundred years later during the liberalisation of the 1960s. The very concept 'society', as distinct from 'state', had not re-asserted its right to exist during that second liberalisation of the 1960s. Whereas the liberalisation of the 1860s under Alexander II was a democratisation, i.e. an increase in society's independence from the machinery of state power, by contrast, Khrushchev's liberalisation of 1954-64 was an attempt to make the regime better than under Stalin, but it in no way signified a growth in society's freedom from the regime.

Although under Alexander I the village and town obshchiny and church parishes were responsible for maintaining schools of the first level, i.e. primary schools, according to pre-Soviet researchers there was already an extensive and real possibility for applying private initiative both in the organisation of schools and in designing their curricula. The state, however, did not oblige the obshchiny and parishes to open primary schools but left the matter to their discretion, and they showed little zeal in this direction until the 1860s. The provincial Gymnasia (classical high schools) and district schools were opened and maintained by the government itself. In 1828 Nicholas I introduced a compulsory statute on primary schools for the urban population, and in 1830 for the rural population, but only for the state and apanage peasants. The education of the serfs remained entirely dependent on the whim of the landowners. It should be noted that the higher strata of society were free to provide their children with independent education at home until they entered university or other institutions of education. I assume that this circumstance had quite a strong influence on Russian culture (and Russia itself) in the nineteenth century and on the world view of the Russian noble intelligentsia. Researchers note Nicholas I's stubborn distrust of private and public initiative in the field of education, even primary education (to which the government itself paid very little attention). Even before the second half of the eighteenth century, however, the educated part of society was striving ever more persistently to gain control of the sphere of education and to impress on it the humanistic ideals that sector so clearly expressed. N. Novikov's activity in the field of Russian schools played no small part in Catherine II's repressive measures against him.

Despite the conflict between the regime and the public, moves towards independent education increased (with ups and downs) until the death of Nicholas I, though the conflict never took the form of a total prohibition or eradication of all non-state educational initiatives, as it did after October 1917.

Society's interest in schools was growing irresistibly by the 1860s, along with all the other public interests, and was displayed by individuals and groups with very different views and tendencies. In the early 1860s several schemes (liberal, moderate, conservative and radical) aimed at reforming school education appeared in journals and as separate publications, most frequently concerning education of the masses (that is, primary education). These proposals examined the experience of a multitude of private schools with various systems of education, some of which had been in existence since the 1820s and had functioned for decades unimpeded and remained known to the comparatively narrow circle of people connected with them. This also applied to the landowners' schools for serfs, whose quality depended on the cultural and moral level of the organisers and teachers. In the first half of the nineteenth century independent pedagogical, statistical and sociological research was already being carried out into schooling in the Russian Empire, including the non-Russian areas, which sometimes evoked an extensive public response.[2]

*

In the 1860s the problem of schools even rivalled the peasant question in popularity. The subject of schools, which for a while had taken second place in topicality to the peasant question, greatly agitated Russian society after the 1861 reform which abolished serfdom. If the juridical emancipation of the people proclaimed by the reform was to be realised, then cultural emancipation was also necessary.

One of the landmarks of the school-educational movement of the 1850s was an article by the noted doctor N.I. Pirogov, 'Questions of life'.[3] Soviet history of pedagogy usually refers to it only in connection with Dobroliubov's criticism of some of Pirogov's pedagogical views, in particular the fact that he condoned 'moderate corporal punishment' for pupils. However, apart from this view, which is unacceptable to a humane educator, Pirogov's article contained a number of interesting psychological and pedagogical observations and recommendations. In its wake an enormous number of articles, brochures, collections of articles and journals appeared, all concerned with problems of teaching and education. This flourish of literary activity was followed by a spurt of organisational activity. The variety of ideas, projects and proposals reflected in the pedagogical journalism of those years found a natural practical outlet in a variety of types and forms of public education and enlightenment. There is much literary evidence of public, voluntary school experiments in the 1860s in Kharkov, Kiev, Ekaterinoslav, Moscow, St Petersburg, Perm, Ufim, Kazan' and elsewhere (often in small district towns or even villages). This was a broad civil movement which could not but alarm the conservative sections of the state administration. The regulations, curricula and work routines of these schools were designed by the same enthusiasts (usually very well educated people) who opened them. This movement (and work) was joined by students, members of the free professions, clergymen, educated and liberal members of officialdom (sometimes fairly high ranking), landowners, etc. One of the first Sunday* schools in Perm was opened by the wife of the governor of Perm. In Kharkov the university helped to establish such schools by placing rooms and educational

* The schools were called Sunday schools but were often active in the evenings and during the week.

supplies at their disposal. There was a very wide variety of curricula, from those at the simplest primary level to ones that included two foreign languages, the principles of public medicine or first aid, chemistry, drawing, etc. The schools were run by councils of their teachers and founders and were financed by donations, aid, various kinds of exhibitions, shows, concerts, and so forth. The enthusiastic teachers who had any other source of income (no matter how modest) worked for nothing. The more well-to-do teachers were often donors as well. According to published data, there were 316 independent centres of primary education (apart from the official school network), mainly Sunday schools. One feature of these schools was particularly remarkable: they had a very high 'density' of teachers, quite unknown in the official schools. In Kharkov, for example, there was one teacher for every three pupils in the public schools. This shows what a large number of teachers, as well as just well educated people, were swept up by this wave of enthusiasm.

This fact is also of interest to the 1980s when the developed Western countries are going through a very grave crisis in education. At the same time, industrial workers in the highly industrialised countries are fighting automation which threatens to put them out of work. Unemployment, or underemployment, combined with the critical state of the schools and educational institutions, bears the seed of grave social instability. Meanwhile, the experience of the Russian (and not only Russian), pre-Revolutionary, independent public schools shows that education alone can absorb the entire labour surplus created by automated production. Research by Soviet educational psychologists in the 1960s came up with interesting conclusions which made a brief appearance in the specialist journals and were promptly dismissed as being impracticable. They recognised that the optimal number of children per group in kindergartens was between five and seven (at present the actual number is 25-30), and the optimal number of pupils per class not more than ten (the present size of classes is 35-40 pupils). If the crèches, kindergartens and schools were to receive the full complement of qualified educators and teachers for every 5-10 children, many problems of modern society would be resolved. Unfortunately, however, we give little heed to the most important problems of our social life.

Alexander II's idyllic non-interference in the activity of the Sunday schools did not, however, last long. There were apparently two reasons for this: the first is noted by official

Soviet histories of education (in the few cases where the public boom in education in the mid-nineteenth century is mentioned at all) and lies in the authoritarian nature of the Russian state administration to whose spirit the innovations of Alexander II and the progressives who surrounded him were intrinsically antipathetic. I shall consider the second reason for the administrative interference in independent school education in the 1860s and 1870s a little later. The Sunday schools were officially authorised in 1857 and shortly afterwards observers from the Ministry of Public Education began to be sent to them periodically. These observers were mostly people who knew very little about this matter which was new for Russia (except for its westernmost provinces). But the main trouble was that the goals of the schools' organisers, and consequently the entire nature and structure of their activity, were utterly alien to the observers. After 1860 the Ministry of Education began to organise its own state Sunday schools. Then it compelled the private and public Sunday schools to adopt the curriculum of the state schools. This, of course, was not done because the observers were rarely present at lessons, but misunderstandings and conflicts became more frequent and repressive measures began to be taken against obstinate organisers and teachers in the public and private schools.

As early as the end of 1860 the Minister of Internal Affairs, Prince Dolgorukov, petitioned the liberal Tsar to increase surveillance of the Sunday schools. In 1862 the organisers of one of the St Petersburg Sunday schools was accused by the police of anti-government propaganda under the cover of school teaching. Similar accusations and incidents became more frequent, and in the second half of 1862 all the independent Sunday schools and public reading rooms where lectures and discussions were held were banned (except in the western provinces which had a long tradition of such institutions). The ban was declared temporary, until a special statute would be worked out, but this did not happen until 1914. True, the schools functioned and continued to appear, but their existence was based on compromises with the official organisations and on agreeing to the official curricula and inspection. Those public schools which tried to act independently continued to be in a state of tension and instability.

At this point I should like to return to the second reason for the conflict between the Russian public schools of the 1860s and the official educational organisations. The Sunday school episode was one of the numerous manifestations of the tragedy of Russian history of that decade. This tragedy is particularly important because in many respects it parallels the Russian tragedy of the second decade of the twentieth century - indeed, the socio-political situation in the world today possesses certain features of the same conflict. The situation which arose in Russia as a result of Alexander II's reforms was difficult and complex, but not hopeless. It allowed for literary and practical discussion by various social groups and disputes with the government (within the bounds of loyalty, but very widely interpreted). In short, the influence of social-reforming tendencies and constructive governmental reforms was paramount. Indeed, an hour before Alexander II was assassinated by members of the People's Will, he had signed Loris-Melikov's draft constitution which opened up a wide field of action for the progressive reform of Russian society. After the death of Alexander II, Alexander III abrogated the bill signed by his father.

Legislative liberalisation also occurred in Russia in the first two decades of the twentieth century. Under pressure from liberal-democratic public opinion and on the initiative of a number of statesmen - above all P.A. Stolypin - the empire was moving swiftly towards a European level of legal emancipation. The events of 1917 (which I shall not discuss here) frustrated the advance of liberalisation. Similarly, in the modern world, radical-extremist forces consider the social situation in the West to be hopeless and provoke explosion after explosion, one terrorist action after another, whereas the situation can be improved gradually only by fundamentally reformist, evolutionary methods for which a considerable length of time is essential.

The extremist movements of the 1860s and 1870s in Russia were in a hurry to turn the public schools into an arena for their conspiratorial, anti-governmental struggle as soon as possible. The radicals turned the schools into a field and instrument of destructive political propaganda and organisation. The literary legacy of the radicals provides ample evidence of this throughout these years (from the 1860s to 1917). All the radical movements, from what, for the sake of convenience, can be called Chernyshevskii's movement to the socialists and Bolsheviks of the twentieth century, conducted their propaganda in the Sunday (and evening) schools. Their goal was always to exacerbate the crisis and not to solve it in a gradual, evolutionary way.

Moreover, the tragedy both of these radical movements and of Russia itself was the absence (as in 1917 and also today) of a constructive social programme, for all their energy, selflessness and self-confidence.

As in all societies, the offensive by left-wing extremism provoked an attack from right-wing, conservative-reactionary extremism. Like all the movements of 1858-63, the democratic beginnings in the sphere of education flourished due to the initiative of the liberal-progressive, 'centrist' and constructive-liberal sector of society, and perished when the movement became the arena of struggle between the two extreme forces, which the middle group was never able to withstand.

*

As the right-wing governmental reaction grew, the same fate (an increase in the authorities' diktat) befell not only the independent Sunday schools but also the primary schools of the Chamber of State Properties and the Department of Crown Domains, the church schools, as well as the ordinary (not Sunday), private primary schools. Nonetheless, despite the periodic ups and downs and the alternating bursts of liberalisation and reaction, the civic activity of the educated sector of society and of the peasantry in the realm of mass, i.e. primary, education indisputably continued to grow in practical and varied ways. Moreover, until 1917 the public schools typically continued to be a field of pedagogical experimentation for the educated and independent part of Russian society, due to the Russian educators' rejection of the narrowly utilitarian trends of European primary education. The aim of the latter was usually only to teach reading, writing and arithmetic. The Russian educating intelligentsia, however, viewed the primary school as a field for the moral and intellectual emancipation of the people, as exemplified by K.D. Ushinskii and L.N. Tolstoi, for whom the significance of literacy, of fundamental knowledge of the world and moral-ethical emancipation increased in that order, from the first to the last.

From the beginning of the 1860s, however, official primary education also had a number of very progressive features: it was free; girls and boys were taught together until the age of 13; in accordance with a statute of 14 July 1864, primary schooling was begun in the languages of the local nationalities, switching to Russian only in the second year. Nonetheless, the Minister of Education, Count D.A.

Tolstoi, following the German educational system in the mid-nineteenth century, aspired to give education a purely practical character, so foreign to the spirit of the Russian educating intelligentsia. In his time, the curriculum of the primary and district (intermediary between the primary school and the Gymnasium) schools was designed in such a way that it was impossible to enter a Gymnasium from a district or town school, while the curricula of the teachers' institutions of education were changed so that they could train just teachers and not semi-scholars.

The reaction in education lasted from the end of the 1860s to the end of the 1890s. The teaching community never reconciled itself to this reaction. In the 1870s renewed efforts were made to increase the role of zemstvo public and private initiative in education. The zemstvo used the financial resources at its disposal to encourage the schools that were to its liking and refused financial aid even to the omnipotent Count D.A. Tolstoi who requested it for the schools run, for example, by the Holy Synod. The zemstvos began to subsidise not only primary schools but also secondary and specialised private or other schools whose curricula suited them. Eventually, the zemstvos at the district level, and later at the provincial level as well, also began to show concern for improving the qualifications and general cultural level of teachers by organising courses, congresses and conferences at their expense.

The scope and aims of this study do not permit me to back up the statement I am about to make with extensive illustrations. Nonetheless, there is much evidence in historical literature that throughout the second half of the nineteenth century a struggle was in progress in Russia over who was to control the mass school, who was to control education: the public or the government and the church. Only in 1907 were there clear indications that in this struggle the public was victorious. In 1912 the author of one of the best detailed surveys of the history of Russian schools that I have studied[4] defined 'the character of the Russian school as a public, not state school. In this, Russian schools are very different from German and French schools and are more similar to English and, especially, American ones.'

*

I shall quote another extract from this same book which discusses a new law on Russian popular (i.e. primary, in modern terminology) education, which was submitted to the government for consideration and, according to the author, was close to being ratified.

> What is most important is that there is no mention anywhere that the inspector has to gather information on the political reliability of candidates for teaching posts. It is to be hoped that this survival of a police regime by virtue of which any representative of the police could, without trial, deprive a teacher of the professional right to teach which he had acquired from another department or by completing a course in a special institution of education, will finally disappear ...
>
> This new order is the result of demands which life itself has been making for a long time: (1) to give the founders the right to direct the instructional side of the schools; (2) to separate the administrative authority from the pedagogical leadership, in which pedagogical authority and not the right to make various instructions should play the main role ...
>
> The increase in allocations for primary education in recent years has been as follows (in thousands of rubles):

Years	For town parish schools	For primary schools	Total	Increase (in thousands of rubles)
1907	1.730	7.197	8.927	+1.370
1908	1.726	13.411	15.137	+6.210
1909	1.908	19.154	21.062	+5.925
1910	2.189	24.865	27.054	+5.992
1911	2.618	35.436	36.054	+9.000
1912	2.966	43.074	46.040	+9.986

> A further increase, until universal education is realised, on condition that the estimate will grow by 10 million annually, gives a picture of the proposed growth of this item of expenditure for the years (in thousands of rubles):

1913	1914	1915	1916	1917	1918	1919	1920
56	66	76	86	96	106	116	126

> The Ministry determined the total cost of introducing universal education as 103 million for 1907 and 132 million for 1914.
>
> Universal education can therefore be achieved by 1921 on condition that the existing rates of allowances granted by the zemstvos and towns for introducing universal education are maintained and additional grants made for population growth.
>
> But the most important change in the life of the school in the near future will be the radical change in its inner content. There has never been such a broad pedagogical movement in Russia, not even in the 1860s, as in our days. This movement has penetrated deep among the majority of teachers. Every summer, public [i.e. primary school] teachers rush in their thousands, to courses or on educational excursions in Russia or abroad. It is far from uncommon now to meet a public teacher who has been to Italy, Greece and Palestine, attended courses in St Petersburg, Moscow or elsewhere in the provinces. The large number of original and translated pedagogical works that appear every year and the growth in pedagogical journals are also evidence of the growth in these writings, while the enormous number of textbooks for primary schools, compiled by public teachers, emphasise even more that those who seek, find! And the time is not far off when the public teachers, and precisely they, will fill with living content what they, along with all Russian society, are working to create - the new school![5]

What conclusions can be drawn from the above about Russian schools before the Revolution? The same processes were taking place in the schools, and tending in the same direction, as in the whole of Russian society from the 1860s until 1917 (with ups and downs and excesses). They were moving in a complex way, slowly but indisputably, towards the type of school that its most highly civilised educators had been fighting for since the end of the eighteenth century: the public, independent school concerned not only with education but also with moral and civic upbringing and enlightenment. There were strong and tenacious conservative tendencies and traditions in the schools, as in all aspects of Russian life, whose bearers resisted the innovations which were democratising and liberalising the schools. There throbbed in the schools, as in all Russian life of that period, the nerve of radical intolerance which aimed at transforming them from a tool of education into an instrument of party struggle. But in the schools, more than in any other sphere of Russian society, it was precisely the liberal tendencies of the teachers which grew and strengthened in the second decade of the twentieth century, and for that reason, as we shall see in the next chapter, the schools resisted the Bolshevisation of 1918-23 for a longer period and more stubbornly than Russia's other social institutions.

It would, nonetheless, be unjust to forget that the overwhelming responsibility for the events of 1917 rests with the two extreme wings of Russian society, both right and left, and that a large number of teachers belonged to extreme left-wing circles. They themselves were soon to be dealt a blow by the very revolution that they had helped to bring about.

NOTES

1. N.V. Chekhov (compiler), Narodnoe obrazovanie v Rossii s 60-kh godov XIX veka ('Public education in Russia from the 1860s'), part of series Pedagogicheskaia Akademiia v ocherkakh i monografiiakh (Vospitanie v sem'e i v shkole) ('Pedagogical academy in studies and monographs - upbringing in the family and the school') 1, edited by Prof. A.P. Nechaev ('Pol'za', Moscow, 1912) p.1.
2. See, for example, the collection of articles O vsenarodnom rasprostranenii gramotnosti v Rossii na religiozno-nravstvennom osnovanii ('On the nation-wide spread of literacy on a religious-moral basis'), published by the Moscow Society of Agriculture in 1848 and compiled by its secretary, S.A. Maslov.
3. N.I. Pirogov's articles appeared in the Morskoi vestnik ('Navy herald') in 1856.
4. Chekhov, Narodnoe obrazovanie, pp. 5-6.
5. Ibid., pp. 210-18.

Chapter Two

THE SOVIET SCHOOL, 1917-1930

It is traditionally accepted in the Soviet Union and the outside world that pre-Revolutionary Russia was a land of universal illiteracy. Certain Soviet sources, for example Bloknot agitatorov ('Agitators' Notebook'), an aid for local propagandists, even puts the number of illiterates in 1916 at 97 per cent. This figure is far from accurate:

> According to the data of a one-day school census, on 18 January 1911 Russia ranked last in Europe with regard to the state of education, with 3.85 out of every 100 of the country's population in school.
>
> However, when studying these unattractive statistics it is necessary to bear in mind that these data describe not the level of literacy in the country but merely the state of primary education, which in Russia consisted of four classes and included children from eight to eleven years old.
>
> The number of children who received primary education was about 43 per cent,[1] in round figures: 6.2 million pupils out of 14.4 million children of school age.
>
> ... These statistics do not include the number of students in Gymnasia, non-classical secondary schools, military and naval colleges, church seminaries, institutes and universities ...[2] [Pisarev's emphasis.]

By the beginning of the 1920s primary education was to have become universal, but the Bolsheviks embarked on their work in the field of education as though it had to be started from scratch. The People's Commissariat of Education was established on 26 October 1917,[3] as stated in the first decree of the Second All-Russian Congress of

Soviets on the formation of the Soviet Government. A.V. Lunacharskii was appointed People's Commissar of Education, and he was the author of a number of extremely important legislative documents in the first years of Soviet power. His style (that of a professional writer) and his concepts (those of a utopian intellectual) are reflected in these documents and relieve them of the abstract dryness of usual bureaucratic jargon.[4]

In his first appeal 'to the citizens of Russia' as People's Commissar of Education, Lunacharskii declared that he expressed 'the will of the revolutionary people' and that his and his commissariat's powers were limited to the moment when the Constituent Assembly would be convened.[5] Lunacharskii did not belong to the group of 'staunch Bolsheviks' and was not one of the organisers of the Revolution of 25 October 1917. The texts of legislative and administrative documents that belong to him are imbued with democratic phraseology and certain ideas that were incompatible with the overall tendencies of Bolshevism. These deviations would soon be corrected by the general Bolshevik policy which was to take firm command of education. What stands out in particular in the 'Appeal' written by Lunacharskii is the idolisation of the 'popular masses', that is, the least educated strata of the people, an approach that is more populist than truly Communist. On the one hand, Lunacharskii justly notes:

> Any truly democratic power in the field of education in a country where illiteracy reigns supreme must first aim at achieving <u>universal literacy</u> in the shortest possible time by organising a network of schools that meet the requirements of modern pedagogy and by introducing universal, compulsory and free instruction, while at the same time setting up a number of teachers' institutes and seminaries that can provide as soon as possible the mighty army of people's teachers needed for the universal education of the population of boundless Russia.[6] [Lunacharskii's emphasis.]

On the other hand, he paradoxically places the task of their own education in the hands of the 'illiterate and ignorant' masses and not in the hands of the 'mighty army of people's teachers' which he is ostensibly aiming to produce:

> The difference between teaching and education should

be stressed. Teaching is the transmission of ready-made knowledge by the teacher to the pupil. Education is a creative process. The personality of a person is 'educated', broadened, enriched, strengthened and perfected throughout his life.

The labouring popular masses - workers, soldiers, peasants - are thirsting to learn reading, writing and all the sciences. But they are also thirsting for education. Neither the government, nor the intelligentsia, nor any force outside themselves can give them this. Schools, books, theatres, museums, etc. can merely be aids. The popular masses will develop their culture themselves, consciously or unconsciously. They have their own ideas created by their social position which is so different from the position of the ruling classes and intelligentsia which have until now created culture. Their own ideas, their own feelings, their own approaches to all the tasks of the individual and society. The urban worker in his own way and the rural toiler in his own way will create their own bright world view imbued with the thought of the working class. There is no spectacle more majestic and beautiful than that which the next generation will witness and participate in: the construction by the workers' collectives of their common, rich and free soul.

Teaching is an important but not decisive element here. The criticism and creativity of the masses themselves are more important, for only some parts of science and art have universal human significance: they undergo vital changes during every profound class revolution.

Throughout Russia, particularly among urban workers, but also among the peasants, the powerful wave of a cultural-educational movement has arisen, workers' and soldiers' organisations of this kind are multiplying endlessly. To meet them half-way, to support them in every way possible, to clear the path before them is the primary task of the revolutionary and people's government in the field of public education.[7] [My emphasis.]

Lunacharskii, who was an idealist intellectual of Communist-populist persuasion, was not a professional teacher and had a very vague notion of the processes of teaching and education. It is sufficient to note that he conceived of the teaching process as a non-creative and almost mechanical operation - the transfer of ready-made knowledge from one head to another. Given such an interpretation of the problem, the teacher's role is naturally reduced to purely technical operations. Nonetheless, Lunacharskii's words which I emphasised contain an attitude which would greatly complicate the life of Soviet schools in the period 1918-30: the priority of those who know less (those being taught and educated) over those who know more (teachers, artists, writers, scientists). For a member of the communist government the reason for this approach lay in the inner[8] necessity to make the dictatorship of the proletariat (the masses) accord with the proletariat's role in education. If the Bolshevik state, according to the official (and, for many Bolsheviks in 1917-20, personal) political and philosophical dogma, had to be governed by the working class and rural semi-proletariat, then education also had to be run by the popular masses - such was Lunacharskii's elementary logic. We shall see below what this trend (the priority of the taught over the teachers) turned into, in what form and for how long its effect would last.

The democratic mood of the first People's Commissar of Education was so strong that one of the main progressive tendencies of the pre-Revolutionary teaching community - the tendency to decentralise schools and free them from state diktat - is brought to an apogee in his 'Appeal'.

> Henceforth the State Commission on Education shall not be the central authority governing schools and institutions of education. On the contrary, all school affairs are to be transferred to the organisations of local self-government. The independent work of the spontaneously emerging class, workers', soldiers' and peasants' cultural-educational organisations, should have complete autonomy in relation both to the state centre and to the municipal centres.
>
> The State Commission's function is to be a link and assistant; to organise sources of material, ideological and moral support for the municipal and private, particularly workers' and class institutions of education on a state, nation-wide scale.[9]

This was the transitory inertia both of the pre-Revolutionary mood of the radical intelligentsia and of the extensive post-Revolutionary civil freedoms. The centralist forms of the new state were perhaps clearly seen by Lenin and Trotskii, but not by the public, nor even by all the leaders of the state. Thus a thesis which declared maximum school decentralisation lies at the source of the most centralised school system in the history of Russia.

The link with the situation before the Revolution was still so strong that Lunacharskii offered to collaborate with the State Committee on Education which had functioned under the Provisional Government. However, the proposals made by the State Commission (i.e. the People's Commissar of Education) to the Committee, for all their correctness, sounded very much like directives. The Committee was instructed:

> ...to convene immediately a special session of the Committee to carry out the following programme:
>
> (1) a revision of the procedures of representation on the committee in order to democratise it even further;
> (2) a revision of the committee's rights with a mind to extending them and transforming it into the main State Institute on drawing up bills on the complete re-organisation of instruction and education in Russia on democratic principles;
> (3) a revision of the bills already drawn up by the committee jointly with the new State Commission, necessitated by the fact that when they were drawn up the committee had taken into consideration the bourgeois spirit of the preceding ministries which, moreover, had impeded them even in this restricted form.
>
> After this revision the bills will be implemented without any bureaucratic red-tape in a revolutionary manner.[10]

The word 'democratise' used in the first paragraph of this section of the 'Appeal' has only one meaning: to include a greater number of representatives of the masses on the committee. The second paragraph proposes a 'complete re-organisation of instruction and education in Russia on democratic principles', but it is not clear what this means. The Committee also has to review all its former decisions, even though, despite Lunacharskii's assertion of the 'bourgeois spirit of the preceding ministries', the Committee had had complete freedom of action in the period February-October 1917. The Provisional Government had never issued such directives to school teachers and administrators as the following instruction issued by Lunacharskii on his third day in power:

> Current matters must for the time being take their course through the Ministry of Education. All immediately necessary changes in its composition and construction will be decided by the State Commission, elected by the Executive Committee of the Soviets and the State Committee. Eventually, of course, the procedures of state leadership in the field of education will be established by the Constituent Assembly. Until then the ministry is to act as the executive apparatus of the State Commission on Education and the State Committee on Education.[11]

However, the State Committee had already been informed that it had to submit to the demands of Lunacharskii's Commission. The latter could not do without teachers, but soon the teachers were also informed that 'henceforth decisions cannot be taken exclusively by co-operatives of specialists. This also applies to reforms of institutions of general education.'[12] No such reforms were possible, of course, without the 'co-operatives of specialists', and in autumn 1917 the question of the Constituent Assembly could not be omitted when addressing the specialists. Lunacharskii writes in his 'Appeal':

> The Constituent Assembly will undoubtedly begin its work soon. It alone will actively establish the procedures of state and public life in our country, including the general character of the organisation of education.
>
> But now that power has been transferred to the Soviets, the true popular character of the Constituent Assembly is assured. It is doubtful whether the course which the State Commission will pursue, supported by the State Committee, can be substantially changed under the influence of the Constituent Assembly. Without pre-determining it [this course], the new people's government considers that it has the right to implement in this field as well a number of measures aimed at enriching and illuminating the spiritual life of

the country as soon as possible.[13]

In other words, it was doubtful whether the course which the Bolshevik government would conduct could be 'substantially changed under the influence of the Constituent Assembly', since the nature of any representative organs would now be determined by the Bolsheviks. The teachers of Russia, who for half a century had provided cadres for a variety of progressive and revolutionary movements and had had a taste of complete freedom in February-October 1917, naturally could not fail to be alarmed by the dictatorial notes that could be heard in Lunacharskii's outwardly perfectly democratic 'Appeal'.

Lunacharskii stated that the Constituent Assembly would 'undoubtedly begin its work soon', but this confidence turned out to be as utopian as the decentralisation of Russian education which he proclaimed. Moreover, he himself dismissed this decentralisation in the same breath: if education were really to be autonomous, free of standardisation imposed from above, it was hardly appropriate for the governmental committee to give instructions to the State Committee on Education and the Ministry of Education. Lunacharskii did not notice this contradiction in his own declarations.

The idyllic tone of the first legislative and directive documents in the history of Soviet education was, however, rapidly replaced by stern, dictatorial intonations. On 20 November 1917, by special decree of the Council of People's Commissars, signed by Lenin, Lunacharskii, Bonch-Bruevich and Gorbunov:[14] 'The State Committee in its present composition is to be dissolved and its work halted until a new committee is formed ...' There now followed, in rapid succession, a stream of absolutely categorical and dictatorial resolutions and decrees.[15]

I should like to dwell on the Resolution 'On the dissolution of the Teachers' Union' of the All-Russian Central Executive Committee of 23 December 1918[16] which established that:

> (1) The All-Russian Union of Teachers, as represented by its leading organs, immediately after the October Revolution joined the counter-revolutionary Committee of Salvation of the Motherland and the revolution; (2) the All-Russian Union of Teachers rendered it assistance, among others, by distributing literature against

Soviet power; (3) it urged teachers to sabotage and strikes, disobedience to Soviet power and non-implementation of its decrees; (4) it opposed the decree on the re-election of teachers; (5) it made every effort to undermine the teachers' confidence in the undertakings of the People's Commissariat of Education in the field of school reform; (6) it adopted a reactionary position on the liberation of schools from the oppression of religious prejudices and chauvinism, insisting that scripture should be a compulsory subject for schools and that the national principle of education be a counterbalance to the idea of internationalism; (7) it attempted to inspire teachers with a distrust of Soviet power and to convince them of the need for utmost opposition to the school reform in order to make the restoration easier, and (8) in the person of the provincial associations, acting on the directives of the centre of the All-Russian Union of Teachers, it participated in the counter-revolutionary restoration and at the locations of the Czechoslovak and White Guard uprisings.

In consequence of the above reasons, the All-Russian Central Executive Committee resolves:

To dissolve the All-Russian Union of Teachers as represented by the central and local organisations.

To close down the printed organs News of the All-Russian Union of Teachers, The Petrograd Teacher, Teacher (published by the Moscow Bureau of the All-Russian Union of Teachers) and other central and local organs of the All-Russian Union of Teachers.

To transfer all the property and financial resources of the All-Russian Union of Teachers to satisfying the professional and educational needs of teachers under the control of a board of the People's Commissariat of Education.

Members of the former All-Russian Union of Teachers shall not be liable to any persecution or restrictions because of their participation in the union.

Chairman of the All-Russian Central Executive Committee

Ia. Sverdlov

Secretary of the All-Russian Executive Committee

V. Avanesov.

Both Resolutions, 'On the dissolution of the State Committee on Education' and 'On the dissolution of the Teachers' Union', are evidence of the implacable hostility of the pre-Revolutionary teachers' organisations to the People's Commissariat of Education. In its very first weeks of activity, the latter centralised the entire political and administrative initiative in the field of education (despite its first declaration).

It should be noted that a reading of the pre-Revolutionary pedagogical periodicals reveals that the charges brought against the Teachers' Union and its printed organs in point 6 are imprecise. The Union did not demand that scripture be made compulsory for all children by administrative means, but that those children whose parents considered it necessary should be free to study it. In Tsarist times, lessons of this kind had been held separately for pupils of all faiths. The Teachers' Union and the State Committee insisted that those pupils who desired to acquaint themselves with the princples of their religion should be enabled to do so. This was absolutely forbidden, despite the decree on freedom of conscience and the promise that school affairs would be decentralised and placed under the jurisdiction of the public, including parents, of whom the vast majority in 1917 were religious. If the first 'Appeal' of the People's Commissar of Education had been consistently implemented, the question of teaching the principles of the various religions would have been decided by the collective of parents and teachers in each particular school. This demand, which had been put forward by organisations which had now been deprived of their press and whose entire resources (collected by the Teachers' Union as membership fees) had been confiscated, was fundamental to modern, democratic relations between parents, school and state.[17]

It should also be noted that the Union included non-Russian schools in its demands, in particular Jewish and Muslim schools, and schools in all the areas of the Empire where religion was deeply rooted and widely practised. The second charge of point 6 related to the Union's demand to preserve the achievements of the February Revolution as expressed in the increased attention to national characteristics and the rights and traditions of non-Russian schools. According to a number of very detailed and critical pieces of research and articles published in the pedagogical and general press in 1860-1917, the situation of national schools in the Empire was very difficult. This was especially true of the small national groups and the peoples of European Russia, Siberia, the Far East and the north etc., who lagged behind the general Russian level of development. The teaching community devoted much attention to this question in the period between February and October 1917. Communist power was imbued with the idea of internationalism, which was interpreted in the Bolsheviks' practical policies not as a gradual drawing together of different nations with equal rights, while preserving their cultural, ethnographical, spiritual and political sovereignty, as is happening in modern Europe (or a spontaneous, free, gradual merging, interpenetration, as in the USA), but as an accelerated discarding of national characteristics and traditions ('prejudices'), including first and foremost religion, and the fusion of all peoples into a new, nationless, socialist ethnos. The poet Maiakovskii called this the 'socialist nation'. Russian naturally was and remained the language of communication among the nations within the Empire (Tsarist and later Soviet), but that did not make the Russian people a ruling or privileged nation: its national and religious values were ignored and erased just like all the others. Moscow, the European part of Russia, was and remained the centre of the Empire - hence the Great Russians' linguistic and administrative role in the unification and national standardisation of the Communist USSR, and also the illusion that the Russian people occupied a special position among the USSR's other peoples. The Russians, their culture and faith, received no economic or legal privileges from the Bolsheviks. But Russian remained the language of the state, army and schools, hence the linguistic, cultural and administrative preponderance of Russians in the life of the entire Empire (and Soviet Union). The young power, which was still fanatically internationalist, was in no hurry to introduce changes 'quickly, without any bureaucratic red-tape', as Lunacharskii wrote in his first 'Appeal'. The Teachers' Union remained firmly in support of handling national-educational and national-cultural problems in a democratic way, and this obstructed the unifying objectives of the People's Commissariat of Education.[18]

In the years 1918-25, the articles and speeches of Lenin, Krupskaia and Lunacharskii, the speeches made by party and Soviet leaders at teachers' congresses (now convened by the Bolsheviks) and the press of the party and teachers (now subject to Soviet censorship) still provide direct and indirect evidence of the teachers' hostility to the new power and its educational, political and ideological innovations.[19]

The 1925 Congress of Teachers was mainly attended by the new teachers who had been hastily graduated from brief courses, seminars and two- to three-month refresher courses for those with inadequate qualifications. The Soviet teachers were joined by some of the pre-Revolutionary teachers who had no other means of earning a living or were partially sympathetic to the Bolsheviks' views. The main reasons for the Russian teachers' prolonged and difficult resistance to the Bolsheviks (in conditions of the most severe hunger and terror) seem to be the following:

(1) The onslaught of Soviet power on Russian teachers' age-old democratic aspirations, which in many ways had been satisfied after the February Revolution. I mentioned two aspects of this onslaught above (see point 6 of the Resolution 'On the dissolution of the Teachers' Union'). This dissolution of the teachers' independent organisation and its replacement with the Union of Internationalist Teachers set up by a directive of the Central Committee of the RKP(b) (Russian Communist Party (Bolsheviks)) and the People's Commissariat of Education abolished the right of professional association that the teachers had enjoyed in the years before the Revolution. The confiscation of the Union's membership fees astounded the teachers, who had become accustomed to the previous legal economic standards and to a respect for the property of others (and here it was a question of the property of worker-teachers). They were also shocked by the political devastation, such as the ban on all non-Bolshevik periodicals, including the teachers' professional publications, which had deep roots in their pre-Revolutionary cultural life. What is more, even those publications which had traditionally been considered liberal, and even left wing, were closed down.

(2) The most cultured and highly qualified teachers were stunned and infuriated by the demands for absolute ideological monism and uniformity with which the Bolshevik government deluged them in 1918-20.[20] The fact that many of Lenin's speeches are devoted to the problem of the ideological subjection of teachers to Communist diktat and to the task of turning them into a channel for inculcating the masses with Bolshevik ideology and a lever for subjecting the masses to Bolshevik policies, is evidence of

the great importance which the RKP(b) leadership attached to these matters. However, most of the pre-Revolutionary teachers did not share this ideology and belonged to liberal circles, the Kadets (Constitutional Democrats), Mensheviks and Socialist-Revolutionaries. Moreover, despite the stock notion (that also exists in the West) that civil freedoms did not exist in twentieth-century Russia before the February Revolution, these freedoms were actually very much alive in 1910-17. Even in earlier periods Russia had never known such ideological pressure and uniformity.

(3) Both Lunacharskii, in his first appeal of 1917 to the public and the teachers, and Lenin, at the beginning of 1923 when he was slowly dying, spoke of the need to pay teachers more than in Tsarist times. Nonetheless, party leaders admitted in their speeches to the 1925 Congress of Teachers that from 1918-25 the teachers had actually not received salaries from the Soviet government and would have been reduced to utter poverty if the peasants had not supported them in the villages - in 1918-21 with immense difficulty and very meagrely, and after the introduction of the New Economic Policy (NEP) more generously and adequately. In the district towns and main cities, however, teachers were actually starving and dying.[21]

The following administrative act was quite in accordance with the intention expressed in Lunacharskii's first 'Appeal' to reorganise Russian schools 'completely':

> On the abolition of marks
> Resolution of the People's Commissar of Education (May 1918):
>
> (1) The system of marks for assessing the pupils' knowledge is abolished in all instances of school practice without exception.
> (2) Transfer from class to class and the issue of certificates will be conducted on the basis of the pupils' progress according to the opinions of the pedagogical council on the fulfilment of school work.
>
> People's Commissar of Education
> A.V. Lunacharskii[22]

It should be noted that once again this uncompromising Resolution contradicted Lunacharskii's declaration on the complete decentralisation of school affairs in Russia with which he began his work as commissar. If schools had really been decentralised, the methods of assessing pupils' knowledge and of informing the pupils of these assessments would have been determined by each school in accordance with its specific conditions.

This Resolution was a shock to the mass of teachers as it deprived the schools of any formal assessment of the success or failure of their work. Of course, 'the opinions of the pedagogical council' also had to be formulated in some way, and this need soon gave rise to the following marks (instead of the five grades in schools before the Revolution): 'very good' ('excellent'), 'good', 'satisfactory' ('fair'), 'unsatisfactory' ('bad') and later 'very bad'.[23]

It can be disputed (and is being disputed throughout the world) whether young children in the first and second years of schooling should be informed of formal marks (especially bad ones). Sometimes this is extended to the first three or four years of schooling to avoid causing young children anxiety and to avoid categorising them formally and permanently (in their own and their friends' eyes) as 'good', 'satisfactory' and 'bad' children. But in this case the teacher has to have a clear, recorded and accepted (i.e. understood by all his colleagues) notion of the children's progress. Without this, that most complex, multifaceted and multi-level process which makes up teaching and education as a whole cannot be organised.

As the pupil grows and his personal responsibility develops, he should also undoubtedly be informed of how the teacher and school assess his work and - what is not always done even to this day - his potential. The pupil should be informed of his achievements and deficiencies, his diligence and neglect in his studies, his potential and prospects, not when he 'transfers from class to class' but on a daily basis, by routine assessment and discussion of it.[24] A child and adolescent is not yet sufficiently capable of controlling his progress without ongoing assessment. When students are left to themselves they often become confused in the large gaps between examinations. Older school-children should certainly be introduced to 'semi-student' independence, to which end a relatively small but gradually increasing number of lecture courses or practical studies without ongoing assessment but with subsequent tests, seminars and essays, is currently being introduced. This is happening in both contemporary Soviet and Western schools, but this complex work, carefully thought out by qualified teachers, should also be accompanied by constant educational influence on all the pupils and control of the weak ones. Lunacharskii, however, spoke of abolishing marks, 'in all instances of school practice without exception', which laid the foundation for the state of sheer chaos which lasted approximately 13 years (1918-31).

It is worth noting that the 'Declaration on the single labour school' of 16 October 1918 (first called 'Basic Principles of the single labour school) still mentioned in passing that 'private initiative' in school education could not be excluded (those same pre-Revolutionary democratic sentiments of the author of the 'Declaration', Lunacharskii). It stipulated, however, that the decisions of Soviet power (the People's Commissariat of Education, at that time still the State Commission on Education) would be binding, as mentioned above, for 'all instances of school practice without exception'. Private schools were not mentioned after October 1918: they died without any public reverberations.[25]

The abolition of assessment of the pupils' current progress was symptomatic of a peculiar combination of the main pedagogical trends which marked the birth of the Soviet school: on the one hand, the growing diktat applied to the previously independent teachers' organisations, culminating at this stage in the dissolution of these organisations and the closing down of the teachers' press; and on the other hand, the increasing withdrawal of disciplinary restrictions on pupils and the relaxation of educational demands in the name of democratisation.[26] The lowering of demands and, in particular, the abolition of marks can be largely explained by the sudden influx of children and young people from the least cultured sections of the population into schools of general education. The aim was to avoid 'discriminating' against them, in the eyes of the better prepared and more cultured pupils, by having to give them poor marks.[27] This method, however, was wrong, as it did not remove the actual inequality of the pupils. The less prepared pupils should have been specially, better prepared for school and not deprived of the opportunity for timely and sobre self-evaluation.

On 30 September 1918 a session of the All-Russian Central Executive Committee adopted the 'Statute on the single labour school of the Russian Socialist Federative Soviet Republic'. The single school also included the kindergartens (children from six to eight years).[28] The following article was introduced into the Statute in the name of that same democratisation, interpreted as primitive levelling:

> Article 7. The division of teachers into categories is abolished. All school workers (Article 8) are to be remunerated according to the rates of the first category of the decree of the Council of People's Commissars 'On rates of pay for teaching work' ('Collected statutes and instructions of the workers' and peasants' government', no. 47, article 552).
>
> Note 1. Payment for teachers' work is made not by the lesson but monthly.
>
> Note 2. Special pay above the established rate is not permitted for officials among the school workers.[29]

At the beginning of the 1930s school workers would once again be paid according to their education, length of service and number of hours worked. Meanwhile, however, the link between qualifications and pay would be broken for a long time.

Article 2 of this Statute established that 'The single labour school is divided into two levels: the first, for children from eight to 13 years (a five-year course), and the second from 13 to 17 years (a four-year course).' Different education had been required for teaching at each of these two levels in pre-Soviet schools (and after 1931 in Soviet schools as well): in the first to fourth grades, specialised secondary education; in the fifth to seventh grades (and sometimes the eighth), incomplete higher education (two- to three-year courses in teachers' institutes and seminaries); and in the senior grades, higher education (four- to five-year courses in pedagogical institutes and universities). Each level had teachers with the appropriate educational qualification who were paid accordingly. This was an incentive for teachers to acquire the necessary education for the particular level and at the first opportunity to improve their qualifications in order to progress to the next teaching level. As there was a clearly defined teaching load (18-24 hours a week, which varied at different times according to the subjects and levels), those teachers who taught more or less hours received more or less money. This achieved (and still achieves) automatic correction to the absolute minimum of expenditure. By making the monthly rate of pay independent of the actual number of hours worked by the teacher, the legislators destroyed this correction. It began to be advantageous for teachers to work the minimum number of hours, as they were not paid less for doing so. The enthusiasm of individuals who were prepared to work more than others for the same pay was not rewarded. This was one of the numerous manifestations of the idea of direct and immediate levelling that was held at that time by all Communists. After this principle had reigned supreme for a few years, the diligence of the majority of teachers had declined drastically. It had precisely the same influence in other spheres of working life, but elsewhere it was abolished earlier than in the schools.

Because of the expected mass influx of pupils from the lowest strata of the population and because many of the older teachers were unwilling to share the school policy of the new regime, the latter was obliged to organise urgently the 'mass production' of new teachers. It was inevitable that their educational and other qualifications were very low.[30] Just as the abolition of ongoing assessment was meant to eliminate 'discrimination' against the ill-prepared pupils who entered the schools after the Revolution, so the abolition of the link between education, length of service and pay for teaching was meant to eliminate discrimination against the poorly educated teachers who graduated from the quick teaching courses after the Revolution. These teachers were mostly recruited from among the workers and poor peasants and the main virtue expected of them was loyalty to the new regime and devotion to its ideological postulates. But, however strange this may seem (superficially), according to records of the 1925 Teachers' Congress, the new teachers were also not always enthusiastic about the Bolsheviks' innovations. High-ranking speakers at the congress expressed ominous dissatisfaction on this score. The heads of the first People's Commissariat of Education were so possessed by the idea of levelling that, according to the second note to Article 1 of the Statute on the single labour school, 'The division of schools into primary, higher primary schools, Gymnasia, non-classical secondary schools, trade, technical, commercial schools and all other forms of primary and secondary schools is abolished.' The pre-February Revolution concept of the Gymnasium as a superior, privileged type of educational establishment and of the primary and higher primary (incomplete secondary), trade and technical schools and colleges as institutions mainly of the common people evidently played a role in this decision as well. It was decided to remove all differentiation between schools at one fell swoop (with one decree), but the various types of educational institutions referred to in this note to Article 1 of the Statute pursued different aims, and pupils graduated from them with different kinds of training. Since the founders of the 'single labour school' were unable to raise every kind of school to the level of the former classical Gymnasia and non-classical and commercial (and also complete secondary) schools, they were consequently obliged to lower the overall level of schools of general education in comparison with the former Gymnasia. This did not take long to bring about.

Article 8 of the Statute on the single labour school echoes the basic sources of Communism and the party programme: 'All school workers, i.e. teachers, school doctors and instructors in physical labour, shall be elected according to the resolution on the appointment by election of all pedagogical and administrative-pedagogical posts of 27 February 1918, and according to the instructions of the People's Commissariat of Education'. I have not been able to find this resolution, as it is not included in the collections of documents known to me, but both Marx and Lenin wrote about 'the complete appointment by election from top to bottom' of all state (public) officials and employees, including school workers, the former in his 'Critique of the Gotha Programme' and 'The Civil War in France' and the latter in his 'State and Revolution'. This principle was also proclaimed in all party programmes up to the 1930s. The year 1918 in general was characterised by a struggle between election and appointment: state employees, including school workers, over whose election there was some confusion, began to be hired and appointed by the appropriate state administrative institutions.[31] Indeed, it was ridiculous to speak of any true principle of election of teachers once all the independent teachers' organisations and press had been closed down. From the early 1920s the so-called 'vydvizhentsy' (activist and Communist workers promoted to administrative posts) were usually appointed as school leaders, often without having completed secondary education.[32]

The 'democratisation' of schools, in the sense of 'emancipating' pupils from all obligations, from any system of education capable of developing their ability to work and perform tasks in an organised manner, and from any sense of duty attached to a culture of independent work, reached catastrophically destructive proportions:

> Article 17. It is not permitted to set compulsory lessons and work for the home.
> Article 18. No punishments are permitted in the school.
> Article 19. All examinations - entrance, transitional and leaving - are abolished.[33]

Thus no disciplinary and restrictive-educational restraints were to be placed on children and adolescents. The authors of the Statute create the impression that their aim is to realise the dream of all children - a school that imposes no obligations.

The Statute also clearly manifested concern for the children's free time, which was to be the responsibility of the school as much as possible (this rule was not - and is still not - always observed), for giving them free meals in the school,[34] and for the medical supervision of schoolchildren (which is observed to this day):

> Article 15. Schools shall be open to the pupils seven days a week.
>
> Note 1. Two days a week, but not in succession, are to be set aside from the overall number of days of instruction, of which one day is to be completely free of usual pursuits, and is to be used for reading, excursions, shows and other independent children's pursuits, for which new pedagogical cadres are to be recruited. The other day is to be a semi-working day with the regular teaching staff and is to be used for club and laboratory activities, reports, excursions, pupils' meetings.
>
> Note 2. Every school worker shall have one free day a week.

*

Two harsh and pervasive restrictions were imposed on the pedagogical staff: an economic one, since the state became the exclusive employer and salary payer; and a political-ideological one (see the bibliographical sources referred to in previous notes). Pupils, in contrast, were not only liberated from very necessary didactic and educational disciplinary measures, but were also placed on an equal footing with the administrators and teachers in running the school.[35] This participation did not only take the form of pupils' organisations, organs of pupils' self-government such as the pupils' committees or meetings of class prefects, or, as they are still called in Soviet schools, 'class organisers', which would have been natural for and characteristic of modern schools in most developed countries. It also involved pupils' representation on the school council and even their attendance at sessions of the pedagogical organ:

> Article 27. The responsible organs of school self-government shall be the school council made up of: (a) all school workers; (b) representatives of the working population in the given school district, numbering one quarter of the number of school workers; (c) the same proportion of pupils of the older age groups, from 12 years of age; and (d) one representative of the department of education.[36]

In the schools of the 1920s, especially at the beginning of this period, characterised by illusions of democratising the life of all the people, pedocratic trends reigned supreme.[37]

Nonetheless, all this democracy within the school (meetings of workers, parents and children) was immediately placed within a rigid framework[38] and made absolutely subject to government directives:

> Article 30. Decisions of the school council on all questions of school life shall not violate the general statutes on the single school or the resolutions of the Department of Education of the Soviet of Deputies and can be objected to by a representative of the department.
>
> Note. An objection shall not halt a decision of the school council, but the matter shall be brought to the attention of the Department of Education.[39]

This meant, of course, that such disputes would be decided by this higher department and not by the school council. The Statute was signed by 'Chairman of the All-Russian Central Executive Committee, Ia. Sverdlov, Deputy People's Commissar of Education, M. Pokrovskii, Secretary of the All-Russian Central Executive Committee, A. Enukidze'.[40]

Along with this 'emancipation' of pupils and centralisation of the ideological principles of the new school, a number of attempts were made to bring about a complete transformation in the curricular and methodological bases of the teaching process itself, which had until then been generally accepted. Schools were becoming an arena for unrestrained experimentation which was mostly dictated from above. The Declaration on the basic principles of the single labour school of 16 October 1918 introduced radical changes into the aims and methods of instruction and education in Russian schools. Although it outlined only vaguely the structural and organisational principles of schools, which were to be elaborated and to take on their true and stable form only at the beginning of the 1930s, the teaching and educational process was dominated by a mood best expressed by the famous lines of the 'Internationale': 'The entire old world' of school life was to be destroyed 'to the foundations, and then we shall build our new world ...'

For the first time labour instruction was introduced into the schools by legislation, and not in the familiar forms, which had also existed in the old schools, of manual labour designed to develop the child's aesthetic taste and habits of practical work, adapted to his physical powers, needs and interests. The lessons in labour were introduced as 'polytechnical training' which Marx had declared as a principle of the Communist school.

> ... the aim of the labour school shall henceforth be not training for a trade but polytechnical education, which acquaints children in practice with the methods of all the most important forms of labour, partly in the school workshop or school farm, partly in factories, plants, etc.[41] [My emphasis.]

What immediately strikes the reader is the utopian nature of the enterprise - to introduce children 'in practice' to the 'methods of all the most important forms of labour'. The school timetable can include only a very limited number of lessons in labour or excursions outside the school. The children could be introduced to 'the most important forms of modern production' by means of a condensed lecture course, with teaching aids such as scientific films, meetings with specialists, etc., while preserving a reasonable number of labour lessons. This would also be extremely difficult, since the aspiration to include in the school curriculum all the most important forms of modern labour contradicts two trends of the modern world: (1) the growing division of labour and increasing specialisation (along with the systemic unification of specialised processes into a complex whole); (2) the aim to divide schools of general education into schools specialising in various subjects, which is essential because of the increasing overloading of pupils and because there is not enough room in the school timetable to teach essential information even in basic subjects. However, such an approach to 'polytechnical training' contradicted the ideal, which in those years was still very much alive, of the dominant role of physical labour in social production. Moreover, this idolisation of labour merged with the desire to borrow from the experience of the West, but the Bolsheviks drew from the powerful and very varied current of this experience - the experience of free, diverse, independent schools - only information concerning experiments that accorded with their frame of mind and concepts.

The result of this one-sided borrowing was that certain trends and episodes in American school experimentation had a very destructive influence on Soviet schools during 1917-31. In 1918-20, out of a timetable of 24-33 hours a week, up to ten lessons a week began to be set aside for 'polytechnical training' (in practice, physical-labour training), which merely amounted to the pupils' physical labour: in the lower grades, in theoretically and practically acceptable forms and frameworks; and in the higher grades, in forms and on a scale which were clearly detrimental to the basic subjects of the school course. In reality, however, even if this 'ideal' could have been approached, and adolescents could have been given all possible working skills, a vast number of the most important professions of the modern world would still have remained outside the pupil's field of vision.

The transformation in the teaching process was not limited to the introduction of polytechnical education. It was proposed to replace the generally accepted method of education, in which the pupil studies a number of subjects in courses which have an internal logic of development and provide the repetition necessary for understanding, with the 'encyclopedic method'. This method was to dominate approximately two-thirds of the school course and was to be replaced only in the higher grades with systematic study of subjects which were being severely constricted by the factory 'polytechnical training'.

In order to make it easier for the reader to understand

the 'encyclopedic' (also called the 'complex') method of teaching in the first grades (one to four), I shall quote samples of the compulsory plans (or curricula) issued by the People's Commissariat of Education to help teachers of the third and fourth grades (groups) in the 1926/7 school year. I shall take one autumn-winter term of studies of the third and fourth groups:[42]

PLAN

of work of the 3rd group .... of school of the 1st level

Autumn-winter term

No.	Complexes	Aim of study	Beginning of work	End of work	Duration
1.	Our village. Our volost; its nature; work in it; social life in the past and present with the themes:	What is around us has to be studied in order to change it. Our backward village has to be transformed into a cultured Soviet village.	25.9	31.12	83 days
	The October Revolution; its preparation and significance.	The October Revolution liberated the town from capitalism, the village from the landowner, it gave the village culture; it gave the village freedom and land; it will give it wealth. It is the beginning of a new life, whose strength lies in the union of workers and peasants.			

	Man and his labour.	To explain that labour is the source of the people's wealth; it is the source of health and happiness if it is based on knowledge of the life of the human body and is protected by socialist legislation.			
		Total:			83 days

PLAN

of the work of the 4th group .... of the school for 192...

Autumn-winter term

No.	Name of complex (main theme)	Why we study	Beginning of work	End of work	Duration
1.	The planning of work: what is planned work; why it is necessary; how to do it; the precepts of NOT.*	Planned work gives meaning to labour, shortens it, raises productivity, is necessary for one's own and the state's economy. NOT liberates the people from the slavery of labour.	25.9	31.10	6 days
2.	The USSR: its production, the	Without knowing about the labour and production			

* NOT = scientific organisation of labour.

workers and their struggle. The October Revolution Holiday, the Holiday of the Struggle and the Victory.	of the USSR, labour in one's own village cannot be improved and organised; when we organise the village, we organise the USSR. The USSR is a very rich country. We have to know how to put our hands to it.	25.9.	24.12	77 days
RESULTS of the work and plan for the following term:		25.12	31.12	6 days
	Total:			83 days

The collection of materials *Plans and programmes of 'complex instruction'*[43] included an elaboration of methodology by M. Osiptsev which explained to teachers where to find materials for the main subjects of the 'Encyclopedia'.[44] I give as examples two or three recommendations on the subject 'The USSR' for the fourth group:

> *8th theme*. The population is the work force of the USSR.
>
> The aims of this theme are to explain the composition of the working population and its cultural-economic level. There is no need to go into detail in view of the complexity of the subject and the shortness of time - two days. Here it is necessary to resort to the division of labour: to divide into groups and to give each group a question to study. The national policy - full autonomy - should be especially emphasised.
>
> The teacher must prepare beforehand the necessary statistical data and distribute them to the children.
>
> This theme has hardly been dealt with in our reading books, and it is necessary to concentrate attention on preparing diagrams and on discussions.

Here there are enough statistics.

Statistical data can be found in any book of economic geography or in the Geography of the USSR by Uvarov and Sokolov.

9th theme. The socio-political organisation of the USSR.

The aim of work is to explain that the USSR is a country with the most powerful and advanced social organisations, which are led by the workers of the USSR in order to improve their economy and welfare.

Among excursions, we shall indicate: an excursion to the local party and trade organisations and study of their history, structure and work.

Among laboratory work connected with statistics we shall indicate: diagrams on the composition of the party; Komsomol; trade unions both in the USSR and in our village.

Among reading materials: Keep pace, comrade; Execution of the Communards; Zhuravushki; We peasant lads; Lenin's funeral march; The International of youth; The young guard! We fell victim; The workers' palace, etc.

There is quite sufficient reading material in these same books, especially in The green noise and The new village. Among written works can be mentioned: What the Communist Party has done for the village; Works of our Pioneers in the village; Works of the Komsomol.

Among the kinds of communal work, we can mention organising a detachment of Pioneers if the school does not already have one.

10th theme. The USSR as the workers' and peasants' state.

The aim of the work is to show that the USSR is really governed by the workers and peasants.

This theme is broken down into nine sub-themes and, in order to make it more concrete, it is necessary to enter more closely into the life of Soviet institutions and to gain detailed and thorough knowledge of the new volost, its tasks and organs. It is therefore particularly desirable to visit the VIK [Volost Executive Committee] and to learn about it in detail. If this is impossible, then not all the group will investigate the VIK, but a special investigatory group will, with the plan of inquiry being worked out jointly with the entire group. Among laboratory work we shall indicate: the preparation of charts; charts of the republics of the USSR; a chart of the USSR administration; a chart of the new volost; a chart of education in the USSR.

Suitable songs and poems: 'Boldly we go into battle'; 'The send-off'; 'Song of the Komsomol girl'; 'Song of labour'.

Reading material can be found in various books, especially in With our own forces and The green noise. But newspapers will also provide answers to many questions. There are no articles at all in booklets on the church and the state and on judicial authority.

Written essays: 'Whom we elected to the VIK and why'. 'What we saw and heard at the citizens' public assembly'. 'Our VIK'. 'Women's rights under the Tsar and the Soviets'. 'What the Soviets should do in the village'.

Among statistics we can indicate: a calculation of the volost budget; of expenditure on education; of expenditure and figures in the struggle against illiteracy, etc.

The last theme (11) in the study of the USSR - prospects for the immediate economic and cultural development of the USSR. This theme is extremely essential, and without studying it knowledge and study of the USSR would remain incomplete.

We shall also allot a week to it and break it down into seven sub-themes. True, given the lack of material, the period can be shortened to two or three days and some of the material transferred to the theme on successes in agriculture, but this would not be desirable.

Reading material on this theme is relatively scarce and talks as a method on instruction will have to be employed. A great deal can be taken directly from newspapers.

We shall indicate some literature that will assist the teacher in work on this theme:

Electrification: (1) Stepanov - Electrification, new edn 1925, price 1 r. 50 kop. (2) Gartman - Electricity in the village, 1920, price 8 kop. (3) Idem. Electricity in agriculture, M. [Moscow] 1921, price 12 kop. Agricultural policy: Semenov - The new peasantry.

Osinskii - The restoration of the peasant economy and our tasks.

Mesiatsev - Agrarian policy.

Darin - Questions of the peasant economy.

Agricultural cooperative societies: Baliev - Machine association, price 8 kop.

Ivanov - Land improvement associations, price 8 kop.

Katonov - Credit cooperative societies, price 40 kop.

Krot-Krival - Control unions, price 20 kop.

Maslov - Agricultural cooperative societies, price 40 kop.

Sinitsyn - Cooperative societies in field-crop cultivation, price 15 kop., and many others.

Economy in the USSR in figures.

Works on economic geography by Don, Timofeev, Dmitriev, Sinitskii, etc.

Agricultural tax and income tax:

Pavlov - The single agricultural tax.

Gurov - The agricultural tax.

Stroev - The single agricultural tax, price 10 kop.

The whole complex of the USSR takes 65 days. If we allot another six days to taking stock of the work and organising an exhibition, then the entire complex will take 71 days, as we have noted in the plan, i.e. it will fit into the first term.

This gives us an idea of what the pupils were to study and where the teachers were to find material for these studies, and also of the scope of the general educational, literary and scientific information which the pupils were to be given and of their ideological tendentiousness.

In order to describe the 'encyclopedic' method of teaching for the middle (fifth-seventh) and upper (at that time, eighth-ninth) grades, I shall return to the same document - the 'Declaration on the principles of the single labour school':

> A somewhat broader cycle of approximately the same knowledge will be covered in systematic historical order, i.e. the children will learn about the history of labour and, on this basis, about the history of the whole of society, in vivid essays and always with the aid of independent work. The evolution of all culture on the basis of the growth of labour possibilities should not only be studied by them from books or the teacher's accounts but also to a certain extent lived through: not only their minds, but also their bodies, and first and

foremost their hands, should periodically be involved as fully as possible in the life of the savage, the nomad, the primitive farmer, the barbarian (epochs of the great river kingdoms, classical antiquity, the middle ages, etc.).

The teaching of this subject, i.e. the encyclopedia of culture, can easily acquire an undesirable superficial character if adequately trained teachers are not available. The study of this subject and its methodology should be immediately introduced into the pedagogical institutes and introduced into schools gradually when trained teachers are available.

The same subject, transformed into a sociology course on the basis of the evolution of labour and the economic forms created by it with incomparably more technically precise and profound, in brief, scientific-technical, study of improved labour devices (machines) and fairly rich statistical and juridical study of modern society and its polarity (labour and capital, socialism and capitalism), will comprise the content of the labour encyclopedia in schools of the second level, where it should also be combined with a systematic study of the history of science, closely connected with economic life, both in the origin of its views and methods and as a source of further changes in the economy.

At the same time the pupils' independent study of elements that particularly interest them should also always be encouraged: individual research, essays, papers, models, collections, etc.

As we have stated above, the higher we climb on the school ladder, the greater is the place occupied by subjects, along with the encyclopedia, i.e. systematic study under the guidance of specialists of: native language, mathematics, geography, history, biology and its subdivisions, physics and chemistry, living foreign languages.

These studies, in turn, should, of course, be imbued with the labour method of learning ...

Recalling the words of Marx on transforming factory child labour from a curse into a source of healthy, integrated and active knowledge, the new school will be closely linked with the neighbouring industries and will bring pupils to the factory and plant, the railroads, branches of industry - to every place to which it has access according to local conditions - and

> it will bring them not only for an excursion, not just to look, but to work ...
>
> Schools of the second level can be very diverse with regard to the kind of labour on which the study of polytechnical culture is based.
>
> It is possible to study it [polytechnical culture] and, vitally connected with it, the entire cycle of natural and social sciences on the basis of almost any branch of production, for today they are all closely interwoven. Textile factories, metallurgical and sugar-refining plants, woodwork workshops, navigation, the broad range of agriculture, railroads and tramways, post and telegraph, etc. can each form the basis of teaching. Given that this is physically possible, it should of course also be varied during the four years of work as much as possible. If such variety is impossible, the particular school which takes local industry as a point of departure should nonetheless not allow itself to become a kind of specialised institution of education, but should aim to give [pupils] knowledge of modern labour culture as a whole, while basing themselves on specific industries.[45]

The 'complex-encyclopedic method of teaching' was, of course, unable to give pupils 'knowledge of modern labour culture as a whole' in schools either of the first or the second level. This is especially evident if we bear in mind that pupils' rights were constantly increasing, and in the mid-1920s a pupil could not be expelled from school without the approval of a general assembly of pupils. However, the school revolution would not have been complete without attempts to undermine such a traditional form of study as lessons. In 1923 Soviet schools borrowed an educational experiment from American schools which was given far more prestige in the USSR than in the USA. At the beginning of the twentieth century, in the town of Dalton, Massachusetts, a teacher by the name of Parkhurst introduced a special form of instruction which became known in the USSR as the Dalton Plan which, in its two forms - individual and group (called the laboratory-team method),[46] was predominant until 1931. Parkhurst rejected lessons as the basic form of instruction and also dismissed the timetable. In the individual form of the Dalton Plan the teacher gave the pupil an individual, solitary assignment, reading lists, briefing and, in periodic meetings with him, noted how his work was progressing and reported his progress to the school council. In the group version, assignments were given to a team of pupils who had to study the material collectively and conduct independent laboratory work. At certain intervals (determined by the teacher and the administration) one of the team members would report to the teacher on the group's work. In each subject (i.e. to each subject teacher) a different pupil would report. The level of the pupils' knowledge declined, of course, disastrously, the curriculum disintegrated and any kind of discipline disappeared from school practice. The school-leavers of the 1920s were irremediably ignorant, while the level of culture, literacy and education of those who had graduated from the pre-October Gymnasia became legendary. In the 1920s and 1930s, when people wanted to describe someone as really well educated, they would say that he had graduated from a Gymnasium.

At the beginning of the 1930s the state was confronted with the challenge of highly accelerated industrialisation. In addition, there was an urgent need for young, literate commanders in the army. The task of strengthening and 'hardening' which confronted the partocratic state was obstructed by the low professional quality of the human resources being turned out by the technicums (technical colleges) and institutions of higher education, whose selection committees complained of the semi-literacy, low overall development and lack of discipline and capacity to work of school-leavers.

The state was now confronted by the urgent need to reform the schools that had been damaged by ten years of experimentation.

NOTES

1. In 1911. By 1916 this number had grown by approximately 24 per cent.

2. V. Pisarev, 'Prognozirovanie proshlogo' ('Forecasting the past'), Golos Zarubezh'ia ('The voice of abroad') (Munich), no. 21 (1918), pp. 19-22.

3. All dates up to February 1918 are given in the book in the Old Style.

4. All legal documents are quoted from Narodnoe obrazovanie v SSSR, sbornik dokumentov 1917-1973) ('Public education in the USSR, collection of documents 1917-73')

('Pedagogika', Moscow, 1974).

5. Ibid., p. 7, 29 October 1917.
6. Ibid., pp. 7-8.
7. Ibid., p. 8.
8. This was an inner motive for many Bolsheviks in 1917-20, i.e. the result of conviction.
9. Narodnoe obrazovanie, p. 8.
10. Ibid., p. 9.
11. Ibid.
12. Ibid.
13. Ibid. p. 10.
14. Ibid., p. 11.
15.

1917	Narodnoe obrazovanie	Page
11 December:	On the transfer of upbringing and education from the department of churches to the jurisdiction of the People's Commissariat of Education. Resolution of NKP (People's Commissariat of Education) adopted at a session of the CPC (Council of People's Commissars)	12
20 December:	On pre-school upbringing. From the pre-school department of the People's Commissariat of Education	327
1918		
2 January:	On the appointment as government Commissars attached to the Commissariat of Public Education of N.K. Krupskaia-Ul'ianova, P.I. Lebedev-Polianskii, V.M. Pozner, L.R. Menzhinskaia and I.B. Rogal'skii. Resolution of the CPC	12
	On increases to public teachers	442
9 January:	On commissions for minors. Decree of the CPC	342
20 January:	On freedom of conscience, church and religious societies. Decree of the CPC RSFSR	12

18 February:	On the Soviet school. Resolution of the State Commission on Education	132
9 March:	On the appointment of N.K. Krupskaia-Ul'ianova as Deputy People's Commissar of Education in Moscow. Decree of the CPC	13
11 April:	On the activity of the People's Commissariat of Education. Resolution of All-Russian Central Executive Committee	13
31 May:	On the introduction of compulsory co-education. Resolution of the People's Commissariat of Education	132
	On the abolition of marks. Resolution of the People's Commissariat of Education	133
5 June:	On the transfer of teaching and educational institutions and establishments of all departments to the jurisdiction of the People's Commissariat of Education. Decree of the CPC	
18 June:	Statute on the organisation of public education in the Russian Socialist Soviet Republic. Statute of the CPC RSFSR	13
26 June:	On norms of pay for teaching-work. Decree of CPC	14
2 July:	On the exemption from requisition of the premises of the People's Commissariat of Education. Decree of the CPC RSFSR	442
2 August:	On rules of admission to institutions of higher education of the RSFSR. Decree of the CPC RSFSR.	403
23 September:	On the fund for child nutrition. Resolution of the CPC	342
30 September:	Statute on the single labour school of the Russian Socialist Federative Soviet Republic. Ratified at a session of the All-	

	Russian Central Executive Committee.	133
5 October:	On the vacation of all buildings belonging to educational establishments and occupied by institutions of other departments. Resolution of the CPC	515
10 October:	On the introduction of the new orthography. Decree of the CPC RSFSR	17
16 October:	Basic principles of the single labour school. From the State Commission on Education	137
31 October:	On schools of the national minorities. Resolution of the CPC	145
5 December:	On the preservation of scientific values. Decree of the CPC	481
10 December:	On the mobilisation of the literate. Decree of the CPC	371

I shall return to some of these decrees below. The decree on 'Freedom of conscience, church and religious societies', which had a number of limiting and ambiguous points that later permitted persecution of the church and believers, is included in this list because it contains a paragraph on the complete separation of the school from the church.

16. Narodnoe obrazovanie, pp. 17-18.

17. In his speech to the 1925 Teachers' Congress, G. Zinov'ev quoted the following example of the 'crimes' of the former teachers' organisations in order to justify the dissolution of the Teachers' Union (which was independent of the new power), and the dispersal of its congresses: according to him, on 13 December 1917 a general meeting of the Petrograd Council of Teacher-Delegates resolved by a majority of votes - 800 to 66 - to declare a strike in support of the following demands:

> (1) the immediate opening of the Constituent Assembly; (2) full immunity for all its members; (3) immediate cessation of the fratricidal civil war; (4) restoration of all civil freedoms; (5) the restoration of the legal rights of all municipal and zemstvo organs of self-government, elected on the basis of universal suffrage.

The ratio of '800 to 66' was very characteristic of the teachers' organisations of 1917-20, and it was this that led to the government's dictatorial actions against the teachers, even though the latter did not go further than the usual democratic, lawful claims.

18. The meaningless formula of cultures 'national in form and socialist in content' arose later. It is meaningless because the concepts of 'form' and 'content' cannot be separated in any field of culture or ethnography.

19. Since schools in the period 1917-20 are not the main subject of my research I shall not quote this very interesting evidence but merely give some reference sources (which by no means exhaust the material on this subject): V.I. Lenin, 'Speech to the First All-Russian Congress of Workers of Education and Socialist Culture, 31 July 1919', in Lenin, Sochineniia ('Works'), 4th edn, (State Publishing House of Political Literature, Moscow: 1950), vol. 29, pp. 494-7, and 'Speech to the First All-Russian Congress on Adult Education', ibid., pp. 308-10; N.K. Krupskaia, 'The Union of Teachers and the Union of Internationalist Teachers' in Voprosy narodnogo obrazovaniia ('Questions of public eduation'), (Gosizdat, RSFSR, 1922), pp. 30-2; the 1925 Congress of the All-Russian Union of Teachers: Speech by N.K. Krupskaia, report by A.V. Lunacharskii, report by G. Zinov'ev, report by N. Bukharin, report by M. Pokrovskii, in the journal Na putiakh k novoi shkole ('On the paths to the new school'), no. 1 (January 1925); 'Teachers on new paths', stenographic report of the 1925 Congress of Teachers (Gosizdat, RSFSR), 1925 and 1932 editions.

20. These demands are contained in the sources of the previous note and in other material. They are expressed with particular clarity in Lenin's speeches 'On the deception of the people with the slogans of freedom and equality', (in Lenin, Sochineniia, 4th edn, vol. 29, pp. 293-350; in his study, 'How to organise competition' (ibid., vol. 26, pp. 367-76); in his speech, 'The tasks of the Unions of Youth' (ibid., vol. 32, pp. 258-75); in his report 'The New Economic Policy and the tasks of the political educators' (ibid., vol. 33, pp. 38-56), etc.

21. M. Pokrovskii said at the 1925 First Congress of Teachers:

> The commercial peasantry, i.e. the kulaks, was also that sector that before other rural sectors valued the progressive landowner - the zemstvo school. And under

> Stolypin's regime the kulak grew as never before. With the flourishing of the kulaks the country saw not only the primary school, technically complete as never before, but also the emergence of the rural secondary school and volost Gymnasia - pro-Gymnasia, which, from the kulaks' children, prepared the new bourgeois intelligentsia.
>
> All this 'flowering' of rural culture, parallel to the development of the private farms, could not fail to enthuse the professional cultural worker that the teacher is...

Report by M. Pokrovskii in the journal Na putiakh k novoi shkole, no.1, January 1925.

But the starving peasants of 1918-21 also did their best to save the village teachers from starving to death. It is incomprehensible why Pokrovskii put the word 'flowering' in inverted commas. He justified the fact that the teachers' work was not paid in 1918-21 by explaining that in 1921 teachers' salaries composed 20% of the former zemstvo one and that by the time the teacher had received the money for December in January, the ruble had decreased in value ten times. But the teacher did not always receive even this money, as the provincial executive committees plugged holes in the budgets of other departments at the expense of the schools. According to Pokrovskii:

> The provincial executive committees rightly considered that the militia would disband itself if not paid, the hospitals would be closed down, but the school would 'somehow survive'. The kulak would support the schools by feeding the half-starved teachers, heating the freezing schools and repairing them just as much as was necessary to prevent them from collapsing.

The 'kulak', as in all Communist propaganda and speeches (except in the first three years of the New Economic Policy) was the capable, energetic peasant or village tradesman - the intermediary between the peasant and the market.

22. 'Collection of decrees', 1st issue, p. 96.

23. The five-grade system was restored by Stalin.

24. The question of discussing assessment with parents is more complex, since the educational, cultural and moral potential of the parents has to be taken into account so that

their reaction to the failures and difficulties of their children does not lead them to punish their children. Pedagogical work has to be conducted with parents as well.

25. There are still private pre-school groups to this very day, but the vast majority operate without making themselves known to the authorities. In any event, I do not know of any private children's groups that operate openly, while the illegal ones operate everywhere. Like the vast numbers of teachers who coach slow pupils in their homes for a fee, they belong to the sphere of private services known as the 'second economy'. True, the private lessons to slow pupils and candidates for admission to institutions of higher education are occasionally given partly openly, that is the district Finance Departments are informed of some of the lessons and tax is paid. But this is the exception, not the rule. I include the children's groups and coaching lessons in the category of the 'second economy' because for the 'employers' (the parents) they are in the sphere of services, in the field of the division of social labour essential to them, while for the workers (educators or teachers) they comprise an additional, and as a rule illegal, source of earnings. However, it would be senseless for the worker to legalise all such earnings as he would immediately be placed on the same footing as 'private tradesmen' on whom the tax is disproportionately high (relative to the earnings of educators and teachers).

26. I shall return to the relation between democracy and regulation in the teaching and education process and to the concept of democracy itself as applied to schools in the conclusion to this book.

27. The same practice arose in the secondary technical schools and all institutions of higher education which began to admit the children of workers and the poorest peasants without entrance examinations or any preparation. Many teachers and scholars tried to fight this demand, in particular Academician I.P. Pavlov - see 'vstupitel'naia lektsiia v 1924-5 ychebnomy godu', in the journal Krasnaia nov' ('Red virgin soil'), no. 1 (1924) pp. 104-19 and S. Kheitman, Put' k sotsializmu v Rossii ('The path to socialism in Russia') (Omicron Books, New York, 1967). The same is happening in Russia today with the students from the underdeveloped countries who are admitted into institutions of higher education with only primary education. Marks were restored in the 1920s, but the principle of admission to institutions of higher education on the basis of social origin

and connections and not academic accomplishments survives to a large extent to this day.

28. Narodnoe obrazovanie, pp. 133-7.

29. Ibid, pp. 133-8.

30. The process which I am describing is well illustrated by V. Tendriakov's story 'Shest'desiat svechei' ('Sixty candles'), Druzhba narodov ('Friendship of peoples'), no. 9 (1980), pp. 91-155.

31. There was talk in 1956-60 of the election of school directors by the teachers' collective and some experiments of this kind were even conducted, but this undertaking was soon abolished.

32. On my arrival in a village school in 1948 I still found such school directors and directors of the teaching department of the school (deputy directors). By the time I left the village school in the early 1960s they had barely managed to acquire higher education by correspondence course. In this period, 1940s-1960s, it was the rural schools which were the most numerous schools in the USSR, with the greatest number of teachers and pupils.

33. Narodnoe obrazovanie, p. 135.

34. This point was impracticable in the pre-New Economic Policy years of hunger (1918-21) and was not restored in any school I know of from the 1940s to the 1980s.

35. I do not want to go into this question, but in his speech to the 1925 Teachers' Congress (see n. 19) Bukharin asserted outright that the Komsomol pupil had priority over the non-party teacher. He admitted that some of the Komsomol pupils (in the villages) were drunk and half-degenerate, but called them the party's reserves and warned that politically they stood above the non-party teachers.

36. Narodnoe obrazovanie, p. 136.

37. Pedocracy (from the Greek): 'the rule of children'.

38. Not only by the 'Statute' under consideration but also by the 'Programme of the RCP(b)' of the early 1920s.

39. Narodnoe obrazovanie, p. 136.

40. Dekrety (Decrees), vol. 3, pp. 374-80, in ibid., p. 137.

41. Ibid., p. 139.

42. Ibid., pp. 115-24.

43. Narkompros (People's Commissariat of Education), Moscow, 1923.

44. 'Plans and Programmes of Complex Instruction', pp. 122-4.

45. Narodnoe obrazovanie, pp. 139-40.
46. The 'project method' was akin to the 'laboratory-team method'.

Chapter Three

SECONDARY SCHOOLS UNDER STALIN

The resolution of the Central Committee of the VKP(b) of 25 August 1931 'On primary and secondary schools'[1] can be considered the beginning of a new era in the life of Soviet schools. However paradoxical this may sound, the school resolutions of the early 1930s literally saved Soviet schools from self-destruction, from the virtual futility of their work caused by the poor standard of instruction in them. The schools of the 1920s also had, of course, talented organisers and good teachers who had led their institutions and classes against the general current of chaos and non-professionalism which had overwhelmed all the schools. But these were merely the exception that emphasised the inexpediency of the whole for a country that aspired to attain the level of the industrialised Western countries of its time. These exceptions were usually found in schools where former Gymnasia teachers had somehow survived as directors and where graduates from pre-Revolutionary Gymnasia and institutions of pedagogical education worked as teachers. On the whole, however, the period in the life of Soviet schools preceding the Resolution of 25 August 1931 was marked by two incompatible features: on the one hand, there was a steady increase in ideological monism and the centralisation of the economic and administrative life of the schools; on the other hand, utter chaos reigned inside the schools: the pupils had uncontrolled freedom, all regulating principles of the pedagogical and educational processes had been destroyed by decree and there was a multitude of ill-qualified teachers who had been hastily produced by the new regime.

Nothing could be taught in these schools. Paradoxically, the schools of the 1920s, which were far more state-controlled, centralised and mono-ideological than before the Revolution, internally contradicted this centralisation (it was difficult for the authorities to manipulate the children's collective, emancipated from all obligations, and the endlessly experimenting teachers); moreover, they were not fulfilling their immediate state goal of providing well prepared cadres of future specialists, officials and soldiers. The Soviet regime needed to educate specialists who were not only ideologically orthodox and devoted to the regime, but also literate, well-grounded in the necessary subjects and professionally educated. In this sense the reforms carried out at the beginning of the 1930s were opportune, essential and (in their basic trends) became firmly rooted in Soviet schools. The later reforms of the Stalin period in particular will be discussed.

School administrators, teachers and parents were delighted by the school reforms of the early 1930s.[2] These changes brought order to the schools, defined the absolute minimum of knowledge to be learnt and committed both teachers and pupils to something definite (in the sense of general educational subjects). Teachers had some kind of curriculum and discipline to support them when faced with the unruly freedom of the pupils. Nonetheless, teachers were still just as deprived of rights, just as defenceless in the face of the state, as in 1918-20. As we saw above, pupils' and parents' collectives also lost the scope of self-government which they had had in the first decade of Soviet power, while nobody stood up for the administrators and teachers who were being subjected to repressive measures and silently removed from the schools, even though sympathy was often on their side.[3] They were automatically replaced by others who, as a rule (especially the administrators), were less qualified, and the teaching process continued on its established path determined by the state (now in the minutest detail).

The first resolution of 25 August 1931 already contained the following elements which to a large degree signalled a return to the organisational and didactic principles of pre-Soviet schools.[4]

(1) Strict regulation of the teaching process by means of the curriculum.
(2) Under Stalin the process of 'polytechnical training' was essentially removed to the background, despite the Marxist-Leninist bias (which Khrushchev would try to

revive). The task of regulating and systematising the teaching of general knowledge now came to the fore.
(3) The economic and disciplinary status of teachers was enhanced to a certain degree, while the opportunity for pure pedagogical experimentation which, as we have seen, had destabilised schools as a whole, while being useful to a few of the most gifted and highly qualified teachers and administrators, was eliminated.
(4) The limits of the initiative of pupils' organisations were strictly delineated and henceforth they would always be controlled by the school leaders (and in the class, by the class leader, i.e. the teacher responsible for the particular class).
(5) The Resolution postulated and legalised the rejection of both 'ultra-left' tendencies (the inertia of revolutionary extremism) and 'bourgeois' tendencies (the purely academic approach, political and ideological pluralism and the teacher's relative professional independence).

The Resolution of the Central Committee of the VKP(b) of 25 August 1932 'On the curricula and routine of the primary and secondary school'[5] expressed even more strongly the objectives present in the preceding one. The fact that both these Resolutions were adopted at the level not of the People's Commissariat of Education or Council of People's Commissars, but of the Central Committee of the party indicates just how much importance the latter - which was the real government of the USSR - attached to them. The idea of training literate cadres of future Soviet specialists recurs throughout the Resolution, and this time the academic (curricula and methodology) and organisational (the comprehensive supervision and control of teachers by the administration, and of pupils by the teachers) sides of school life were stressed.

These were natural tactics for a state that was becoming stabilised and aspired to industrialise and acquire modern military strength. The ideological and political sides of this control were a continuation of the trends of the preceding period and inevitable in a partocratic state system. The reference to Lenin in the first part of the Resolution was probably merely a political formality (so as not to lose the link with the great name); this resolution was one of the most businesslike ones in the history of Soviet schools. It was also epoch-making for Soviet history in general, as it was instrumental in providing the USSR with the necessary number of specialists and commanders who had both a completely Soviet world view and an adequate level of professionalism. These specialists would have neither dangerous pre-Soviet erudition in the humanities nor habits of intellectual independence and revolutionary free spirit. They would be prepared partly in time for the war and partly in time for the post-war period when they would replace the manpower which had been destroyed by the first waves of the 'great terror', lost in the war or sent to the camps. If not for this Resolution the partocracy might not have coped with the military and industrial challenges of the next two decades.

The document under discussion rehabilitated the class as the basic sub-division of pupils and by so doing played an important role in imposing the necessary order on the process of instruction and imparting Soviet political and ideological views. An equally important feature of the Resolution was its return to traditional methods of teaching: (a) the lesson; (b) the teacher's explanation of the material and homework; (c) checking and assessing the pupils' progress; (d) control of their independent work; (e) transitional and leaving examinations. State control of the schools was strengthened by this Resolution which introduced standardised and far more clearly defined forms of accountability than previously. Discipline was tightened, with pupils being made responsible to the school and parents responsible for the pupils' conduct (not criminal, but moral and social responsibility, as it were). The schools were instructed to incorporate parents in a framework of pedagogical education.

The economic and legal status of teachers was also enhanced by comparison with the preceding Resolution: the 1931 Resolution had placed teachers on an equal footing with workers (with respect to the allocation by ration cards of food products and other essentials) and not with white-collar workers, whose position had somewhat improved in the hungry years of 1931-3. The second Resolution gave the children of teachers the same rights as workers' children with regard to admission to institutions of higher education and technicums, whereas children of other white-collar workers and specialists were, in the tradition of the 1920s, severely discriminated against. This was a significant bonus which the state gave the teacher in his capacity as a junior or senior (school administrative) officer in the state's educational and ideological army. The cost of specialised literature was also reduced for teachers, although their salaries were still low compared with those of many other professionally qualified specialists.

The schools were thus regulated and firmly placed within the system of other centralised state institutions and recognised as one of the most important contributors of the state's production of specialists. These two resolutions, adopted in the years when the partocratic state was waging an extremely cruel all-out war on the independent peasants (1931-2), greatly enhanced the prestige of Soviet power in the eyes of the urban (especially the educated) population.

The Resolution of the Central Committee of the VKP(b) of 23 April 1934 'On the overloading of schoolchildren and pioneers with social-political assignments'[6] was also very symptomatic. It was a peculiar blend of state interests ('Cadres solve everything!' was the slogan in those years) and ideological interests. The ideology necessary to the state had to be provided during schooling. A number of special resolutions were adopted to this end by the USSR Council of People's Commissars and the party's Central Committee on the teaching of the humanities and social subjects: for example, 'On the teaching of civil history in schools of the USSR' (15 May 1934)[7] and 'On the teaching of geography in the primary and secondary schools of the USSR' (15 May 1934).[8] The ideology was to be provided without any deviations in any direction in all the subjects taught (even in arithmetical problems and sentences for parsing), but nothing was to distract pupils from their main task of learning, just as nothing was to increase and stimulate their individual political activity more than necessary. The ardent revolutionaries of the 1920s had to give way to the efficient, diligent and moderately active (on the school's orders) pupils of the 1930s - the future Soviet specialists and soldiers were not to be revolutionaries. It is interesting that five years later schools would be forbidden to teach the history of the VKP(b) and this subject would be taught only in institutions of higher education.[9] Pupils, including older ones, were being deliberately diverted from excessive political activity and from paying too much attention to what was happening inside the party, for in these years (1934-9) party functionaries of the first three decades of the twentieth century, and then of the 1930s too, were being eliminated.[10] Schoolchildren were not to be involved in these processes, even though, from the fifth grade, they were forced to vote for the execution of the idols of yesterday and renounce their parents.[11]

At a time of proliferating administrative documents, a Resolution of the USSR Council of People's Commissars and the Central Committee of the VKP(b) was issued on 15 May 1934 'On the structure of primary and secondary schools in the USSR'.[12] The main features of this structure would survive until the mid-1980s (after certain modifications in the Khrushchev era, which we shall discuss later). In 1984 a new reform of secondary education was announced (see Chapter 7).

It is particularly significant that this Resolution omitted any reference to 'social origin' (children of workers, peasants, white-collar workers, etc.). The need was for skilled workers with a Soviet conception of the world and the amount of knowledge necessary to perform their tasks. This was the type of person that schools were obliged to turn <u>all</u> their pupils into. Moreover, by 1934 the children of surviving members of the former upper classes had grown beyond childhood; the individual peasant farmers who had refused to join the kolkhozes (collective farms) had been exiled to the north and north-east along with their children; and the children of urban residents who had been subjected to repressive measures, enormous numbers of whom would turn up somewhat later, would mostly be sent to special children's homes (or take refuge in the homes of relatives and keep silent about their parents).

Another striking feature of this document is the increased standardisation and regulation of every detail. For example, schools were forbidden to issue any certificates of education except documents of a strictly prescribed model on special forms of which inventories were made. It was noted that schools were carrying out the Resolutions of 1931-4 too slowly and rigidly and with insufficient skill, and for this reason the directive documents issued from 1934-5 began to sound increasingly imperious and threatening.

The Resolution on the structure of schools declared that pupils could be expelled on the recommendation of the school director by a decision of the town and district Department of Education, even though they had the right to enter other schools and were not given a 'wolf's ticket'.[13]

Universal complusory primary education was introduced in 1930 and on 13 March 1934 the USSR Council of People's Commissars adopted a Resolution 'On preparations for the introduction of seven-year compulsory polytechnical education' (universal compulsory seven-year - and, from 1959, eight-year - education was not marked by a special resolution but assumed to be necessary from the end of the 1930s). In connection with universal compulsory education, at first in primary schools and from 1934 in incomplete (seven-year) secondary schools, the Resolution on the structure of schools included paragraphs which stipulated that parents should be compelled to implement the law on vseobuch.[14] Schools were set up for handicapped and difficult children, the latter being perfectly normal children showing 'anti-social behaviour', as the Resolution put it. All tests and, first and foremost, school-leaving examinations were extremely standardised:

> (6) To cease the existing incorrect practice of 'individual question-papers', in which the teacher marks beforehand different questions for each pupil and prepares the pupil accordingly to answer these questions. To ensure that in final and transitional examinations the pupils' knowledge in various sections of the curriculum is checked.
>
> The subjects for written papers in native language and mathematics for the final examinations in secondary schools are to be established by the provincial and regional (in the large towns, the city) Departments of Education and are to be communicated to the school directors well in advance. The school directors will inform the teachers of these subjects on the day of the examinations.
>
> (7) Pupils who successfully complete secondary school will be issued with a certificate which will include marks in all subjects. When passing from class to class the pupil will be issued with a transitional testimonial which will give marks for progress and conduct. Those who pass the final and transitional examinations with the best results will be awarded certificates of merit. Those who complete secondary school with the mark 'excellent' in basic subjects and a mark not lower than 'good' in the remaining subjects (drawing, draughtsmanship, singing, music, physical education) will be eligible for admission to an institution of higher education without entrance examinations, which is to be specially noted on the certificate.
>
> The schools department of the Central Committee of the VKP(b) jointly with the People's Commissariats

> of Education are to devise a single model certificate and transitional testimonial for the USSR (in the various national languages) and submit it for ratification to the USSR Council of People's Commissars.
> (8) To establish in schools the following five degrees of assessment of the pupils' progress (marks): (1) very bad; (2) bad; (3) fair; (4) good; (5) excellent.
> To instruct the schools department of the CC VKP(b) to enlist the People's Commissariats of Education of the Union republics to work out standards for assessing pupils' progress which will be compulsory for all schools in the USSR, so that the same level of knowledge will be assessed equally in all schools.[15]

It was permitted to gain a school-leaving certificate (attestat zrelosti, 'certificate of maturity') through external studies. Schools were divided into three 'concentric circles':[16] grades one to four, primary school; grades five to seven, incomplete secondary school; and grades eight to ten, complete secondary school. School regulations and rules for pupils were created and pupils' cards (identity cards) and a school uniform (which was hardly worn until the end of the Second World War) were introduced. Personal files were kept on the pupils. Stalin was conducting what might be termed a certain 'Gymnasification' of the schools.

On 2 October 1940 the USSR Council of People's Commissars issued a Resolution 'On the establishment of payment for tuition in the upper grades of secondary schools and in institutions of higher education in the USSR and on the change in the procedure for awarding stipends'.[17]

> Considering the growing standard of material welfare of the workers and the Soviet State's considerable expenses on the construction, equipping and maintenance of the constantly increasing network of institutions of secondary and higher education, the Council of People's Commissars of the USSR recognises the necessity to lay some of the expenses on tuition in secondary schools and institutions of higher education in the USSR on the workers themselves and resolves in this connection:
>
> > (1) To introduce from 1 September 1940 payment for tuition in the eighth, ninth and tenth grades of secondary schools and in institutions of higher education. ..

> (5) Payment for tuition by correspondence in institutions of secondary and higher education is to be charged at half the rate.
> (6) To establish that from 1 November 1940 stipends will be awarded only to students and pupils in technicums who have displayed outstanding progress.

The annual tuition fees varied from 150-200 rubles for secondary education to 300-500 rubles for higher education. In the chapter on the post-Stalin 'thaw' and the Khrushchev era of 1954-64 I shall describe in detail the economic significance of this Resolution for the families of pupils and for students. Here I shall merely note that in 1939-40 the Finnish War was in progress and economic conditions had deteriorated drastically: food products were beginning to disappear; there were queues; and in some places rationing was being introduced. There was a joke going around the country at the very beginning of the war: 'Nothing has happened yet, and already there's nothing. So what will happen if something happens?'

Stipends began to be awarded only to students who achieved excellent marks and the majority of students found themselves without means of livelihood - 300-400 rubles was the monthly income of many urban families. After the concern shown in the 1930s for training competent specialists, it is difficult to understand what prompted this harsh measure, especially as it contradicted the VKP(b) programme, which clearly stated that not only tuition but also clothing, food and textbooks for pupils were to be free of charge (a goal which was never realised).

Now, in retrospect, it seems that fees for tuition were introduced so that some of the older pupils would leave school and go to the army and the construction projects. It was in the 1930s that numerous military schools and secondary militarised 'special schools' for boys were opened. Tuition in the military schools was free. Many students transferred to the evening and correspondence departments of institutions of higher education and technicums and went out to work.

The following very strange and unexpected Resolution, which took everyone by surprise and was rumoured to have been personally inspired by Stalin, also contradicted the Marxist-Leninist directive on the full equality of men and women in education and at work, in the family and public life (it was published twice, as a thesis and in elaborated form. I give here the short text):[18]

> <u>On the Introduction of Separate Education for Boys and Girls in the 1943/4 School Year in Incomplete Secondary and Secondary Schools in Oblast and Krai Cities, Capital Centres of Union and Autonomous Republics and the Main Industrial Cities.</u>
>
> Resolution of the USSR Council of People's Commissars
>
> 16 July 1943
>
> Considering that the co-education of boys and girls in secondary schools creates certain difficulties in instructional-educational work with the pupils and that in co-education the special characteristics of the physical development of boys and girls, the training of both for labour, for practical activity and for the army cannot be given due consideration, the Council of People's Commissars of the USSR <u>resolves</u>:
>
> (1) to introduce from 1 September 1943 separate instruction for boys and girls in the first to tenth grades of all incomplete secondary and secondary schools of oblast and krai cities, capital centres of union and autonomous republics and the main industrial cities, and for this purpose to organise in these cities separate male and female schools (a list of the cities in which separate instruction for boys and girls is being introduced is attached);
>
> (2) to conduct instruction in the male and female schools in the 1943/4 school year in accordance with the plans and curricula of the incomplete secondary and secondary schools;
>
> (3) to oblige the People's Commissariats of Education of the union republics to complete the allocation of premises for male and female schools and the allocation of teachers and pupils to these schools by 10 August 1943.
>
> (4) to make comrades Kosygin and Potemkin responsible for implementing the separate instruction of boys and girls in incomplete secondary and secondary schools in the cities of the RSFSR enumerated in the attached list from the beginning of the 1943/4 school year.
>
> (5) Since the Council of People's Commissars of the USSR attaches great state importance to the introduction of separate instruction in schools, it

> obliges the oblast and krai executive committees and the Councils of People's Commissars of the union and autonomous republics to ensure that the present Resolution is implemented, to proffer the necessary assistance to the education organs and to submit a report to the Council of People's Commissars of the USSR by 20 August 1943 on the preparatory measures that are being taken to implement separate instruction for boys and girls.

If we exclude Stalin's personal views and whims, then this Resolution can be explained rationally only by the intention to militarise the schools as much as possible. With this I conclude my brief survey of the changes which Soviet schools underwent in the Stalin era: the process of standardisation , stabilisation and absolute centralisation of schools which was achieved in those years.

NOTES

1. Some editions give 5 September, i.e. the day it was published and not the day it was adopted.

2. In 1936 the schools would be hit by a wave of the 'great terror' and large numbers of the new administrators and teachers, especially those in the field of the humanities, would be sent to prisons and camps. The art of denunciation would be cultivated in the schools and it would be demanded that pupils from families who had been subjected to repression renounce their parents. In the purely professional sense the curve of development of Soviet schools plunged drastically, and in this state the schools entered the disastrous and tragic period of the Second World War, after which a new period of terror began - against the 'rootless cosmopolitans' - which imbued both administration and pupils with a 'Black Hundreds' mentality. But the reforms of the early 1930s survive to this day.

3. Nadezhda Mandel'shtam writes bitterly in her first book of memoirs (Hope against hope) about the indifference and even hostility of schoolchildren to the school workers who were being subjected to repression and to the pupils whose families suffered such repression in the 1940s. My memories are somewhat different, perhaps because I was a pupil in this period in one of the central schools of a large Ukrainian city where the parents of a high percentage of the pupils had been subjected to repression: we not only

wholeheartedly, although purely emotionally, sympathised with the school's teachers and administrators who were victims of the repression, not understanding why they were being punished, but we also tried to boycott those who came to replace them, although it is doubtful whether the latter realised to whose posts the Education Department had assigned them, being completely passive in this matter. We refused to answer during Russian literature lessons given by the semi-literate wife of a great soldier who had replaced our wonderful teacher, L.V. Nikolai, whose husband had been subjected to repression and who had been forced to work as a conductor on the tram route that ran not far from our school. The same happened when our first school director (whose name I do not recall, I was in grade seven) was arrested in 1937 and we tried to show our lack of respect for her successor. In any case, our sympathies lay with the persecuted.

4. Narodnoe obrazovanie, pp. 156-61.

5. Ibid., pp. 161-4.

6. Ibid., pp. 165-6.

7. Ibid., p. 166.

8. Ibid., pp. 166-7.

9. See ibid., pp. 176-7, the Resolution of the USSR Council of People's Commissars of 10 December 1939 'On the violation of the established procedure in the teaching of the history of the USSR'.

10. In 1928-32 rural schoolchildren actively participated in collectivisation. See the novels by Vasilii Grossman, Vse techet ('Everything flows') and Iuz Aleshkovskii, Ruka ('The arm').

11. As I was a schoolgirl in the 1930s (1930-40), I can testify to these documents not only on the basis of the materials which I have studied but also, so to speak, from the inside, on the basis of my personal experience.

12. Narodnoe obrazovanie, pp. 167-72.

13. The name in Tsarist times for the certificates of expulsion from a Gymnasium which did not allow admission to any other Gymnasium.

14. Vseobuch: vseobshchee ob"iazatel'noe obuchenie (universal compulsory schooling).

15. Narodnoe obrazovanie, p. 171.

16. The programmes of instruction in these concentric circles will be discussed on pp. 103ff.

17. Narodnoe obrazovanie, pp. 176-7.

18. Ibid., pp. 177-8.

Chapter Four

SCHOOLS IN THE KHRUSHCHEV ERA

> Question: What are Khrushchev's socio-economic reforms?
> Answer: The injection of medicine into a wooden leg. (Anecdote from the series 'Armenian Radio' at the beginning of the 1960s)

1. SCHOOLS AT THE CROSSROADS, OR THE ERA OF THE HUMANISATION OF THE STALINIST SCHOOL

The portraits of Stalin began to be taken down from school walls and his countless statues and busts removed from corridors and halls after the famous secret letter of the Central Committee of the CPSU of 1956 'On the cult of personality and its consequences'. It seems to me that this event was perceived in two ways: on the one hand, there was a growing sense of liberation and expectation of change, as though the weight of a heavy hand had fallen from one's shoulder after many years; on the other hand, thinking people were irritated by the servile readiness with which officials, who only recently had grovelled obsequiously before Stalin's name, hastened to carry out the new demands and throw yesterday's icons onto the scrap heap. Not everyone by far heard of the secret letter. Rumours proliferated. Children and adolescents who had recited verses about beloved Stalin since the cradle were given an object lesson in unscrupulousness and perfidy. At that time I was the director of a village secondary school. The group instructor of the party district committee who read the secret letter to us (without commentary or discussion) and who was a narrow-minded, compliant and cautious man, took down the portraits of Stalin with his own hands and put them in the store-room. The next day he assembled the teachers and said that in Russian reading lessons teachers of the first to fourth grades should replace Stalin with Lenin in the famous quatrain which all Soviet children learnt in kindergarten: 'I'm a little girl, I dance and sing, I've never seen Stalin, But I love him!' It then turned out, however, that Stalin's name appeared in many other stories and poems as well as in all the textbooks, with the possible exception of mathematics books. The instructor was at a loss and said: 'I wasn't instructed about that, but change it in the rhyme.' And they did ...

Official pressure led to increasing renunciation of the recent idol in the years 1954-61 but had nothing to do with a rethinking of experience or increased national self-awareness. For the masses of rural and urban workers and residents this was a passive change of forms of behaviour, a kind of verbal ritual carried out under pressure from without. Stalinism had so successfully crushed all independent poltical thought and civic-mindedness that the mass of people were willing to change ritual political formulae like gloves. The main thing was what 'they', the authorities, demanded and commanded. This rule applied even more to the schools than to other state institutions. The totally politicised phraseology of Soviet schools was - and is - combined with a profound inner indifference to the words uttered and with a profound lack of political interest and civic spirit of school workers. There were, of course, exceptions to this rule, but we shall return to their fate in a separate section.

The gradual retreat from deifying Stalin was combined in the schools with a reform of school legislation. At first this consisted of acts of <u>repealing</u> some of Stalin's school laws and not the introduction of new statutes, and as long as these were acts of repealing and not innovation, they passed without disturbance and were accepted as essential improvements. In general it is easier to abolish than to create something new.

Co-education, which had been abolished in city schools in the 1943/4 school year, was restored by a USSR Council of Ministers Resolution of 1 July 1954.[1] Two years later, a USSR Council of Ministers Resolution of 6 June 1956 abolished payment for tuition in institutions of specialised secondary and higher education and in the upper grades of secondary schools, which Stalin had introduced in 1940 and which had existed for 16 difficult years - before, during and after the war.[2] The first Resolution pleased the teachers, the second pleased parents. The best teachers had always opposed separate education (the less able ones were won over by the relative ease of keeping order in girls' schools). Until 1954, of course, the teachers' real opinions were heard only in private conversations among themselves. Tuition fees, however, disturb teachers less than parents everywhere: when parents have to pay for schooling, the children are more conscientious about their studies, so teachers think. Many of them assume that free and compulsory schooling drastically lowers standards in the last three grades of secondary schools of general education (this also applies to teachers in Western countries where secondary education is free of charge).

The abolition of tuition fees delighted parents and students alike, because their gain in this case was greater than is usually thought. The overall standard of living of the masses in the country in 1940-56 was so low that even a small payment for the studies of an older pupil or student was a heavy burden and sometirnes a decisive factor in his choice of a future career. Free education was one of socialism's fundamental trump cards which had always been so much vaunted in the Soviet press that Stalin's cavalier abolition of this 'conquest of socialism' had shocked even the silent society which had grown accustomed to anything in the 23 years of Soviet power. Even the programmes of the pre-Revolutionary RSDRP(b) (Russian Social-Democratic Workers' Party - Bolsheviks) had included not only universal, free education but also the provision of pupils with free food, textbooks and clothing. As we saw in the previous chapter, tuition fees consisted of:[3]

(1) in technicums and secondary schools (per year): 200 rubles in towns and 150 rubles in villages;
(2) in institutions of higher education (depending on the type): 300-500 rubles a year.
(3) in correspondence-extension institutions of education - half the rate (the Resolution prudently omitted mention of evening courses; the various institutions of higher education and technicums decided this matter individually).

Let us compare these modest sums with the population's income.

(1) Kolkhozniks were not guaranteed pay at all. Throughout the war and post-war years the vast majority of kolkhozniks (those who were not 'under occupation') did not receive money for workdays (the unit of payment on collective farms). Payment in kind was extremely meagre while the entire money payment was 'loaned' to the state.

During the time I spent as a village teacher in a 'Stalin' school (1948-55) I observed how 150 grams of wheat and about the same amount of rye were issued as 'payment in kind' for one average kolkhoz workday which was not less than a ten-hour day (and at harvest-time and in stock-raising far more). In the busiest month this could amount to nine kilos of grain per worker which did not cover his needs for bread. And what about his dependants (the old people and children), the pigs and hens, and the winter months when there was hardly any work for ordinary kolkhozniks who did not have permanent duties? In 1965, when I was working in a town, I happened to see the certificate of one of my former pupils who at that time was a student, which recorded the income of his mother who lived on a kolkhoz (he needed the certificate of income to be entitled to a stipend: in his institution of higher education stipends were given to children of 'highly paid' parents who earned more than 25 rubles per family member a month, only if they excelled in their studies). In 1964 his mother had earned in one of the huge kolkhozes of the Kharkov area an average of eight rubles a month (she earned 40 rubles a month at harvest-time but was paid kopecks for the remaining eight months). Naturally, whether the son continued his studies depended on his receiving a stipend, since it is not permitted in the USSR to work while attending the daytime department of an institution of higher education. And what if he had to pay tuition fees as well? As it was, even though he had been seriously ill as a child, he had no choice but to spend all his holidays working in the northern students' construction detachments in order to clothe himself in the winter.

The kolkhozniks paid excessive money taxes on their individual plots in addition to supplying the state with their produce. The family's entire resources had to be mobilised to pay the money tax. The ordinary kolkhoznik simply could not afford to pay for a child's schooling or a student's technicum or institute and, in addition, keep the student in the town (the beggarly stipends of 130-150 rubles a month in 'old money' in an institute and eight to ten rubles in a technicum were not enough for urban living). Village schools, however, still comprised 80 per cent of all schools, and rural families, unlike most urban ones, often had several children. This was why most young people from rural areas who intended to continue their studies went to military, fire-protection, police, etc. institutions of education, where they not only did not have to pay but were also provided with everything, including guaranteed work, accommodation and high salaries on graduation (high by rural standards). It was mostly, however, the children of the rural 'aristocracy' (or rather plutocracy, intelligentsia and bureaucracy - the word plutocracy being used in the Russian sense of the word plut = 'cheat/swindler') - chairmen, brigade leaders, storemen, machine operators and officials - who went to institutions of higher education and technicums. I am not talking about the districts near the towns where people lived from selling the produce of their individual plots at the town markets. As a rule, however, it was rural school-leavers who made up the future army and police cadres. Moreover, a privileged rural stratum was being created: the parents were 'country bumpkins' while the children were specialists with specialised secondary and higher education who frequently did not return to the villages. The parents tried to save them from their own fate at all costs.

(2) The minimum salary for white-collar workers in those years was 300 rubles in the towns and 200, later 250, rubles in the villages (there was no minimum pay for peasants). Kolkhozniks did not receive old-age or (non-military) disablement pensions, while ordinary workers and white-collar workers (except former officers, scholars and those entitled to special pensions) received a pension of 150 rubles a month after working the full number of years. It is therefore evident that a low-income family with only one wage earner who had to pay for the tuition of one older pupil had to live a month without income, a pensioner's family two months, and so on.

As previously shown, the Resolution of 2 October 1940 had made stipends in institutions of higher education and technicums the exclusive privilege of students with excellent marks. The fund for stipends had been drastically reduced, and a student could always be given a 'four' instead of a 'five', especially one who had come from a rural school (even a good senior pupil in a rural school is usually not as good as his average urban counterpart as the quality of teaching in the villages is far lower and the schools' resources poorer). At that time teachers in institutions of higher education and technicums had begun to complain among themselves that they were being subjected to administrative pressure not to increase the number of students with stipends and not to give too many 'fives', since the stipend fund was not large enough.[4] From 1956, however, students who failed were virtually the only ones who were not eligible for a stipend, while students who received excellent marks began to be given larger stipends (about 20 per cent higher than the usual one).

The rejection of tuition fees and the increased number of stipend-aided students were perceived by the public as a real, practical democratisation and humanisation of the educational system, which these measures indeed were, as they eased the situation of the majority of low-income rural parents and extended the opportunties for the children of these population groups.

2. KHRUSHCHEV'S INNOVATIONS IN THE FIELD OF SCHOOL EDUCATION; THEIR ECONOMIC FEASIBILITY AND PEDAGOGICAL VALUE; THEIR PLACE IN KHRUSHCHEV'S STATESMANSHIP AS A WHOLE

Venture No. 1: The Boarding-School Boom

The period of Khrushchev's school reforms began very clearly with the 'Resolution of the CC CPSU and the USSR Council of Ministers on the organisation of boarding schools' of 15 September 1956.[5] When discussing the resolutions connected with boarding schools, we should not forget the main functions of Soviet schools in general. Like all schools, their goals were bound up with the very existence of a human society which changed over the years in accordance with the changes in the general situation inside the USSR and in its foreign relations. Sometimes, if the state had a particularly urgent need for skilled workers with secondary specialised and higher education, the schools would be encouraged to send their pupils to continue their studies in institutions of higher education and technicums. When there was a sharp increase in the competition for admission to these institutions, this indicated that the number of students who wanted to continue their studies exceeded the number of places which were planned approximately according to the need for specialists. Moreover, in periods when most pupils were being sent to institutions of higher education and technicums, the need for workers and other employees in industry and agriculture without specialised education increased. Since Soviet schools are purely state, centralised institutions, their orientation and goals depend primarily on the demands of the authorities. In the situation described above, the schools rapidly re-oriented themselves to preparing their pupils morally and, as far as possible, with the appropriate curriculum, not to continue studying in institutions of higher education and technicums but to go and contribute to the national economy. This, of course, led to a contradiction: despite all the demagogic claims that secondary education is essential to both the worker and the collective farmer and that it helps them in both their professional and their social life, the interest in studying would immediately decline, as the industrial and rural workers do not really have any need, professional or social, for secondary education, either in the USSR or anywhere else in the world. This is especially apparent in the light of D.M. Bardin's data: 46 per cent of workers in the USSR are employed in auxiliary, storage, loading and unloading and repair work 'which is performed mainly manually'.[6] In 1985 the figure of 40 per cent for manual workers appeared in the Soviet press and we shall return to this point below.

Apart from these functions of education which, with certain reservations, are common to many countries, Soviet schools have one further objective which never changes: to form the 'Soviet man', i.e. a citizen with the Soviet type of social behaviour and Soviet ideology. We constantly use this cliché 'Soviet ideology' and I do not intend to discuss it in detail here, especially as I have not yet described the specific methods of educating Soviet schoolchildren in the Khrushchev era. However, in order to understand the boarding-school experiment which was embarked upon in this period, I have to give a brief description of the concept 'ideological upbringing' and I shall do this with the aid of Soviet fiction. In 1956 the journal Novyi mir ('New world'), nos. 11 and 12, published a story by Liubov' Kabo V trudnom pokhode ('On a difficult march'). The author was a literature teacher in the upper grades of a secondary school and knew what she was writing about very well. I shall return to her literary work and pedagogical views and quests in the section on the teaching community in the 1950s and 1960s. This story has several very vivid portraits of school teachers and administrators, including a very likeable secondary hero (who is by no means among the worst in his profession), a former front-line soldier who, in a moment of bitter self-analysis, comes to the conclusion that he always acts as though his mind and conscience are firmly under the command of 'someone else'. This 'someone else' is outside his consciousness and superior to his own will and, though not named in the story, is unambiguously defined by the context: it is the party leaders who devise binding directives on everything - world view, conduct, curricula and other professional matters - and bring them to the teacher through the administration of the education organisations. 'Soviet ideology' regardless of its actual content, course and nuances at any particular moment, assumes first and foremost unwavering conformity to the directives of the highest party centre at any given time. For each individual the will of the centre is embodied in the party, Komsomol, administrative, academic, military etc., superior who is closest to him.

When Khrushchev mentioned schools in his speeches to various fora and for various reasons, he often drew a parallel between the military schools, institutes for daughters of the nobility and other pre-Soviet private institutions of education on the one hand and the boarding schools which were being opened in the USSR, on the other. He saw the parallel in the fact that both the former and the latter were deliberately class institutions of education, the former of the nobility, and the latter belonging to the working classes. The former had existed in order to raise children in the 'reactionary' ideology of the monarchy and the nobility, while the latter were being established in order to imbue children more successfully and fully with the 'Marxist-Leninist', 'Communist', 'Soviet' ideology, to form the builders and future members of the Communist society. Khrushchev explained that this was done more easily and better in the boarding school than in the family, because there were still various kinds of families in the Soviet Union. Thus, the boarding schools were not only to promote better education, tuition and upbringing, but also an even more completely unified ideology.

I certainly do not suspect Khrushchev of having read Plato or Fourier, and I fear that he had hardly read Marx either. Nonetheless, the desire to separate children from their families and raise them in state institutions is characteristic of all literary centralist or tribalist conceptions and has been present in Communism from its origins. Centralist or tribalist thinking, whether on paper or in real life, naturally aspires to subordinate education as completely as possible to the criteria and goals of the state centre or tribal assembly which stands above the individual. Although centralism and tribalism (democracy by popular assembly) are to a certain extent opposed to each other,[7] they are equally opposed by the so-called 'small groups' that give the individual some support in his opposition to the dictates of the centre or assembly. The family is one of the most important of the 'small groups' in a society divided into families, as it forms the primary foundations of character, the deepest source of world view and the elements of a person's consciousness which are imbibed along with the rituals of family life in the pre-critical phase of development of his reason and attitudes to the world and other people. The desire to protect children as early as possible from the formative influences of the family (or at least to counterpose equally strong influences to them) is therefore natural for Plato, ancient Sparta, the utopian socialists, Marx, Soviet power and even the Israeli kibbutzim.

As long as Stalin's successors were content to abolish some of his innovations, they achieved some results. When, however, they began to reconstruct and introduce something new, they immediately came up against insuperable difficulties. Many reasons could be given for these difficulties, but two reasons were decisive:

(1) Serious reforms required large capital investments, but under Khrushchev the Soviet economy did not alter its basic principle of absolute state monopoly and did not become more productive.

(2) A profound re-organisation of education demanded the re-thinking of a number of fundamental principles of Soviet life, and even under Khrushchev the party did not retreat from the principle of the absolute ideological dictatorship of the Central Committee.

Without the necessary additional capital investments, for which there were no sources, and without permitting the mass of people connected with schools to re-think the basic principles of their work and goals, the reforms were doomed to become either a fiction or a brief diversion on an unswerving path.

According to Khrushchev's original declaration, by 1965 the boarding school was to become the 'main form' of secondary education in the USSR, incorporating 2.5 million schoolchildren[8] as opposed to 180,000 at the end of the 1956/7 school year. According to official data, however, in the 1959/60 school year there were 33.4 million pupils in general education schools, and in 1965/6 43.4 million pupils were attending mass day-schools of general education. Thus 2.5 million pupils at the end of 1965 were approximately 5.7 per cent of the total and were far from the majority. But we pay so little attention to official pronouncements that this figure was never seriously examined and, at a wide variety of teachers' and non-teachers' conferences, millions of people seriously discussed the transformation of boarding schools into the 'main form' of secondary education by 1965.[9] In reality, the aim was fairly modest: to admit to boarding schools within nine years about six per cent of those pupils in general education secondary schools.

It was quite clear, however, even in that first Resolution of 15 September 1956 (see part 1, paragraphs (c) and (d) quoted below)[10] that there would be no reliable financing of the proposed construction of boarding schools, since there was a constant demand to economise on other financial investments in capital construction. Meanwhile, the latter was the smallest item in the Soviet education budget and it was impossible to squeeze anything out of it for construction by economising.[11] This meant that from the outset it had been calculated that the project would be financed by sponsors[12] or the local Soviet organisations and organs, but their budgets were also too strained to enable them to economise on other items and scrape together the means to construct boarding schools which cost millions of rubles.

According to data of the Central Statistical Board, the number of pupils in primary, incomplete secondary and secondary schools increased from 1960 to 1965 by ten million or approximately 30 per cent of the number of pupils in 1960. In the same period expenditure on all kinds of general education schools, including schools for adult education and correspondence-extension schools, grew by 2.5 million rubles, or approximately 70 per cent of the 1960 level. In other words, the increase in investments in education was apparently more than double the increase in the number of pupils (in percentages). Capital investments, i.e. in construction, comprised only an insignificant proportion of this increase - around 4.5 per cent.[13] It was senseless to open boarding schools without capital investments: the construction of a model boarding school cost six times more than an ordinary rural school (I discovered these figures during my struggle to build a new school in 1956-62).

The budget, however, hardly provided for any increase in capital investments in school construction: out of an overall increase of 5,333 million rubles[14] in investments in all education throughout the country from 1960 to 1965, only 231 million rubles were allocated to capital construction. It was only to be expected that from year to year party and government resolutions stressed more and more the need to take the money for school construction and repair, for equipping workshops, subject rooms (kabinety), laboratories, teaching-experimental, sports and meteorological grounds and other needs of polytechnical education from other departments quite unrelated to the budget of the Ministry of Education.

These are the relevant paragraphs of the first Resolution of 15 September 1956 'On the organisation of boarding schools'.

> Part 1.
>
> (c) additional building for hostels and auxiliary premises in accordance with the plan of development of the network of boarding schools is to be financed not out of the funds allocated to the construction of school buildings but from special allocations for housing construction and other purposes;
>
> (d) the adaptation and extension of buildings for hostels and other premises for boarding schools are in 1956 to be financed out of the total amount of capital investments established by the Councils of Ministers of the union republics and also by economising [on other items of] the republics' budgets ...
>
> (3) To recognise the necessity of enlisting ministries and departments in the construction of boarding schools.
>
> The ministries and departments are to implement the construction of boarding schools by means of the construction organisations subordinate to them at the expense of their own resources and funds.

I should like to stress the point that the 'ministries and departments' were to 'implement the construction of boarding schools' not with the aid of specially allocated additional funds but by 'economising'. In practice, however, nothing compelled or stimulated them to economise from their eternally over-stretched budgets. From the outset the entire project came to depend not on funds specially allocated to this purpose but on ever-problematic and impracticable inter-departmental charity. Moreover, there were high hopes for revenue from the schools' own subsidiary farms and workshops[15] (see parts 5 and 6 of the same Resolution). The following resolution is exhaustively precise on this subject:[16]

> On the ratification of the Statute on the Boarding School
> Resolution of the RSFSR Council of Ministers
> 13 April 1957
> The Council of Ministers of the RSFSR resolves:
>
> (1) to ratify the attached Statute on the boarding school submitted by the RSFSR Ministry of Education.
> (2) to add a list of the special funds of institutions maintained by the budgets of the autonomous republics and local budgets (appendix no. 2 to the RSFSR Council of Ministers Resolution of 11 November 1953, No. 1373) in a paragraph with the following content:
> Sources of special funds:
> '... the boarding schools' income received for pupils' work in workshops, subsidiary farms, enterprises and on kolkhozes.'
> Destination of special funds:
> 'To cover the boarding schools' expenditure on improving the nutrition, daily and cultural needs of the pupils, on extending study workshops and subsidiary farms and also on incentives to the pupils.'

Tuition fees were also to cover some of the expenses of maintaining the boarding schools. This calculation, however, was also not justified from the outset, and the contradiction already existed in the following paragraphs of the 1957 'Statute on the boarding school':[17]

> (9) Children shall be enrolled into boarding schools exclusively upon the wish of their parents or of persons taking their place.
> (10) Boarding schools shall admit in the first place children of single mothers, war and work invalids, orphans and also children whose families do not have the necessary conditions for raising them.
> Parents shall pay for their children's upkeep in a boarding school an amount depending on the parents' wages in accordance with the established rates.
> Full state provision shall be made for children who

> do not have parents and also in certain cases for children from families with many children and families in poor circumstances, according to a decision of the town and district Soviets of Workers' Deputies (in the children's place of residence).

All this would appear logical, but the fee for keeping a child in a boarding school came to 25 per cent of the family's income. These figures were not published but were not - and could not be - concealed from anyone who worked in schools or educational organisations.[18] The government was planning that the boarding schools would include children from well-to-do families, who would pay a large sum for their child, along with children who would not be paid for. However, for a number of reasons - the high fees, poor nutrition (60-90 kopecks per day per child depending on age,[19] which meant that children in boarding schools, like patients in the general hospitals, never had enough to eat unless they were sent extra food from home),[20] the mediocre and frequently very poor quality of instruction and education, the reluctance to part from their children, etc. - only in extremely rare cases did well-off families send their children to the ordinary boarding schools financed only by the educational organisations. The ordinary boarding schools became filled with orphans and children with one parent or from poor families and difficult children with complicated characters and histories.

The absence or small number of paying pupils increased the financial burden on the state. Willy-nilly, they became more like children's homes (orphanages)[21] than boarding schools and placed orphans in a difficult situation, especially in the best schools of the central cities where there were many children with homes to go to. On days off, national holidays and school holidays the school kitchens and canteens did not work and the staff had a rest. The children without families were left alone, on dry rations. Unlike the children's homes, the boarding schools did not provide all the children's clothing, relying on the families as well, not to mention such 'trivialities' as pocket money for inevitable personal expenses and transport which was not provided for in the boarding schools' budget. Adolescent girls of 15-18 were not given brassieres or other female accessories and wore the standard, factory-made children's clothes. In short, the usual poverty of the children's homes was aggravated for the orphans, first because the boarding schools' budget did not provide for their needs and second, because of the constant contrast with children who had parents. This was partly remedied only by the commercial initiative of directors of boarding schools, which led to abuses on the part of some of them and to the authorities finding fault with all of them.[22] The situation was better only in boarding schools which were constantly subsidised by their own sponsors and organisers: the Novosibirsk Physics and Mathematics School and similar schools in Moscow and Leningrad. The only advantage which orphans gained from being transferred to boarding schools (but a very important one) was that there was far less tyranny and cruelty on the part of the educators in the latter than in the children's homes, and the criminal terror waged by the older children against the younger ones, so widespread in the children's homes, did not exist.[23] Nonetheless, the orphans were still constantly reminded of their misfortune in comparison with children from normal families, and this could be somewhat mitigated only by a very good team of educators (a rarity, as everywhere).

The boarding schools were many times more expensive than ordinary schools because of the need for living accommodation, kitchens, service complexes, etc., because the staffing needs were quite different (educators, service and technical staff, additional administrators) and because of the food and clothing. As mentioned above, the cost of building a boarding school was six times as much as that of a rural secondary school, while it took ordinary schools years to obtain funds not only for building but even for decent repairs because of the shortage of materials and lack of resources. Major repairs were approved and provided with funds and materials only when the buildings were on the verge of collapse.

On 26 May 1959 the CC CPSU and USSR Council of Ministers published a document entitled 'On measures to develop boarding schools in 1959-65'.[24] Compared with Khrushchev's speeches on this subject and the intention he expressed in 1956 to make boarding schools the 'main form' of secondary education, this document was extremely modest: the intention here was only to have 14 times as many pupils in boarding schools by 1965 (i.e. to bring the number to 2.5 million, as stated above) 'so that in the future all who so desire will be able to educate their children in these schools'. It stressed that orphans brought up in the boarding schools should be given all the 'privileges established for the wards of children's homes when they are sent to work and for a period of instruction in institutions of secondary and higher education'. The following recommendation in this document was very symptomatic:

> It is recommended that the CC of the Communist parties and the Councils of Ministers of the union republics examine and decide, taking into consideration local conditions and possibilities, the question of gradually re-organising children's homes into boarding schools in the course of 1959-65.[25]

In practice this meant that two forms of education - without the family and outside the family - would be amalgamated, and this was achieved at the end of the 1960s when the vast majority of boarding schools were closed down and the remainder (with a few exceptions, such as the Physics and Mathematics Schools and other special schools) turned into children's homes in the guise of boarding schools, after which the interest which the press and pedagogical institutions had evinced in them died down. The same document emphasised that:

> The CC CPSU and the USSR Council of Ministers have approved the initiative of advanced kolkhozes which have built boarding schools at their own expense. It is proposed that the CC of the Communist parties of the union republics and the oblast and krai committees of the CPSU support and propagate this valuable experience in every way possible and that the Councils of Ministers of the union republics give kolkhozes the necessary assistance to build boarding schools and organise the sale to the kolkhozes of building materials and equipment for this purpose.[26]

To sell the kolkhozes materials and equipment so that they could build <u>state</u> boarding schools, whose establishment was decreed by the <u>state</u> and every detail of whose life was dictated by the state, certainly conformed to the spirit and style in which the state treated the kolkhozes. When something is taken from the kolkhozes, they are regarded as organisations subordinate to the state, but when they are <u>given</u> something, they are regarded as independent co-operative societies and therefore nothing is 'given' free of charge: everything is <u>sold</u> to them, even the schools which were attended not solely by the kolkhozniks' children (the Departments of Education sent other children to the boarding schools, often from far away). They are even sold the education and medical services which the rest of the population receives free of charge,[27] as hospitals, too, are built with their help.

The collapse of the 'boarding-school boom' of 1956-8 is expressed even more clearly in the RSFSR Ministry of Education Order of 27 July 1962 'On measures to improve the work of boarding schools and for more economic expenditure on their upkeep'.[28] As we can see, the very title of this Resolution expresses the aim of lowering the cost of Khrushchev's penchant for indulging in hare-brained schemes. It was quite obvious to us, who observed the boarding-school saga in the flesh, so to speak, that the number of boarding schools was being reduced under the guise of amalgamating them: '(1) To implement measures to amalgamate the existing small boarding schools by 1 September 1963 in order to create eight-year and secondary boarding schools with the full complement of classes'.[29] The smallest boarding schools were those built by the kolkhozes and their 'amalgamation' meant that boarding schools for the entire district and even for several districts of the oblast would be established in these buildings.

The insistent demand expressed in paragraphs 2 and 3 of the 1962 Order to increase the role of the boarding schools' subsidiary farms and workshops came just before the curtailment of their independent financial activity in 1963-6. There is no contradiction here: on the one hand the schools and education organisations were interested in the revenue from these sources, while on the other hand the Finance Ministry, the Council of Ministers and the CC were afraid of the development of commercial initiative. The KRU (Control and Auditing Directorate) and OBKhSS (Department of the Struggle Against the Embezzlement of Socialist Property) and other 'supervisory organisations' stressed the abuses connected with this initiative (known to be undesirable in Soviet conditions). It was unavoidable that in this conflict victory was won neither by the schools nor by the Departments of Education.

The need to economise and increase the aid of sponsors and parents was again stressed in this 1962 Order. The following words will mean nothing to a reader who is not familiar with the real situation: 'The Planning and Finance Directorate and the Main Directorate of the schools are to make provision in the annual economic plans for a broader development of extended-day schools and groups'.[30] This, however, was an indication that a new and far more viable and practical system was being introduced of admitting to schools children who, after lessons, remained most of the day outside the control of their working parents. It was a signal for the boarding school to be ousted by the extended-day school. The extended-day groups were (and are) attended mostly by children of grades one to eight (especially one to four) who, under the teachers' supervision, prepared homework, went on walks, ate and played until five and six o'clock in the evening. They were given one meal which had to be paid for, but was cheap. The fee for attending an extended-day group was not high. Parents are very willing to use this form of occupying their children in the time after lessons, and for the teachers this was additional employment which paid no less than regular teaching work and demanded much less responsibility: there was hardly any responsibility for the pupils' progress in these groups. There is no doubt that the system of extended-day classes which triumphed in the 1970s signified the increased realism in the organisation of school affairs after Khrushchev in comparison with Khrushchev's wild ventures.

The following paragraphs of the Order are also of interest:[31]

> ... The Council of Ministers ...
>
> (c) has established that children who live with their families can attend boarding schools, in which case the fee for their upkeep is reduced by 5 per cent;
>
> (d) has introduced from 1 September 1962 new norms of issuing and lengths of time for wearing the various kinds of clothing, footwear, soft stock [i.e. bedding etc.], according to the appendix;[32]
>
> (e) has established that parents can be exempted from payment for their children's upkeep in boarding schools in full or up to 50 per cent only in exceptional cases by a decision of the executive committees of the Soviets of Workers' Deputies of the districts and towns on whose territory the boarding school is situated, within the limits of no more than 25 per cent of the number of pupils with parents.[33]

The following Resolution of the RSFSR Council of Ministers of 27 April 1963, 'On the further improvement in the work of boarding schools and extended-day schools and groups',[34] openly unites the three forms of raising children outside the family: the boarding school, extended-day school and extended-day group. As is always the case in Soviet 'bureaucratese', 'further improvement' means that things are going badly and that what follows will point to significant errors and failures and make fresh demands. The following statistical gambit is also worth noting: it combines the boarding schools and extended-day schools and groups in the same index, pointing out the 'significant work in developing the network of boarding schools and extended-day schools and groups and in improving the organisation of instruction and upbringing of the pupils in them. At the present time about one million children are being educated in these schools and groups'. As we may recall, in 1956 it was stated that boarding schools were to become the 'main form' of general education schools, and in 1959 that the number of pupils in <u>boarding schools</u> was to reach 2.5 million by 1965. In 1963, there were, however, 'about one million children' in boarding schools and extended-day schools and groups <u>taken together</u>. Thus, in the style legitimised by Soviet bureaucratic tradition, one policy or paragraph of the authorities is silently replaced by another. A policy which has failed or which has not justified itself is gradully ousted by new formulas which at first co-exist with it. The new Resolution urged economy and cuts in expenditure on boarding schools. This was no longer merely a matter of 'self-service' (cleaning and maintenance performed by the pupils), but also of the pupils making their own clothes and growing their own food (and this was just before all the independent farming and commercial activity of the schools was beginning to be cut, restricted and banned). This is how the shortcomings of the boarding schools were interpreted in the Resolution:

> In a number of autonomous republics, krais and oblasts, the extended-day school network is being developed slowly and work on amalgamating small boarding schools is being conducted poorly.
>
> The organisation of labour instruction and education of the pupils in many schools continues to be unsatisfactory. Many boarding schools do not have joiner's, metal or sewing workshops, while those that do

> have workshops do not make sufficient use of them for the sewing of underwear and outer clothing by the pupils. Too few subsidiary training farms have been set up. The positive experience of schools that provide for their own needs with vegetables, potatoes, milk, meat, which they receive from the subsidiary training farms, has not been widely disseminated.
>
> In many boarding schools the necessary measures on the economic expenditure of funds have not been taken.
>
> ... excesses in the acquisition of equipment are tolerated and the rules for preserving material values are violated. The full and punctual payment by parents for their children's upkeep is not ensured. In 1961 non-payment of fees came to about four million rubles in the RSFSR and in 1962 the plan has also been considerably under-fulfilled.[35]

And finally there is a paragraph which can only mean that this is a veiled order to curtail the entire boarding-school venture:

> (2) To permit the Councils of Ministers of the autonomous republics, the krai and oblast executive committees and the Moscow City Executive Committee to use the buildings which are being constructed for boarding schools for extended-day schools, special and general education schools and children's homes.[36]

This means that in 1963 the state had already rejected the idea of boarding schools, i.e. when Khrushchev was still in power. An enormous amount of resources had been wasted on opening them, which the mass of teachers had viewed with hostility from the outset: the (comparatively) luxurious equipment of the model boarding schools had stood in sharp contrast to the extreme poverty of most of the rural schools and many of the urban schools. Even in the mid-1970s 80 per cent of Soviet schools were located outside the boundaries of towns. The overwhelming majority of them were crammed into premises not intended for that purpose without even the absolute minimum of living space, equipment or educational aids. Moreover, the expenditure on the boarding schools was not limited only to material resources, which in any case are at the disposal of the Ministry of Education or Social Security. The work of pedagogical faculties, the Academy of Pedagogical Sciences, institutes of advanced training, pedagogical newspapers, journals, publishing houses, the methodology departments of the educational organisations, teachers' conferences and commissions on methodology had been largely devoted to this ill-founded venture since 1956. Dissertations, articles and books had been written about it, careers had grown round it, and lances had been broken over it in discussions whose inertia was felt for a long time after the signs had appeared that the boarding-school boom was being curtailed. All this had cost money, work hours and the strength and nerves of the numerous people connected with it, who suffered yet another disillusionment over the possibility of achieving any meaningful change by means of their own work and personal energy in the object to which that energy was applied - the Soviet school.

Venture No. 2: The Transition to a New System of School Education

This period officially began with the publication on 29 December 1958 of a Resolution of the RSFSR Council of Ministers 'On the eight-year school, the secondary general education labour polytechnical school with production training and the evening (shift) secondary general education school';[37] a detailed 'Statute' on these types of schools was published on 26 December 1959 ('By resolution of the RSFSR Council of Ministers').[38] Two years later, following the pattern we have already seen in the boarding-school saga, another document appeared: 'On improving the production training of pupils of secondary general education schools' (Resolution of the RSFSR Council of Ministers of 30 May 1961).[39] In the history of the polytechnical schools, this document was analogous to the Resolutions 'On the measures to develop boarding schools in 1959-65' (26 May 1959) and, even more so, 'On measures to improve the work of boarding schools and for more economic expenditure on their upkeep' (27 July 1962)[40] published by the CC CPSU and the USSR Council of Ministers.

As in the first case, the initial Resolution was distinguished by its broad sweep and its confident and categorical tone combined with the grandiose changes it introduced. The second one, two to three years later, had quite a different tone: a restrained evaluation of progress made, emphasis on grave shortcomings, and a considerable retreat from the previously projected 'revolution'. In each case the need to economise and seek funds outside the education budget was stressed. Finally, in both the boarding-school and the polytechnical reforms, came resolutions that signified a shamefaced rejection of the radical changes announced so sensationally and which had entailed such outlays. In the former case, this was the Resolution of the RSFSR Council of Ministers of 27 April 1963 which gave clear preference to the extended-day schools and groups which it reviewed in the same breath as the boarding schools; in the latter case, this was the Resolution of the CC CPSU and the USSR Council of Ministers of 10 August 1964 'On the change in the period of instruction in secondary general education labour polytechnical schools' which restored the ten years of schooling (previously extended to eleven) in secondary day schools.

Khrushchev was removed in October 1964, and the Khrushchev period in the development of Soviet schools can be seen as having ended legislatively on this date. I emphasise the word 'legislatively' because the inertia of that era would still be felt in schools, as in other spheres of Soviet life, for quite a long time to come.

Before examining the above Resolutions, we should note that the following pattern of Soviet decision-making processes applies not only to the Khrushchev era or Khrushchev's school reforms: a grand declaration of intent (as if to strike the most decisive reforming 'blow') -------> a gradual slowing down and curtailment of reforming operations (the sovereign palm, raised to deal a crushing blow, strikes thin air or becomes bogged down in a bottomless mire) -------> a secret rejection of the authorities' project -------> the launching of a new campaign (as though the old one had never existed). I exclude from this pattern the fields of foreign expansion and state security, external and internal: the decision-making of Soviet rulers in this sphere is governed by other laws and stimuli; but the pattern is very characteristic of the fields of national and social life.[41]

When we compare the Resolutions on boarding schools and polytechnical schools, we can see the same desire to have the construction of expensive school study-production complexes financed by the enterprises and institutions of the district in which the schools were located (including kolkhozes) and not by the state. Similarly, the kolkhozes, enterprises and institutions were themselves obliged to provide this polytechnical instruction for the pupils. On the one hand:

> Secondary general education labour polytechnical schools with production training may be opened only if appropriate school premises and a base for the pupils' production training and productive work are available and if educational equipment and other resources can be provided and the newly opened schools can be provided with teaching and leading staff with higher education.[42]

On the other hand, responsibility for providing these conditions was laid on organisations which had nothing to do with education and which knew that their own ministries and central directorates* (and even the party organs) would be concerned that first they carried out their usual assignments, and only as a last priority take care of educational needs. The heads of organisations and institutions inevitably included the schools among their least important business. Exceptions were made only under the influence of personal contacts and interests, most frequently for schools attended by children of 'powerful' parents. As director of a rural secondary school, I fairly frequently came up against this unbreachable indifference to the problems of schools on the part of these managers who were overburdened with their own unresolved problems. They were not impressed by the obligations enumerated in the Statute on 'creating suitable conditions for the pupils' vocational training and productive labour'.

Moreover, the Statute's declaration of these obligations was not accompanied by a parallel legislative formulation of the financial relations between schools and enterprises or organisations. Nor was any change made in the legal procedures which regulated the enterprise's or organisation's use of their financial and material resources, while the

---

* Central directorate = the department of a ministry that controls either the branch of industry falling within the competence of the ministry or establishments in a particular area - tr.

existing procedures left no room for schools and their needs. Moreover, the actual needs of polytechnical training - with regard to materials, financing or even curricula - were not defined by law or elaborated. A new form of very complex (financial and other) relations between schools and production, two spheres of social-state life which until then had been almost unconnected, came into being. The system in which it arose was, and still is, based on the strict centralisation and formalisation of every kind of financial and economic activity of state institutions. Such a far-reaching innovation, without any concomitant or, even more important, preparatory regulating measures, only compounded the sense of confusion in this ever-increasing disorder.

The 'Statute' also listed the physical requirements of these schools, specifying the rooms and equipment to be available. The schools in which it fell to my lot to implement this Resolution, like the overwhelming majority of rural secondary schools, even large ones (ours had 600 pupils, which was quite large for a village), did not have any of the material and technical resources for polytechnical training enumerated. The 'special funds' (were these special accounts of the schools or budget allocations, which I certainly never saw throughout the years of the polytechnical saga?) and the ability to be self-supporting appear only as the result of workshops and farms that already exist; but how were they to be set up? As for subject rooms the rural schools and many of the old, cramped urban school buildings simply had nowhere to put them and no money to equip them. A couple of cupboards containing some equipment would be installed, and tables and wall charts hung in the first available classroom and this would be called a subject room. Things were different in the new urban model schools which did have subject rooms, even though of very varying standards.

Just two years after the 1959 'Statute' had been brought into effect, a Resolution of the USSR Council of Ministers, 'On improving the production training of pupils of secondary general education schools' (30 May 1961), contained such paragraphs as the following:

> (d) To oblige the State Committee on Vocational-Technical Education of the USSR Council of Ministers, the Ministries of Education of the union republics, the Ministry of Communications, the RSFSR Academy of Pedagogical Sciences to work out and publish by 1

> August 1962 programmes of production training in schools for the most common and leading occupations, model programmes for certain groups of less common occupations, and also to establish procedures for compiling programmes in the provinces on the basis of the model ones; to select, in conformity with the above programmes, the best available manuals on training workers in the most common occupations, to rewrite them according to the needs of the secondary schools and to publish them in 1962-3 in large editions, and also to prepare and publish by the same date the study manuals that are lacking.[43]

Meanwhile, polytechnical instruction had been in progress, in some places since 1959, in others since the 1957/8 school year, without curricula or textbooks and in subjects selected by the schools or the district Department of Education.

> (14) To charge the State Committee on Questions of Work and Wages of the USSR Council of Ministers, jointly with the USSR State Planning Committee, the USSR Ministry of Finance, the State Committee on Vocational-Technical Education of the USSR Council of Ministers, the All-Union Central Trade Union Council and the RSFSR Ministry of Education to prepare and submit within two months to the USSR Council of Ministers proposals on the remuneration of workers in the training-production workshops of secondary schools and also on the necessary changes in procedures of remuneration of engineering-technical workers, other specialists and skilled workers who are being enlisted to conduct production training and practical work with pupils of grades nine to eleven of secondary schools.
>
> (15) To establish that the numbers of skilled workers, engineering-technical workers and other specialists employed in the production training of pupils of grades nine to eleven of secondary schools in enterprises, construction projects, sovkhozes and other organisations, and the funds from which their wages are to be paid, are to be included in the work plans of these enterprises, construction projects, sovkhozes and other organisations.
>
> The sums spent by enterprises, construction projects, sovkhozes and other organisations on the wages of these workers shall be paid by the secondary

> schools out of the funds provided for in the estimates of these schools.
>
> The wages of the agronomy and technical personnel of kolkhozes enlisted for the production training of pupils of grades nine to eleven of secondary schools shall be paid out of the funds provided for in the schools' estimates.[44]

The 'schools' estimates', however, do not even cover the bare minimum of the schools' own expenditure on 'polytechnical education' or their own compulsory lessons in the theory of the vocational subjects chosen by the school, let alone funds to compensate enterprises for their expenditure on training pupils. In this case, too, the lessons and practical training in production had been in progress since 1959 at least, while it was only in May 1961 that a directive even mentioned the forthcoming elaboration of an estimate of the outlays on these lessons.[45]

This Resolution reflected another important aspect of the polytechnical training that Soviet schools tried to carry out in the period 1958-64 which, for the sake of convenience can be called: polytechnical training and the subsequent vocational self-determination of pupils; the school and social production. This document clearly expresses the ambition to put an end to the chaos and lack of co-ordination in the schools' teaching of the various vocational occupations. The contradiction underlying this ambition goes much deeper than the mere lack of co-ordination between the vocational structure of polytechnical training and the needs of the industry in the school's district for specialists with secondary education who have been through a course of this training. To a large extent this contradiction applies to all the developed countries which aspire to expand general secondary education and, ideally, extend it to the entire rising generation. Nonetheless, the content of that secondary education is usually the same as when relatively few pupils attended secondary schools with the aim of going on to higher education (or, if they had another source of income not connected with an educational qualification, of simply acquiring a high school certificate). In the developed industrial countries of today social prestige and status are connected with higher education.[46] Secondary education formally entitles the pupil to seek admission to an institution of higher education, but the need for specialists with higher education is extremely limited even in the most highly developed countries. The following table indicates the situation in the USSR with regard to the population's level of education.[47]

Table 4.1: Changes in the educational structure of the population from 1959 to 1970 (in % of the total population over ten years of age)[a]

	1959	1970
Completed higher	2.3	4.2
Unfinished higher	1.1	1.3
Secondary specialised	4.8	6.8
Secondary general	6.1	11.9
Incomplete secondary	21.8	24.1
Unfinished incomplete secondary and primary education	63.9	51.7
Total population above 10 years	100.0	100.0

Note: a. Calculated on the basis of Narodnoe obrazovanie v SSSR (Public education in the USSR), Moscow, 1972, p. 36.

In the period between the two population censuses of 1959 and 1970, the number of people with higher education increased from 3.8 to 8.3 million. The largest increase in this period was in the number of people with secondary general education - from 9.9 to 23.4 million. Even with this fairly low level of educational qualifications (without comparing it to the underdeveloped countries or nineteenth-century Russia which Soviet sources give as the standard to this day):

> 70-80 per cent of boys and girls who finish secondary schools aspire to higher education, while the percentage of parents who desire them to have higher education is even higher. According to our calculations, about 18.2 per cent of the total number of graduates of secondary general education schools in our country were admitted to institutions of higher education. Consequently, the population's needs for higher education are only partially satisfied at the present time.[48]

The attempts to satisfy these needs by expanding 'informal post-secondary education' are fruitless, because from among all the kinds of 'post-secondary' education (not higher, not secondary specialised nor even incomplete higher edcuation) only a certificate from typing and shorthand courses holds out the hope of finding a job in these occupations.

> In recent years the people's universities have begun to play a significant role in providing informal post-secondary education in the USSR. In the period 1965-9 their number increased more than five times and their students more than three times. A large number of students in the people's universities acquire knowledge in the field of culture (literature and art), teaching, law and medicine. In order to satisfy the great desire of young people to learn foreign languages and of girls to learn shorthand and typing, state fee-paying courses in foreign languages and shorthand and typing have been set up.[49] [My emphasis.]

The point is that the 'population's needs for higher education' are not being thwarted by someone's ill will or even by inefficiency, but by the actual structure of employment, the actual need of the country's economy for a particular educational qualification of its citizens. In this case, errors in planning and 'voluntarism' play an extremely insignificant role compared with this need, and all Khrushchev's talk about achieving universal secondary education in the USSR within the following five to seven years was an example of the purest kind of voluntarism. However, the actual structure of employment in Soviet industry presented the following picture of the educational level of the most common categories of workers even in the post-Khrushchev era (data for 1972):

> A system for the instruction of young workers is being developed. It should be borne in mind that, despite the huge increase in the population's general educational level, until now 41.2 per cent of workers have education below incomplete secondary education of six grades. Most of them have not yet been involved in evening instruction.[50] [My emphasis.]

Among agricultural workers the educational level is even lower than in the towns, but this is only natural. If, at the beginning of the 1970s, about 50 per cent of workers in Soviet industry were employed in unskilled manual labour, in the sovkhozes this figure was 75 per cent and in the kolkhozes 80 per cent.[51] Given this employment structure, do the state, society and the large majority of the workers objectively need a high educational level for the entire population, especially as the present forms of secondary education are designed with a view to higher education? (I shall return to this problem in Chapter 7 on schools in the 1980s).

I should now like to discuss briefly the actual content of the term 'polytechnical education' and its historically evolving interpretation in the Soviet (Marxist-Leninist) education system. Although this may seem to be a digression into a field extraneous to our subject, this is not the case. It should be borne in mind that Soviet schools exist in a state which is saturated with ideology. From the outset the founders of this state intended - and then attempted - to govern it according to a definite goal - the construction of socialism and later Communism. In order to achieve this goal, they had to create a 'new man', a term that appears in the very first writings of Marxism. The idea of the poly-vocationalisation of the 'producer', that is, the 'new man' is as fundamental to 'scientific Communism' as the idea of the 'elimination of classes'.[52] Now, when all that remains of Marxism in its widest application is mostly its political slogans and not its basic principles, the following is usually overlooked: Marx and Engels assumed that the techniques of production and communication in their time, the nineteenth century, would enable the division of social labour into management and execution to be abolished. Thus, Engels wrote in his book Socialism: utopian and scientific that the abolition of classes

> becomes practicable, not by men understanding that the existence of classes is in contradiction to justice, equality, etc., not by the mere willingness to abolish these classes, but by virtue of certain economic conditions. The separation of society into an exploiting and exploited class, a ruling and an oppressed class, was the necessary consequence of the deficient and restricted development of production in former times.[53]

Or, as he wrote in The housing question:

> It is, therefore, the law of division of labor that lies at the basis of the division into classes ... But if, upon this showing, division into classes has a certain historical justification, it has this only for a given period, only upon given social conditions. It was based upon the inefficiency of production. It will be swept away by the complete development of modern productive forces.[54]

> As soon as the productive power of human labour has risen to this height, every excuse disappears for the existence of a ruling class. After all, the ultimate basis on which class differences were defended was always: there must be a class which need not plague itself with the production of its daily subsistence, in order that it may have time to look after the intellectual work of society. This talk which up to now had its great historical justification, has been cut off at the root once and for all by the industrial revolution of the last hundred years.[55]

Later in the same work Engels writes about the necessity and possibility (with the level of development of forces of production in the nineteenth century!) of forming producers for the new society (i.e. the direct creators of the material product in the most varied fields of production) who would simultaneously engage in 'such general social matters as management of labour, affairs of state, justice, science, art, etc.'[56]

The term 'polytechnical education' occurred in the speeches and writings of Lenin and the educational leaders of his time literally in the very first days of Soviet power. Stalin, with his characteristic political pragmatism, removed this fiction from the agenda without polemics or declarations (he did not argue with Marx). It was only natural that Khrushchev, who once again started talking quite seriously about building Communism, would also begin to talk about *poly* (= multi)-technical training. Communism needed people who were capable of doing 'everything' (in theory, of course, or, more precisely, in a profoundly literary sense, as all this had very little to do with science). Otherwise, how were the divisions of social labour which gave rise to classes to be removed, and the classless society with its 'new man' - the universal producer-manager - to be built? However, these divisions of social labour were not only not eradicated by 'the industrial revolution of the last century' (i.e. the nineteenth), in Engels' words, but neither by the scientific-technological revolution of our twentieth century, which did not eliminate the division of society into governing and governed in any sphere of social life. It not only failed to eliminate occupational specialisation within each of these two fields (management and production) but, on the contrary, intensified and diversified specialisation. *Poly*technical education instructed us Soviet school teachers, school leaders at all levels and the scholars and production workers connected with schools to engage in the rapid moulding of the 'new man' for the Communist, i.e. classless, society which Khrushchev promised to the 'new generation' (Lenin had promised it to the younger generation, Khrushchev promised it to the entire generation).

At the 1960 All-Russian Congress of Teachers, after announcing the USSR's fabulous economic victories which, his audience was to understand, had been achieved under his brilliant leadership, Khrushchev said:

> We are now resolving two historical tasks - the creation of the material-technical base of Communism and the formation of the new man. This is essentially a single process. If we lag behind in educating and forming Soviet people, the entire building of Communism will inevitably be delayed ...
>
> The most important thing in the restructuring of the school is to combine instruction with socially useful productive labour and to strengthen the educational (vospitatel'nyi) work of the school. The struggle for the victory of Communism requires the all-round harmonious development of the Soviet man. And this means not only to master the sum total of scientific knowledge on nature, technology, society, but also to learn to use this knowledge practically for the direct participation of labour in Communist construction.[57]

But by then, in 1960, it was already clear that, only two to three years after all the talk, writing, experiments, conferences, dissertations and other forms of wasting time and money connected with polytechnical training, the venture of forming 'the all-round harmonious' 'new man' who had mastered the 'sum total of knowledge on nature, technology, society' and was also capable of 'using this knowledge' directly for 'Communist construction', was doomed to failure. There arose instead a kind of ugly hybrid of general secondary education and elementary, superficial, narrow vocational education. Although it had seemed that the schools, which were disastrously short of enough time to teach even their general curriculum, had been given an extra year of instruction, in fact this year had been added not for polytechnical training, but for narrowly technical and very primitive vocational training. Even in Khrushchev's speech to the 1960 Congress of Teachers, underneath all the bragging, buffoonery and demagogy, underneath all the stirring declarations about the 'new' 'harmonious' man who knew and could do everything, another aim could be discerned: to orient shcoolchildren not to higher education but to production. To be more precise, some pupils were, of course, to continue their studies in institutions of higher education. In particular, the 'production' training in the few privileged schools with a bias towards physics and mathematics and a few others was of a high enough quality to assist the future students and specialists with higher education: these schools had classes in computer programming, accounting, shorthand, typing, etc. The ordinary schools, however, taught only the most common and primitive occupations. This gave rise to a paradox which we have already mentioned: future students had no use for the trades and skills of the plasterer, bricklayer, locksmith, seamstress, lathe operator, crop grower, tractor driver, livestock specialist, etc., while the future workers and collective farmers, employed in the most primitive, routine kinds of labour, had no use for general secondary education.

The orientation referred to above (directing the majority of school-leavers towards production and not higher education) was also hinted at in Khrushchev's following comments made at the same Congress:[58]

> We are all delighted by the work of schoolchildren in the numerous pupils' production brigades, training farms, in enterprises, kolkhozes and sovkhozes. It's a good thing for schoolchildren to produce a socially useful product.
>
> But the labour of pupils is important not only in itself, not only for its product. The main thing is to use the production studies in a correct and all-round way to educate in the young a love of labour for the common good.
>
> The schools should foster in their pupils the ability

to work collectively, that is, in the final account, the ability to live and work in the Communist way. [Prolonged applause]

Remember what Vladimir Il'ich Lenin said about Communist labour in 1920. He stressed that it is voluntary labour, without norms, labour rendered without expecting a reward, labour according to the habit of toiling for the common good, labour as a need of the healthy organism. This is the kind of labour that we should prepare our children, our young for! [Applause]

Life has shown that involving schoolchildren in productive labour does not lower the level of their general educational training at all. On the contrary, with correct guidance, the schoolchildren begin to have a more responsible attitude to their study obligations. The experience of life and production which they have acquired helps them to master the fundamentals of science more profoundly, more consciously. The school should help the young boy and girl to determine their vocation in life, to find a place in our toiling family.

Unfortunately, not all parents and teachers by far understand correctly the significance of education for choosing a profession, for labour activity in which the very meaning of life lies. Many are quite unable to renounce the old views of secondary education and consider that the obligatory result of such education should be some command post, even a minor one, but a commander's, or a 'clean', 'easy' job.

Some people argue 'what does a milkmaid need trigonometry for, and a metal worker and electrician biology?' In their opinion, you don't need much education for physical labour and, consequently, it's not worth troubling children with science if they're not guaranteed a place in an institution of higher education.

This is absolutely wrong. I recall a friend of my youth, Pantelei Makhinia. He was a miner and used to read a lot. In the old days a miner's work was exhausting, hard labour. In those days people had the following idea of the usefulness of studying: studying to be a doctor's assistant was useful as you'd make people better, or to be a foreman-miner ... was also useful. So when they saw Makhinia with a book - and he was always reading - they used to say 'Pantelei's studying to be a foreman-miner or a doctor's assistant'. And

Makhinia would laugh: he wasn't studying to be a doctor's assistant or a foreman-miner - he was studying in order to acquire knowledge, in order to know the meaning of life better. [Applause]

Both the milkmaid and the shepherd need such knowledge. I ask you not to be disrespectful towards the occupation with which I began my labour activity. [Applause] And a worker in any work in which he is placed needs above all knowledge, with knowledge life is easier and happier.

To oppose labour to learning is an aristocratic, not a worker's attitude to education. This is essentially a distortion of the idea of the re-structuring of the school.

... Over the past three years thousands of boys and girls with secondary education have poured into the oblast's[59] kolkhozes and sovkhozes. And so what? It turns out that a knowledge of physics, chemistry and trigonometry has come in very handy to milkmaids too.

The high educational level of the new intake has had a very convincing impact on the oblast's successes, on the increase in the productivity of labour.

... I once had the great satisfaction of visiting a kolkhoz and talking to a pig tender. You remember how this occupation used to be regarded? They used to say, 'look what she's come to, she's become a pig tender'.[60]

In our time notions have changed completely. You can be talking to a pig tender and she'll tell you that she's in the third year of a livestock institute. You can be talking to a milkmaid and she'll tell you, 'I'm graduating from an agricultural institute'. Another time you can be listening to a talk by a team or brigade leader and you'll be delighted with what good and practical knowledge of farming the man has. And you'll be told that he's graduating from an agricultural institute and works on the kolkhoz. Just look what times have come, just look what we've come to! [Loud applause]

It is difficult for Khrushchev with his extremely 'non-theoretical mind' and more than modest cultural level to perceive how graphically he refutes his own argument: all those pig tenders, milkmaids, team and brigade leaders who had been prepared for chatting with him[61] were completing their higher education for the sole purpose of raising their social status. I remember very well how difficult it was for graduates from the school which I headed in the village at that time to work in the kolkhoz. In those days we still believed that it was at least to a certain extent possible to make kolkhoz work and life more civilised and we seriously gave the children both elementary knowledge of the fundamentals of agricultural production and, most important, an honest attitude to their obligations, a sense of duty. The result of all this was that not a single one of our best graduates who had had experience of the school's animal-breeding farm, experimental nurseries, market gardens, accounting, etc. was able to remain on the kolkhoz. For the majority of rural and urban schools, however, 'polytechnical', i.e. production, training was just another fiction, just another fake government campaign which, as always, begins with a thunderous, officially inspired 'nation-wide' commotion and ends with the silence of the grave.

3. THE TEACHING COMMUNITY IN THE YEARS OF KHRUSHCHEV'S REFORMS

In the 1950s, long before the beginning of the 'thaw', the agonising problems which complicated the purely professional side of school life were discussed officially, semi-officially and unofficially. The last wave of Stalin's Terror was directed against those strata of the Soviet population which eked out a bare existence in the depths of the country and the district centres. In these places it was pointless to stir up an 'anti-Zionist' commotion, and reverberations from the 1948-53 purges of the top party leadership were practically unfelt there. For the villages, all these matters existed only in the newspapers, which were little read. This was why people talked to each other somewhat more freely in 1949-52 in the remote areas of the country than in its centre.

March 1953 was a boundary, a turning-point in my personal life as well. At that time I was in an oblast hospital for TB patients where I spent the chaotic days after Stalin's death (coinciding with my thirtieth birthday) and where I felt in full measure the difference between the rural and urban realities of Soviet life. Rural life, for all its hardships and poverty, was spiritually freer than urban life. It was less distorted by the disinformation that saturated every pore of urban life. It was not flung from one extreme to another by the lopsided semi-education which is an inevitable result of this disinformation. Having lived this life during my most active years (from age 25 to 40), having worked in four villages and visited many others, having associated with colleagues at a great variety of district and oblast conferences, and having maintained some of my village contacts up to the second half of the 1970s, I cannot consider my experience fortuitous. I can therefore state that the broadest strata of Soviety society, which in those years resided in the villages, do not have either the positive or the negative features which it became fashionable to attribute to the present-day Russians or the eastern Slavs as such. These people do not suffer from the morbid xenophobia of those who speak in their name. They have no craving for a Master, nor yearning for a strong hand, having suffered from the strong hand more than anyone else. Their cognitive mode is inductive, not deductive, and they have a very wide field for induction. I therefore encountered evaluations and thoughts in the opinions of my rural friends which filtered through to narrower circles much later. Thought that is not constrained by ideological directives or by a traditional, deductive, a priori criterion, that is not subordinated to biased judgement or a particular ritual; a generally benevolent disposition towards strangers, a realistic approach to events, an inner standpoint expressed in few words, without the posturing of a malcontent, and an ironical approach to all verbosity - these characteristics, in my view, make the villagers, in particular the older generations (the young people leave the villages early and most of them, unfortunately, fill the ranks of the administration and semi-educated strata of society) akin to the best part of the intelligentsia. It was no accident that my closest rural teacher friends, who still belonged to the hereditary, pre-Revolutionary intelligentsia and had by some happy chance survived in the village, mostly found their friends among the older generation of villagers. This section of village society formed the focal point and fullest expression of the popular type in our century of a priori ideological stereotypes of thought and standard reactions derived from the schools and instilled by the mass information media. Among these people who have not suffered from superficial education, the communal element of thought has weakened considerably, while the official element was never strong. Consequently, the individual, empirical element of reactions and attitudes to people has remained stronger than categorical prejudices.

It was probably all these considerations that intensified my surprise at the hysterical reaction to Stalin's death on the part of people in the towns. There were many war invalids with pulmonary diseases in the clinic where I was being treated. TB patients in general are highly emotional, and during the days after Stalin's death, a mass psychosis of loss developed. The reaction to Stalin's death of the former soldiers and some of the patients, who mostly resided on the fringes of towns and industrial areas, was such as to make the Jewish doctors and patients shrink in horror. It was difficult and painful at that time for Jewish doctors to work with the 'Doctors' Plot'[62] hanging over their heads. Their patients blamed them for everything: the advance of the disease, the lack of medication,[63] the overcrowding and understaffing in the hospital, the fact that they (the Jewish doctors) were relatively numerous. It did not occur to these patients that the Jewish staff had not enjoyed any preferential treatment on being admitted to the medical institutes and that they had been drawn to medicine only by the age-old tradition of their people, which other ethnic groups of the population did not have. They were also criticised for their desire and willingness to treat seriously ill, infectious patients with hypersensitive reactions. I, who was accustomed to the respect accorded the decent doctor and attentive teacher in the villages, whoever they were, found this undercurrent of emotions stunning, frightening and overwhelming. The rehabilitation of the 'doctor-murderers' was the first breath of fresh air in this suffocating atmosphere. But I became completely at ease only when I returned to the village, to a district that was new to me and to a new school. Later, I frequently experienced this physical and emotional tranquillity on alighting from the train and walking through a field, along a dirt road, among a crowd of commuting workers and kolkhozniks returning home from the town. In the village there were no hysterical reactions to Stalin's death and the subsequent events, but rather an attitude of guarded expectation. As early as 1954 a number of measures were carried out which eased the kolkhozniks' situation. But even at that time the sigh of relief was checked by distrustful waiting. Teachers were no exception, although the range of matters discussed with friends became broader. It was most likely at that time that I became convinced that the concepts of intelligence and education, culture and education are not identical. This could be seen in my colleagues too, as well as in our pupils and the people around us. The lack of education, which was felt particularly keenly and was almost insurmountable in the 'intelligentsia' of the first Soviet generation, was plainly seen when the average teacher was compared with the few surviving members of the hereditary provincial intelligentsia about whom I wrote earlier and whom I shall always be grateful to have met. But this lack of education did not preclude civilised feelings and acute perception, and was supplemented by moral experience. No breach occurred between members of the old intelligentsia and their local colleagues who had been born in the villages. The conversations in teachers' rooms, at home and even at district conferences on teaching methods (at the latter, especially after 1953) were rich in content, and franker than in urban schools where I also had many friends.

What, then, were the questions which agitated the district and rural teachers on the threshold of Khrushchev's reforms? First and foremost, the impossibility of imparting to the pupils even the narrow and limited knowledge which the teachers themselves considered essential and which was required by the curriculum of primary and eight-year schools. I emphasise 'which the teachers themselves considered essential' because the level of education, maturity and professional knowledge of the rural teachers themselves (who make up the great majority of the teaching body) was extremely low. In the first place, in the early 1950s there were still many unqualified teachers in the villages and even in the main district towns a few dozen kilometres away from the main oblast town - and the further away, the more unqualified teachers there were; secondly, the qualified teachers had usually graduated from the correspondence departments of pedagogical technicums (colleges for training primary teachers) and institutions of higher education where the education received was almost negligible (unless they worked by themselves on their own initiative and as they saw fit, their degrees were meaningless). Thirdly, the main contingents of rural teachers-by-correspondence had come to the technicums and institutions of higher education from the same villages that they later worked in, from the same poor and crowded schools without subject rooms and with pitiful libraries, from the same intolerably hard semi-peasant life. The huge reserves of industriousness, conscientiousness, ability and experience remained unexploited because of their overall low cultural and professional level. This was painfully obvious to the few who possessed an extraordinary will to develop or who had come to the villages and rural district centres from another environment or had survived there as relics of the old provincial intelligentsia. The local teachers themselves noticed the difference between themselves and the latter, and the more able ones would often try to help their colleagues. But most rural teachers had no time to develop culturally and professionally on their own. Not only did they have to contend with the hardships of family life in the villages, but they were mercilessly overloaded with party, kolkhoz and village council 'assignments' - propaganda, agitation anti-religious activity, subscriptions to state loans, helping in the fields and vegetable plots and conducting various government campaigns (even to the extent of taking part in collecting taxes and payment in kind from the kolkhozniks' individual plots).

Although I could relate many anecdotes to illustrate the low level of education among the teachers, I shall merely note here that the mathematics teachers found the problems in the examination papers sent by the oblast Department of Education difficult to solve (the entire group of neighbouring schools was usually covered by the few teachers, known to everyone in the surrounding area, who were able to solve such complicated problems). They also had great difficulty in solving problems of the higher grades, not only those sent by the district Department of Education, but even those in the textbooks. Help would come from colleagues and sometimes from capable older pupils or from young specialists who would visit the villages on their holidays (the new town dwellers who had left the village for ever but frequently came to visit relatives there). During the 15 years I worked in the village, in which period I changed schools four times and worked as both deputy director and director of a school (eight years in all) and as an inspector of the district Department of Education (not on the permanent staff) for my group of schools, I do not recall one instance when all the teachers of a school I was inspecting wrote without mistakes the test dictation sent specially for them, or coped easily with the test mathematical problems. These tests for teachers were carried out whenever the inspectors sent to check out a school by the district or oblast Departments of Education came across an intolerably low quality of lessons, errors in the pupils' exercise books that were constantly overlooked, wrong corrections or the inability of most of the pupils to cope with the inspectors' assignments. In these cases the teachers would be tested, but what measures were taken after the tests? Thunderous orders would be written, people would be reprimanded; if the teacher's educational documents were in order, he would be obliged to 'raise' his professional and ideological standards immediately; if he did not have the appropriate education, he would be obliged to take a correspondence course of studies. Sometimes, if there was a replacement for him, he would be transferred to lower grades or to a more distant school, but usually this was impossible. It became possible only in the second half of the 1950s, when the districts which were closer to the large towns began to become saturated with qualified teachers. In the remote peripheries of the country, however, the situation has not changed to this day.

Nonetheless, even these inadequately educated teachers were keenly aware of the impossibility of imparting their knowledge to their pupils. The following three reasons were usually given for this: (1) universal education; (2) the notorious 'protsentomaniia' (percentage-mania), i.e. the demand made on the teacher to achieve a high percentage of successful pupils and to reduce the number of bad marks given, or better still, not to give any; (3) the cyclical structure of the curricula, which meant that there was never enough time to learn the material.

Today, when enlightened people throughout the world are fighting fiercely for universal compulsory secondary education, an examination of the Soviet experience might prove very useful. Although in the 1950s universal compulsory education was extended only to the seven-year, and later the eight-year, school, the teachers regarded even this as a scourge which hampered their work. Universal incomplete secondary education had been made compulsory in the second half of the 1930s. The RSFSR Council of Ministers Resolution 'On the state of universal compulsory education in the schools of the RSFSR' was published on 21 December 1939.[64] As this law was not carried out in many places, in July 1943 a Resolution[65] of the RSFSR Council of Ministers ratified an instruction 'on the organisation of the registration of all children and young people from eight to 15 years old and on the procedure of control over the implementation of the law on universal compulsory education' (in September 1943 this was extended to children from seven to 15 years).[66] The instruction stipulated that children of school and pre-school age be registered with long-term considerations in mind. All areas were divided into micro-districts and an army of teachers was engaged in registering each child in the micro-district assigned to each teacher. The lists of children were submitted to the schools, and by the schools to the district Departments of Education and the local Soviets of Workers' Deputies at the end of August-September of every year and were corrected (by the teachers themselves) in December-January of every year, a job that took up most of the January holidays. The corrections were immediately transmitted by the schools to the above authorities. The teachers compiled the lists by surname with a mass of data, and the teacher was responsible to the school, district Department of Education and Soviet for each child in his micro-district, a responsibility that was shared by the class teachers. The school's administration was responsible for all of them to the district institutions, and the latter to the oblast authorities. The pupils' surnames remained at the district level and only figures were transmitted to higher levels. Responsibility flowed downwards and its full weight fell on the exhausted, overworked teacher, worn out by his everyday burdens and never-ending 'social' work. It is hardly necessary to mention that the teachers were not paid a single kopeck for their efforts. If a pupil left school before the seventh (and later the eighth) grade and was not found to be mentally defective by a special oblast commission (as far as I can recall, among the village schoolchildren only downright idiots were ever found to be sufficiently defective), the teacher was obliged to issue a certificate stating that the pupil was entering another institution of education that provided incomplete secondary education: another day school, college, a correspondence or evening school, a children's home. The teacher was charged with the duty of carrying out educational work with the pupil who had left school and with his parents in their home in order to force him to continue his studies. Pupils who 'dropped out' were often quite incapable of doing that because of neglect, backwardness (according to the mental norm) or simply because they were too old (a pupil who repeated a year several times could reach the age of 15 without having gone further than the fourth grade). They already lived, worked and drank like adults but continued to be the responsibility of the teacher, the school and the district Department of

Education.

One solution was the evening schools and classes and the advisory centres of correspondence schools whose pupils were eligible to take the examinations of the seventh (eighth) grade and which were being opened in the large rural schools and the main district towns. The 'drop-outs' were hurried through courses, the tests were written for them, the problems solved with them, their mistakes corrected, they were allowed to rewrite everything several times over, and were finally crossed off the list as having received incomplete secondary education. Some of these youngsters, once they had grown up, settled down, got married and acquired the skills of a rural technical occupation, but who still, as we used to say, made four mistakes when writing a three-letter word, would go to correspondence-extension technicums. They had learnt their trade by practising it, and a degree was just a piece of paper that sometimes meant higher wages or made them eligible for a more responsible position, which was even more dangerous ...

The teachers thought that if they could only give bad marks and expel from school all those who deserved it, the position would improve: only those who wanted to learn would remain in school, the path to improvement would be closed to the rest, and gradually everyone would begin to study. But this was not the case. The need for universal incomplete secondary education for modern man and modern society can hardly be disputed, but it seems to me (and this opinion is shared by many of the colleagues I had during my 29 years of pedagogical work) that this form of education is badly designed. Incomplete secondary education (which it would be more appropriate to define as complete primary education if it is compulsory for all) should optimally:

(1) arouse in the child a sustained interest in learning, reading and culture in its various manifestations;
(2) teach how to learn, with the help of a teacher and independently;
(3) instil in the child and young person moral and ethical principles of individual and social conduct;
(4) give the adolescents who leave the school a fund of scientific and cultural knowledge, abilities and skills which would allow some of them to learn over different periods of time the specialities, professions and kinds of activity that interest them

and which do not require higher education, and others to continue their studies in secondary schools where they would be prepared within three or four years for admission to institutions of higher education.

(5) Admission to secondary schools should be by examination, as in a number of Western countries and in the Russian Gymnasia before the Revolution.

There is no need in complete primary schools to overwhelm the pupils with factual information and huge quantities of detailed scientific knowledge. At this level there is a need for the more fundamental, general and difficult elements of upbringing and education which determine the ethics, intellect and goals of the individual. Instead, Soviet schools were dominated by a cyclical structure of courses which did not allow most of the pupils to learn properly any of the courses of any of the grades, despite the fact that the teaching process is more regulated, the pupils more disciplined and the teachers more demanding and more tied down by their work (in school, outside school, at home) than in the average Western school.

What then was this cyclical structure of education to which teachers were so opposed in the 1950s? How did it arise and what form did it take?

Between the 1930s and the 1960s the complete school programme in the USSR was divided into three cycles: grades one to four; grades five to seven (and later eight); and grades eight to ten (later nine to eleven and then nine to ten). This division into cycles apparently arose because until the mid-1930s only four years of schooling were compulsory. The authors of the first stable school curricula tried to squeeze into this primary education as much fundamental (in their view) knowledge as possible. Incomplete secondary and secondary education were later added, stage by stage, to this basic structure. Aware that most pupils would not go on to a complete secondary school, the authors of the curricula of the seven-year (eight-year) school tried to squeeze into it both a broader and a deeper version of the course in the first four grades and a simplified, superficial and condensed version of as much as possible from the course of the upper grades. The ambition of fitting a basic overview of almost the entire course of incomplete secondary education into the curriculum of the first four grades could still be excused in the first two decades of Soviet power by the need to eradicate illiteracy in older pupils and adults. Hence the aspiration of including as much general educational material as possible in the course. This may have been justified in the case of older pupils and adults: adults with a mature, if untrained, mind may have a poorer memory than children but they do have a better understanding of complex material and a better ability to learn it. For children, however, this approach was completely unproductive, despite the belief that 'repetition is the mother of learning', especially repetition which deepens and broadens the material learnt. In practice, however, this belief proved to be an irremediable error on the part of teachers. A person learns nothing in a neutral way. What has been learnt becomes, as it were, woven into the fabric of consciousness, becomes part of it, 'germinates' in a person's practical work, in his habits and way of thinking. What has been learnt can be deepened, broadened and improved, it can be extended and new habits can be based upon it, but it is extremely difficult to change it retroactively, to erase it from consciousness and replace it with something entirely new. The younger the child, the more deeply he assimilates what he has learnt, for in childhood (especially in early childhood) information is assimilated not so much by reason, which is still immature, as at more profound and subjective psycho-physiological levels: emotional, motor, etc. In order to improve a habit or concept which has been formed at such deep and conservative levels, action must be directed towards reinforcing, rather than changing it. However, the most frequent result of instruction using an overloaded, over-concentrated curriculum in the first four years was wrong habits, reflexes and concepts which had to be broken later by the subject teachers (in grades five to ten/eleven) and not the class teachers (grades one to four), just as a surgeon breaks fractures which have knitted wrongly in order to join the bones together anew.

We seriously underestimate the teachers of the first four grades, those encyclopedists who bear the most difficult and responsible task of any school: that of laying the foundations of interest in learning, of the desire for knowledge, of giving direction to thought and character, of forming the pupil's methods of work - in short, of laying the qualitative foundations of the personality which is being instructed and formed (which is instructing and forming itself). Only one, even more important, group of educators is valued less - kindergarten teachers. The attitude of society and the state (throughout the world) to these professions largely explains the reluctance of talented young people to work in them.

I shall give as an example of the cyclical structure of Soviet education the Russian language course with which I am most familiar (as the reader will recall, I am discussing the curricula of the 1950s and 1960s, before the new curricula were introduced). This entire course was 'done' very rapidly (and superficially) in grades one to four and confirmed bad habits of writing and speech. The situation was particularly serious in the national schools, especially in rural areas, where Russian was introduced only in the second grade to children who either had a poor practical knowledge of the language or none at all, but where it was taught using the same methods and the same amount of material as in the Russian-language schools. The result was that pupils were still semi-literate and still made mistakes in both the written and spoken language when they entered the fifth grade. The children of nationalities who did not use Russian in their everyday life suffered the most. The language teacher in grade five found himself in the position of the surgeon in my earlier analogy, and there he stayed until the end of the course. He had to erase old habits (and it is impossible to learn a language without habits) and create new ones, and this was impossible since there was simply not enough time: as in the first four grades, new subjects followed one another in a constant stream and the course which had already been mutilated once by this haste, was rushed through again, while the gaps in knowledge piled up and failure was added to failure. As a consequence, the pupil lost faith in himself and interest in learning, while the teacher lost patience and hope. Thus an impasse was reached which could only just be overcome by the endless, free, supplementary lessons for backward pupils which every Soviet teacher of language or mathematics conducted in his free time (for hours every day). However, the aim of these supplementary lessons was not to help a pupil achieve a satisfactory knowledge of the subject but to 'cram' him so that he could scrape through the examinations or termly tests with a 'three' ('satisfactory' mark).

The teachers proposed abolishing this cyclical structure in grades one to eight and making the curriculum strictly sequential, so that there would be time for more thorough, meaningful instruction. This extra time could be created by removing the necessity of correcting wrong habits and of battling with firmly rooted wrong 'knowledge' (in supplementary classes or in time 'stolen' from the curriculum and meant for new material - to the detriment of that material). As we shall see below, however, the actual reforms of this era not only failed to solve this problem but even failed to show any official concern for it.

Two conflicting trends can be discerned in the discussions and reflections by teachers on the future of the school which, as the 1950s progressed, became more frank and widespread: a 'majority' trend, among the average teachers, and an 'elite' trend, among the best teachers and schools. All were unanimous in their opposition to the 'percentage-mania', but the first, more powerful, group of teachers was mainly concerned about the lack of time for teaching the existing traditional school curricula, while the second group was also concerned about the inadequacy of the very material prescribed by the curriculum. It was primarily the teachers of the natural and exact sciences, and not the humanities teachers, who complained that the curricula themselves were too narrow, conservative, incomplete and out of touch with contemporary scientific knowledge. This was probably because the school course could not reproduce an adequate picture of the world without giving some notion (if only in principle) of the revolutions which had taken place over the previous fifty years in the natural and exact sciences. On the other hand, in order to teach pupils to speak correctly in their native tongue or a foreign language, to write correctly and to express their thoughts clearly, all the while remaining within the boundaries of the very clearly defined supreme ideological and aesthetic criterion (it was impossible to do otherwise in the humanities), it was hardly necessary to draw upon the latest achievements in structural linguistics or academic literary criticism. Teachers of history and literature rarely disputed or discussed changes in the literature courses of the different grades or a serious revision of the history course, outside their closest circles of colleagues, as these matters were rarely a matter of indifference to the authorities.

In this sense, there could be no serious liberalisation. One experiment I know of to devise and implement a completely new curriculum in Russian literature was carried out with the help of the Kharkov philologists I. Gol'denberg and V. Pertsovskii and developed specially for the

Novosibirsk School of Physics and Mathematics. It ended tragically, despite the support of influential Novosibirsk academicians, liberals and free thinkers. A teacher and some pupils signed one of the letters circulating in samizdat at that time either in defence or in support of dissident writers. Gol'denberg, one of the best teachers of Russian literature whom I have had the fortune to hear, was deprived of the right to teach for ever. Two or three of his closest pupils went through a court trial, imprisonment and even a psychiatric clinic. They were only saved by those same ties with Novosibirsk members of the USSR Academy of Science.

The potential flaw in the new school curricula which began to be developed in the 1960s can be traced to the divergent interests of the majority and elite groups of teachers and the enormous gulf between them in education and interests: among Soviet teachers there were and are people who were capable of devising the most interesting and diverse curricula, but among the majority of teachers, because of their mostly low level of education[67] and general culture, there were not enough people who could teach these curricula satisfactorily. I well remember how, at the end of the 1960s and beginning of the 1970s, teachers (particularly in rural schools) complained that the new curricula and textbooks were too complex and difficult for the pupils. I remember equally well the stories of my friends and acquaintances in Kharkov, Moscow, Novosibirsk, the western Ukraine, Perm and Petropavlovsk (teachers and workers in pedagogical departments of universities, scientific research institutes, institutes for the advanced training of teachers, etc.) about how the majority of teachers could not cope with the new biology, language and mathematics curricula.

The appropriate administrative departments of pedagogical and scientific institutions were charged with working out new curricula in conjunction with the most active and, in the opinion of the government agencies of the 1950s and 1960s, qualified specialists (teachers and academics). Most teachers, in particular the rural teachers, expected that the new curricula would give them greater opportunities to teach the existing course as it should be taught. They wanted more time for the class and each pupil to master the existing course. They wanted the pace of work to be slowed down and the various sections of the course to be shortened and simplified rather than brought up to date. They wanted to get rid of the false 'percentage-mania' and the pseudo-universal education which tormented and corrupted pupils and teachers alike.

The sophisticated reformers and erudite pedagogues, however, representatives of the scientific-pedagogical and civil elite whose ideas were profoundly opposed to the established school practice and curriculum, wanted to make the curricula more scientific, modernise the methods of instruction and accelerate their pace. Drawing on their experience of the experimental and so-called 'base' (model) schools or simply the better schools in the main cities (or those under the tutelage of liberal academicians), observing their enlightened teacher friends, and most frequently seeing the children of their own circle who were surrounded from birth by the active intellectual life of their parents and grandparents, they wanted to increase the children's load, to stimulate all the latent potential of their minds. All these intentions had been brilliantly borne out experimentally when carried out by the enlightened experimenters themselves in their classes. However, when they passed from theory and experiment to organising seminars and lectures on the new curricula among teachers and to experiments in ordinary schools - and even more so in schools in peripheral or rural areas - they were horrified how difficult the new curricula (and even their terminology and phraseology) were for the teachers and the inspectors from the Departments of Education.

*

In the following paragraphs I shall attempt to acquaint the reader with writings in the pedagogical press and journals from 1959 to the end of the 1960s.

On first sight it might seem strange that discussions on education in the specialised pedagogical publications - Narodnoe obrazovanie ('Public education'), Uchitel'skaia gazeta ('Teachers' newspaper'), etc. - were more boring, monotonous and meagre in content, even in the most liberal periods, than, for example, those in Novyi mir ('New world') or Literaturnaia gazeta ('Literary newspaper') or at conferences organised by the latter. However, this is not as strange as it may seem.

The specialised pedagogical publications usually print articles by officials in the Soviet educational system. They also publish all the government statements and speeches by party and government leaders which often have nothing to do with education directly. As a rule, teachers are represented in them by articles which have been ordered or 'organised' (i.e. prepared) by the editors. Publications such as Literaturnaia gazeta and Novyi mir were quite a different matter in the period 1954-65, as this was where the most active and educated members of the intelligentsia sent their works. Even the articles, reports and discussions prepared or ordered by these publications were usually more interesting than those in other magazines and newspapers. Viktor Perel'man, the editor of the emigre journal Vremia i my ('Time and we') published in Israel, was right when he called Literaturnaia gazeta 'Hyde Park under socialism' (in his book Pokinutaia Rossiia ('Russia abandoned')): to the small extent that Soviet socialism is able to permit something like independent thought, it did this in that newspaper and also in Tvardovskii's Novyi mir. Here too, of course, the boundaries were clearly delineated: there was to be no encroachment upon the reigning ideology and the bases of the regime. Specific problems were examined within the framework of the compulsory world view and system; but the specific criticism was fairly fundamental and radical, which was inconceivable before the mid-1950s.

Novyi mir, no. 9 (1955), opened with the section 'Today is the 1st of September'. From page 32 there was a report of a meeting of teachers and literary contributors to the journal held in its editorial office. What did these urban and rural teachers speak about? About the fact that literate rural youth did not want to stay in the kolkhozes even after the seventh grade; that rural graduates from institutions of higher education did not return to the villages even when suitable employment was available. They said that students chose institutions of higher education at random, without having a vocation, wherever it was easier to be admitted. Here is a summary of the main themes discussed at this 'round table':

(1) the need to educate in pupils the inclination towards 'productive' labour (in most cases this meant physical labour), for which purpose it was proposed to introduce a two-year period of work experience before higher education;
(2) the need to redesign the secondary school curricula with an emphasis on reducing the volume of factual material in the curricula and increasing instruction in habits and methods of independent analytical thought;
(3) the terrible position of the class teacher who was overworked because of the need to combine full-time

teaching in his particular subject with general educational work with the pupils in his class. In the speaker's opinion, this situation was inevitable, since the pay for being a class teacher was nominal - 50 rubles a month at that time[68] - while teachers' salaries were too low to permit them to work less than full time;

(4) all the editor's guest speakers, who were connected in some way or other with school administration, were disturbed by the hopeless state of school construction (the lack of funds and building materials) despite the frequently hazardous or unhygienic state of school buildings, especially in the villages;

(5) the need to regulate the work of the schools and classes of rural youths which frequently operated almost fictitiously, mostly in order to issue the appropriate document to those who had dropped out of the day schools but continued to be registered in them because of the law on universal education;

(6) the need to keep new rural teachers, who did not always work the required three years after completing higher education, in the jobs to which they were assigned and which they tried their utmost to leave for town schools;

(7) the need to improve general conditions in the schools: to develop the initiative and creativity of teachers and pupils, to make school buildings, thinking and life more aesthetic;

(8) the poverty of the schools, which was a subject that concerned all the speakers: many spoke of the financial restrictions which fettered the initiative of school directors, of the absurdity of the rigid division of the budget into items which meant that the school directors were not free to use as they saw fit even the very meagre funds allocated to them by the budget;

(9) the subject of the family: teachers and workers in the education organisations spoke at length about 'difficult children' as the products of failed or broken families; they described types of failing families and sought forms of work with parents that would enable the school to influence the family and the child's upbringing in the family;

(10) the difference in the position of schools in towns and rural areas and in the quality of the schools in these two areas.

(11) The subject of creating living and individual

school traditions, which would be unique to each particular school, was interwoven with criticism of the nature of the work of the Pioneer and Komsomol organisations in the school. Behind this criticism, which was very widespread and popular in those years, another idea could be discerned which was no less typical of what the intelligentsia was discussing at the end of the 1950s: the hypocrisy of the bombastic phraseology used in schools in the Stalin era. This is a topic to which anyone sincerely interested in the ideological processes in the USSR in this period should pay more attention. It was depicted particularly clearly and convincingly in Kabo's Na trudnom pokhode ('On a difficult march') (published in Novyi mir, nos. 11 and 12, 1956) and was touched upon in her somewhat later work, at the beginning of the 1960s, Povest' o Borise Bekleshove ('The story of Boris Bekleshov') and in Anatolii Kuznetsov's Prodolzhenie legendy ('The continuation of the legend') (published by Roman-gazeta, 1956). The essence of what was said and written at this time about the hypocrisy and formalism of all Soviet school rhetoric (including in the Pioneers and the Komsomol) can be expressed as follows:

(a) The main ideas which the Soviet school advocates and professes are infallible, irreproachable and correct, but they are advocated in a bad way: formally, in dead, dry words, in a standardised, trite, soulless manner. These defects make children distrustful of, disgusted by or indifferent to the words of their elders and to everything that derives from them.

(b) The education given is purely verbal, not practical, and the children are tired of words, especially such monstrous and banal ones. They crave for romantic deeds which would reveal to them the sublime essence of the truths proclaimed by the school.

(c) The school, which presents the sublime truths of the Communist world view and Communist morality badly and in an uninteresting way, also allows itself to lie - about trivial and specific matters, about the relations between children and adults and between subordinates and their superiors.

We can therefore see that for the participants in the open discussions which were held at the end of the 1950s and the beginning of the 1960s the problem was not the victory of untruth or wrong conceptions in the schools, the rhetoric and ideology of the preceding and present periods, but merely the poor presentation of the truth and particular, specific distortions of that truth in individual cases. This approach was characteristic not only of the schools, but also of literature and all public manifestations of ideology in general, of the humanities, the cinema and the theatre. A different approach emerged only in samizdat, which does not concern us here.

The open approach gave society (including the schools) some scope for more or less critical self-analysis (for a while); but it also set an inevitable limit to social self-awareness in the era of what is called the 'thaw': as soon as social critical thought had exhausted the concrete, specific, secondary aspects of the problems it was considering, it came up against general and fundamental problems. At this point, since the authorities, the system, refused to make any concessions on these matters of principle, critical thought had either to halt or to cease being obedient to the authorities and move into the realm of uncensored creativity.

This is indeed what happened, in particular in the realm of pedagogical thought and activity, to which we shall return below. I shall merely note here that the schools, as legal, state institutions (that were also funded by the state) were wholly and hopelessly dependent on the state. But just as literature created samizdat, which absorbed those who were not satisfied with investigating specific aspects of life, there emerged, parallel to the state schools with their 'chilly' Soviet official climate, an increasing number of forms and patterns of self-education which did not coincide with any of the forms of official education. This phenomenon, however, is beyond the scope of the present study.

Thus, the writings on the school in the 'thaw' period presented the situation as though schools in Soviet conditions could in principle be different from what they were (irreproachably truthful, non-formalistic, highly moral and scientific) but were not different only because of local, internal shortcomings.

The well known and very orthodox Soviet writer Anna Karavaeva responded to complaints and critical reflections which she had received from young people, in an article 'O priamoi doroge i proselkakh' ('On the straight road and byways'), subtitled 'An open letter to my correspondents', published in Novyi mir, no. 2 (1956). Her main idea can be summarised as follows: there is no point in going into abstractions and laying the blame on other people, the environment, or defects of principle. Everything depends on the individual himself: he has to build his life by himself, to choose, to fight, to carry out 'our Soviet ideals'. Life is made up of what 'we all' do. This attempt to channel society's growing analytical activity into the trivialities of 'small deeds', specific details, is inevitable when the general, the whole, is beyond analysis. The impression is that the participants in discussions on the school published at the end of the 1950s did not clearly understand the still profound general contradictions of the ideocratic Soviet school with its obligatory single world view which dictates that the Soviet system be considered the best system in the world.

The same issue of Novyi mir contained a brief article by S. Ezerskii, a teacher in the Leningrad School of Working Youth No. 28, 'Poeziia vospitaniia' ('The poetry of upbringing'). He noted what to him was a surprising paradox: since Makarenko, there had not been enough serious books on the school. 'Are there really no pressing problems?' he asked, and asserted that this indeed was the commonly held opinion, that writers did not see the pressing problems of school life. True, the publishers did not allow writers to depict 'bad' teachers, but Ezerskii criticised the literature on the school for the triviality of the conflicts it portrays, for its over-simplified topics, heroes, characters, for the author's indifference to his subject, etc.

Three or four months after this article was published, Liubov' Kabo, in the same journal, tried to touch upon some deeper questions of principle than Karavaeva or Ezerskii had. She began by speaking about the formalism, hypocrisy and supreme party diktat in the schools before which pupil and teacher were defenceless. She spoke mildly and indistinctly, hardly touching upon these questions and dwelling at far greater length on the mediocrity of purely rhetorical school upbringing. She did not step outside the framework of the concept that the trouble lay in the poor presentation of the truth and not in the fictitious and false nature of the pseudo-truths being propounded. Nevertheless, at the end of the 1950s she was to find herself on a 'black list' of writers who had trespassed into the forbidden zone of investigating general, fundamental problems.

It was very typical that this blow (very mild for the Stalin era, but still severe for the era of the 20th Party Congress) was directed against several authors simultaneously, thus closing the path to further investigation of the question or at any rate to investigations carried out at this pace, at this level and with this degree of analytical objectivity.[69] The works whose authors were abused in the press, by professional criticism, in 'letters from workers' and even at various meetings and gatherings were:

(1) in the sphere of scientific-technical problems: V. Dudintsev's Ne khlebom edinym ('Not by bread alone') and D. Granin's Sobstvennoe mnenie ('One's own opinion');
(2) in the sphere of agricultural problems: A. Iashin's Rychagi ('Levers');
(3) in the sphere of art and literature: S. Kirsanov's Sem' dnei nedeli ('Seven days of the week');
(4) in the sphere of education: L. Kabo's Na trudnom pokhode.

Official criticism and the authorities seemed to be saying 'Stop! Don't you dare go any further', and it was certainly not their fault that they were unable to stop the flow of thought.

Further comments by school workers were published in Novyi mir, no. 7 (1956) in the section entitled 'Essays of our days' under the general heading 'Let us continue talking about the school'. All speakers began with a reference to the 20th Party Congress. It became obligatory to open all critical and polemical speeches and articles with such references for several years - as later to the 22nd Party Congress - and they served as a kind of passport that legitimised what was said and vouched for the reliability of the person saying it. Any of the speakers at the 20th Party Congress could be referred to (among the contributors to this section, a certain E. Pomerantseva, in a note entitled 'The beginning of a great path', referred to K.E. Voroshilov's speech and quoted an extract from it). However, despite these positive references and quotations, a note of weariness and perplexity could be detected in what the devotees of polytechnical training were saying in 1956. Thus, Pomerantseva noted the budgetary difficulties of polytechnisation: the fact that the sponsor enterprise or institution could give schools only machines that were no longer in use or were outdated and that neither the sponsors nor the schools had the right to pay workers and technical teachers (mastery) for the pupils' instruction. Everything depended on the enthusiasm of both sides (sponsors and schools) and on their ability to circumvent the laws. The author noted the despair and fatigue (so soon!) of school directors who had pioneered polytechnisation, and the formal nature and leisurely pace of academic work in this field. Indeed, as we noted above, until there would be some kind of financial legislation in this sphere, 'polytechnisation' and all the school reforms of the Khrushchev era in general would come to nought.

Even though Pomerantseva was a completely loyal writer, she could write of the Academy of Pedagogical Sciences: 'This is a small academy that plays at being a large one - an Academy of Sciences. Institutes, sectors, all these are not all that essential. What is needed, first and foremost, is experimental schools with workshops and laboratories, a good staff of teachers and a collective of research assistants!'[70] We tried to show above just how feasible it was to set up such schools, given the economic possibilities which the USSR State Budget affords the Ministry of Education. The author of this article naturally complained of the impotence of all discussions and talking. 'It would seem that the courageous school directors should have been better equipped for their journey and supplied with "provisions". In practice, however, they set out empty-handed. It is no wonder that only a few resolve to carry on, regardless of the obstacles, along unexplored paths, while the majority stop half-way.'[71]

But who was it who sent them 'along unexplored paths'? Here lay the paradox of polytechnisation whose beginnings revealed (yet again) the main principle of socialist 'progress': the strictest order of the authorities, as in the old folk tale, is to 'go there, I don't know where, and bring it, I don't know what!'.

The same section contained an article by L. Aizerman, a literature teacher in Moscow Secondary School No. 278, entitled 'Zhivoe i omertvevshee' ('The living and the deadened'). This writer also began with a reference to the 20th Party Congress, but the very sub-headings of this article were instructive and anticipated the ideas in Kabo's Na trudnom pokhode. For example, in the section entitled 'Alone with my thoughts' the writer asked the rhetorical question: 'Is not the reason why our pupils' words are sometimes at variance with their deeds that these same words are uttered in school bombastically, but not weightily, with pathos, but not with deep feeling?'[72] It would be interesting to know what effect the author expected his article to have when it itself exuded lies. The words of educators are not only at variance with their deeds, but also with their thoughts - otherwise the author would have spoken first about how the words are at variance with reality, and not about flaws in the educator's intonation. The second section, 'Word-shells', contained another rhetorical question: 'Where do pupils acquire this high-flown monotony of speech, why is their speech so colourless and uniform? It was only some time later that I became convinced that these qualities of speech develop under the influence of the teacher's stories that the pupil hears in the lessons, of the books and articles that he reads, of the lectures and talks that he has to attend.'[73] Later the author referred to 'discussions' during which the teachers 'conduct' the pupils.

No answer was given to this question, for any quasi-answer would have inevitably led to another question: 'Why are the teacher's speech, the books and articles monotonous, high-flown and colourless? Why are discussions "conducted"?' And only one answer would be possible: 'Because the words are at variance with life. Because the teacher is also "conducted": he says and teaches the children to say not what he thinks but what they "ought to, what they are ordered to think".' Despite the 'thaw', however, such an answer was impossible. There was no legal place for such an answer in the whole of Soviet history.

Here are other headings from the same article: 'Fettered initiative', 'From the main entrance', 'Teaching the teacher'. But what should he be taught? Whom did this author, who claimed to be sincere, mention as a teacher of teachers? Kalinin, the irreproachable, featureless and narrow-minded Stalinist.

The journal Iunost' ('Youth'), no. 10 (1956), published a story by M. Bremener 'Pust' ne soshlos' s otvetom' ('Let the answer not tally'). Novyi mir, no. 12 (1956), responded with a critical article by E. Gal'perina 'Vospitanie pravdoi' (Education by the truth)[74] which extended, not too pointedly, but still clearly, the conflict in Bremener's story to the whole of society. 'Formalism, "sham life" are frightening everywhere.' The pupils, in the words of the critic, 'learn that it does not always pay to fight lies with truth, sometimes "it makes sense" to settle for a compromise and be rid of it as soon as possible.' The epigraph of the story: 'The future will not come by itself, if we do not take measures' (Maiakovskii). Let us examine this review in more detail: '... Valerii and his friends seem to be supported by the strength of the party and, in the person of the procurator, by the strength of the Soviet state system. And this, of course, is very good ...' The review contained many such comments; and this was immediately after the 20th Party Congess when Khrushchev's famous 'Secret Speech' to the Congress was being read to teachers. In the wake of these recent, shocking disclosures of the party's crimes and impotence, the reviewer, like the author of the story, considered that 'the strength of the party' and, 'in the person of the procurator', 'the strength of the Soviet state system' could be trusted. This is the price which both the story and the review paid for being published. This, indeed, was 'settling for a compromise'.[75] Teachers were trying to get their thoughts past the censor, to prod their colleagues and pupils to reflection and critical conclusions by means of analogies, examples, parallel directions of thought: out loud they spoke about the distant past, to themselves about the recent past and the present.

This same Aizerman wrote in Novyi mir, no. 1 (1959): 'The most terrible enemy of the literature lesson is cold indifference' and gave as examples analysis of the characters of Tolstoy's Tat'iana Larina and Andrei Bolkonskii. Later he asked 'What is it, then, that always moves the reader?', a question that Stanislavskii always asked himself, and he gave the latter's reply: 'What he sees around himself in life.' Consequently, literature lessons should correlate with reality and not resort to witting falsification. But how is 'The fourth dream of Vera Pavlovna' (about the realisation of socialism in Russia) in N.G. Chernyshevskii's What is to be done?, which is so carefully studied, to be related to the socialism with which the Soviet ninth-grader is familiar? How is Andrei Bolkonskii to be related to reality if the Soviet teacher in Kabo's Na trudnom pokhode feels as though his 'mind and conscience have been forever handed over to someone else' who stands above him, always infallible. In this story, its main positive hero, the Russian literature teacher Viktor Vasil'evich Lopukhov, who propounds the loftiest ideals of Communist morality and adherence to principles, retreats on the questions which are of the greatest importance to his class under pressure from the administration and party functionaries and is almost expelled from the party. What is the conclusion? Is the teacher and writer, as portrayed by Kabo, free, at the height of the 'thaw', to conclude that a teacher's honesty is compatible with handing over his mind and conscience to any higher authority, no matter which? He is not. The pupils are shocked that their favourite teacher is transferred to another school and almost expelled from the party and their conclusion is different: 'To us you are the party!' they say.[76] The party remains the symbol of wisdom and honour in the very year that it exposed itself in the most ignominious way!

Literature and the school are both doomed either to lie or to fight, which neither the writer nor the teacher can do legally. This is why the very first steps taken by critical writings of the 'thaw' contain the germ of the future split into conformists and dissidents. And this is why 'now, at a certain distance' (as Pasternak wrote in his 'Vysokaia bolezn'' ('Sublime sickness')) we can see so clearly the impotence of the best teachers who aspired to speak to their pupils 'about the beauty of man and his true values'[77] immediately after the cynical and half-hearted self-exposure of the party butchers at the 20th Party Congress. The mere fact that no one dared to demand from his own government and from himself at least the degree of responsibility that was, and is, demanded of the Nazis demonstrated criminal hypocrisy and cancelled all the attempts of Soviet schools to start being honest with their pupils.

Aizerman wrote that the dispute of the author and Luka (in Gorky's The lower depths) was the dispute between 'the philosophy of servile humility, of passive waiting and the world view of active creation and re-making of the world - turning over a page of history'. These words contained the hope, intelligible only to contemporaries and compatriots, that the 20th Party Congress had turned over pages for Russia which had been only half-opened by Khrushchev's speech. But at this point a shout rang out 'from above' and the bearers of the 'world view of active creation and re-making of the world', i.e. of the Soviet world - Granin, Dudintsev, Iashin, Kirsanov, Kabo and others - received a warning rap on their knuckles.

Democracy is not the chaos of total permissiveness which can lead to the emergence and victory of totalitarian tendencies. Democracy is the legitimacy of analysis and struggle by open, humane means: words, debate, rejection, non-participation, choice. The limits of the democracy of the 'thaw' were very narrow, very tight: these were limits which forbade any encroachment upon the absolute power of the 'soft' post-Stalin oligarchy, upon the regime and its ideology.

The teacher quivered in the net thrown over him and tried to draw an allegory even from the lines of the proletarian anthem - to urge their pupils to an independence which they themselves hesitated to adopt. 'No one will bring us deliverance, not God, not the Tsar and not a hero',[78] quoted Aizerman, dragging in for camouflage 'bad' 'popular capitalism'. And he noted (with regard to his analogies and comparisons): 'All this, when used in the classroom, tranforms the lesson.' But in what way? With the plausibility of the false conception that arises when literary facts are compared with the pseudo-reality that the Soviet teacher is compelled to pass off as reality? Some of my pupils, who would meet me at home after school and courses, told me that, as they understood things now, the most terrible part of their school experience had been the good, even brilliant, teachers who had believed in the lies they presented, or who had faked such belief with great expertise. It is hardly necessary to mention that the work of a teacher who did not have this belief or did not fake it entailed constant risk. In practice this was impossible: the lies inevitably filtered through into what the legal Soviet teacher propounded.

The second part of Aizerman's article, 'The boundaries of the lesson', considered the bitter irony of history itself when compared with the teachers' ignorance of life. An urban intellectual, a teacher, is constantly compelled to present his pupils with the party interpretation of the peasant question. Aizerman wrote: 'It is surely no accident that the most intelligent, sensible replies during study of Sholokhov's novel <u>Virgin soil upturned</u> can be heard from the pupil who has spent several summers working on a kolkhoz, and the most contradictory, incomprehensible ones, from the ninth-graders who have come across kolkhozniks only at the market.'[79]

I should like to transport the author to my rural classes of 1959 when, having educated a young livestock specialist on the school's stock-raising farm, we triumphantly 'delivered' him to the kolkhoz after the holidays. A couple of weeks later he came to us shocked, stupefied and confused, having seen for the first time (and this was a village boy!) the whole truth of the everyday reality of kolkhoz stock-raising. This was in 1959, after the measures of 1954, which eased the situation and were extremely important to the villages but in 1949-53 this conflict between Soviet fiction and rural reality was even more shocking. It was simply impossible to discuss the topics in the school curriculum which dealt with the kolkhoz with rural pupils. The urban teacher was saved by the fact that neither he nor the children had any knowledge of rural life.

I shall give two examples: in the 'good' times of Khrushchev, when the game of tag with American stock-raising had over-strained the entire potential of that branch of Soviet farming, a friend of mine, an urban teacher, brought his ninth-graders to visit our kolkhoz. We brought them to the farm without having previously arranged the visit with the heads of the kolkhoz. We came to a model cowshed which had already been described in the district and oblast newspapers. It was a clean, solid, well-equipped cowshed in which the cows, collapsing from emaciation, were held up with canvas breast-bands fastened under their bellies and to the stall partitions!

Kabo recounts the following episode in the above-mentioned story of 1956: during a lesson, in the presence of the inspector and school director, a pupil begins to argue with the teacher that the works of literature on the kolkhozes which have been awarded Stalin prizes are unlifelike and implausible. The boy had spent the summer with relatives on a kolkhoz and had returned stunned. The teacher cannot manage to avoid answering. He is forced to agree with the pupil and says that, if it were up to him, he would not have awarded Stalin prizes for these works. The inspector and director leave in ominous silence and the teacher, looking during the break at the shining eyes of the pupils around him, remarks about himself with bitter irony: 'And Iurka Shnyrev did not know that he had just ruined somebody.' Maybe not ruined, but his question had certainly ensured some unpleasantness.

If we consider that entire chapter in Soviet history known as collectivisation, then it turns out that the innocent school lessons on the kolkhozes (both in history and literature) are designed by the authorities to cover up the abyss in which millions of peasants, murdered by starvation and acts of repression, lie buried. Teachers try, as it were, to hypnotise history - which for them, as for all legal Soviet professionals in the humanities, is embodied in the will and logic of the party - to suggest to it how it should behave. The writers of the 'thaw' behaved in exactly the same way.

In his prose poem, Sem' dnei nedeli (Novyi mir, no. 8, 1956), Semen Kirsanov speaks in the name of the 'Country of the Soviets': '... I shall not spurn the request, even though it should mean delaying my festival ... I shall deny no one defence: ponder, try, seek ... May your future day be justified.' And he concludes in his own name: 'So you will speak, Country, and that is the truth!' In other words, 'And that must, is obliged to be the truth, to become the truth!' The teacher (in this case Aizerman) utters the same magic spells and suggests to 'History' (i.e. the party, the authorities) how it should develop: 'And I think that tomorrow, in the new school, it will be more interesting, to a certain extent easier, to teach literature not only because many unpleasant obstacles have been removed (cramming medal winners, the pursuit of a high success rate, the blinkered fault-finding of inspectors, the restrictions on teachers), but because the intrusion of life into the school, above all of labour, will make the pupil spiritually richer, richer in experience and more responsive.'

'So you will speak, Country, and that is the truth.'

The rhetorical method of Soviet literature is common to the writer and to the teacher of literature and history - to the educator as such: this method compels him to replace the image (the reproduction of the real) with the model (the reproduction of the desired or prescribed). Aizerman goes so far as to merge the pedagogical, educational process with the literary, creative one in the third section of the same article devoted to pupils' essay-writing and entitled 'An essay on essays'. Pupils - like writers - are required to be honest, fresh and original in their essays, within the bounds and framework of the most rigid conceptions and compulsory ideological prescriptions. It is quite inconceivable for the examination commission of a school or institution of higher education to appreciate even the best essay which defended, for example, the cultural bourgeois Shtol'ts (in Goncharov's Oblomov) against Chernyshevskii's heroes, or the 'kulak' Tit Borodin against Makar Nagul'nov (Virgin soil upturned), or the 'apolitical' Grigorii Melekhov against the Bolsheviks Koshevoi and Shtokman (Sholokhov's Quiet flows the Don), or Mechik against Morozka (Fadeev's The rout), etc. This rule applies to all periods of Soviet history. In any essay the pupil solves the problem according to a pre-established conceptual answer and is more or less free only in the choice of words. The plan of the essay is also usually imposed ('Introduction', 'Exposition',

'Conclusion', with a few sub-headings) as well as the genre (discussion essay, individual character study, comparative character study, group character study, essay on problems, study essay). The worse the teacher, the more rigidly formalistic he is in these requirements. But Aizerman, like the majority of other teacher-publicists in the period of the 'thaw', sees another reason for the insipid nature of pupils' essays: the trouble lies in the way the pupils 'handle habitually and lightly words that signify lofty social concepts that we hold dear'. it is as though the teacher is not aware that by propagandising these 'social concepts' he incessantly demands of the pupil plausible lies, thoughtful thoughtlessness, sincere falsification, that is, what he himself engages in during the lessons in literature and history.

However, it is even more frightening if the teacher is sincere about what he is doing. Aizerman writes: 'Now I understood why pupils' essays contain so many trite formulae and hackneyed expressions. Verbal clichés do not require time for thinking, time that the pupil does not have, as he has to expound in the course of two hours the material of the subject in a grammatically correct way, without errors of style.'[80] Are we to conclude that it is easier for the child or adolescent to speak in clichés, in the words of others, in trite expressions, than to be sincere? On the contrary: the trouble is that the pupil knows that he has to 'expound the material of the subject' and not write something of his own, and this is easiest to do with the clichés belonging to that subject.

But not everyone is capable of writing essays, of expressing themselves on receiving a signal. Many people, and often the most thoughtful, are incapable of expressing their thoughts and feelings on paper according to schedule (or are incapable of doing this at all), especially thoughts which they know to be imposed on and dictated to them but which they have to pass off as their own. 'My attitude to Tat'iana Larina' was the subject of one of the examination essays in the 'thaw' period. It was assumed that the pupil would explain conscientiously and sponteaneously, vividly, convincingly and sincerely, that he liked in Tat'iana Larina' all the traits for which the teacher and author had liked her. One of my best pupils refused to submit an examination essay on this subject, which he thought to be half-blasphemous, half-mocking: to express in the time of two lessons his personal attitude to one of the most complex heroines of the Russian classics - not to mention the absurdity of demanding fourteen- and fiteen-year-old schoolchildren to evaluate the characters of other literary heroes such as Onegin, Lenskii, Chatskii, Sof'ia, Pechorin, etc. What, apart from clichés and ready formulae, can save the pupil from having to solve a problem that is beyond his powers?

As soon as the pupils really began to trust me (in school or on courses), I was deluged with letters, instead of the usual cliché-ridden essays. These hastily and inconsistently written monologues, these confusedly sincere and uniquely spontaneous outpourings of thoughts and feelings cannot be termed anything other than personal letters. I had to write replies or have long conversations in private with their authors and explain that the 'essays' (epistles to me) in our dialogue were one matter and the essays for the transitional, school-leaving or entrance examinations were quite another, during which it was above all absolutely necessary, in Aizerman's words, to expound 'in the course of two [four] hours the material of the subject in a grammatically correct way and without errors of style'. I had to remind them that an examination was not the place either for confession or research.

*

Literaturnaia gazeta devoted as much attention as Novyi mir to the subject of the school. Now, at a distance of 25-30 years, the publications of the 'thaw' period have acquired an additional nuance: two faces of the author can be seen simultaneously - what he was then and what he is now.

The uncritical, lyrical acceptance and enthusiasm with which Khrushchev's schemes were greeted after the 21st Party Congress at the end of the decade typify the attitude accorded to his schools program as well. Literaturnaia gazeta, the best newspaper in the Soviet Union and a tribune of the intelligentsia, was full of odes to polytechnical training, to 'the magician, labour' (as though study is not work and as though physical labour, in which humanity has been engaged since time immemorial, had only now become a factor in education, thanks to the genius of Khrushchev). The essays on workshops, on production brigades, garages, greenhouses, were fashionable, transient themes which would quietly disappear from the pages of the newspaper when the 'school reform' was curtailed. The newspaper had nothing but apologia for polytechnical training, and when this training began to be curtailed, before it had had a chance to develop, there would also be nothing except apologia for the new line.

In issue no. 83 (1959) of Literaturnaia gazeta, M. Isakovskii strongly attacked the poet A. Markov[81] for his 'Russophilism', a code-word for a combination of chauvinism and anti-semitism, in an article entitled 'This should be talked about decisively and forthrightly'. Four issues later Markov thanked Isakovskii for his criticism and promised to turn over a new leaf. An article entitled 'History is a great teacher' was published in no. 85 (1959). Its subtitle was 'On the new textbook of history of the CPSU' and it read like some monstrous farce written in the spirit and style of Orwell: in this article, after the party's recent exposures of the crimes which it had committed and which, both in time-scale and in the total number of victims, had even exceeded the crimes of Hitler, two of the criminals calmly exchanged academic notes - A.I. Mikoian and I.I. Mints, one of the highest-ranking figures in the CPSU and one of its court pseudo-historians. Mints stated: 'In his speech to the 20th Congress, Comrade A.I. Mikoian said of our brother historians: "If they had had a good rummage among the archives and historical documents, and not only in the sets of newspapers, they would now be better able, from a Leninist standpoint, to shed light on many of the facts set forth in the "Short Course"."' And Mints added to what Mikoian had said: 'As you can see, life itself has laid before us the necessity to create a new textbook which will be more complete and historically authentic.'[82] He stressed that the main task facing the authors of the new course of party history was to reveal more fully Lenin's role in it. The Western reader cannot fully grasp the cynicism of the participants in this editorial discussion. It turned out that at the same congress as that at which Khrushchev had read his stunning speech, Mikoian had paternally taken Soviet historians to task for distorting the historical truth in their writings, because of laziness and because they were reluctant to rummage through the archives! As though the historian could deviate even a hair's breadth from party directives! As though he were free to rummage about in archives and use them at his own discretion! As though even one single history teacher had ever entered the classroom without the approval of the party district committee!

The fact that society calmly accepted such performances in the newspapers proves just how superficial the 'thaw' was. People did not refute such statements because they did not believe that this could be done legally, while only a few individuals had matured to the point of using illegal methods of expression.

From mid-1959 the correspondents of Literaturnaia gazeta carried out more frequent inquiries into extraordinary instances of abuse or insensitivity on the part of various administrative bodies, usually not very high-ranking. Articles on schools also became more frequent (maybe because of the new editor, S.S. Smirnov). The ideological chief of the CPSU, Suslov, and the heroine of countless anecdotes of the Khrushchev era, the Minister of Culture, E.A. Furtseva, appear in the newspaper in the role of mentors of Soviet teachers. Her statements are imbued with the narrow-minded ignorance that it is ridiculous even to reproach someone for: she wouldn't understand, so what's the point! This leader of the cultural life of a gigantic country declared to the 21st Party Congress, quite in the spirit of the Chinese 'Cultural Revolution' and the cultural policy of the RKP(b) of the 1920s:

> Surely, for example, it cannot be considered normal for young people with literary and musical talent to enter a literary institute or conservatoire straight from the school bench and after completing higher education to become 'free artists'. What can an author who has essentially seen nothing but a school desk, teach? Of course, he will not enrich his reader, viewer or listener with anything. Having received a member's card in a creative union, this kind of young arts worker already demands that a literary, musical or some other 'fund' take care of him.

Literaturnaia gazeta promptly reprinted the entire speech and under it an obsequious caricature by D. Tsikovskii with the caption 'Beloved fund': a robust young oaf with a dummy in his mouth has chained himself to the doors of the Literary Fund and, sitting at a school desk that is too small for him, is writing a request to the Fund: 'Pishu paemu, proshu avants' ('I'm writing a poim and request an advanse'). Musical and literary talents are to be perfected by means of physical labour among the people - such is the idea of Furtseva's speech.

Not a single article can be found in any issue of Literaturnaia gazeta and Novyi mir, not to mention the specialised pedagogical newspapers and magazines, that is even partially devoted to the tragic exposures of the 20th and later the 22nd Party Congresses. There is no explanation why Stalin, who had occupied pride of place in all school courses and readers, had disappeared from the textbooks and why his portraits and statues had disappeared from the classrooms, corridors, halls and courtyards of the schools. This operation - the banishment of Stalin from the schools - instead of being a lesson in the need to think independently and critically, became a lesson in blind acceptance of any world view dictated from above. The schools agreed, without the slightest attempt at resistance, to follow the authorities' slogans which Semen Kirsanov embodied so brilliantly and sorrowfully in his _Sem' dnei nedeli_: 'We need hearts that are useful, like iron locks, uncomplicated, convenient, capable of carrying out everything...'[83] The pedagogical and literary community, having kept silent about the murders, crimes and lies _admitted to by the government_, having let slip a word about them and immediately having cried 'Stop!', when writing about the school swiftly passes to trivial and superficial minor themes and details. Thus, in _Literaturnaia gazeta_, Vladimir Nemtsov wrote about the need to bring up older schoolgirls to be 'inaccessible' and affectingly quoted the trite maxims of the ultra-orthodox Bolshevik, Makarenko: 'A girl should be taught to receive even young men who are agreeable to her somewhat caustically. It is precisely these girls who enjoy the greatest respect, and this maidenly pride must be encouraged in them by every possible means.'[84]

The utterly politicised jargon used by the newspapers and magazines when dealing with the subject of schools is combined with complete neglect of the vital political events of the recent past and present. Everything had been fine, everything had become even better, and the rivers of innocent blood were hidden in occasional obtuse allusions, unintelligible both to children and to most teachers, especially the ones in rural and primary schools who, because of their low level of erudition, were incapable of perceiving the concealed meaning behind these allusions.

Meanwhile, society's passive, silent resistance to the enforced informational and aesthetic 'rationing' was growing. S. Polivanskii, head of 'Mosknigotorg' (the Moscow Book Trading Organisation), wrote that out of two million readers' letters not one had expressed gratitude for the range of books available ('A "State planning committee for literature" is needed', _Literaturnaia gazeta_, no. 32, 1959).

He described how there were mountains of unpopular literature and a shortage of what the people needed. His conclusions were startling: to increase the centralisation of book publishing, to 'plan' it better. All the facts cited by Polivanskii seemed to indicate that the existing system of book publishing was bureaucratic and that the reader's role was reduced to passive acceptance of what Glavlit allowed him to read. The persecution of the 'thaw' writers had apparently already demonstrated that the party would not permit any deviations from its diktat in this matter - but the author of this article proposes even greater centralisation! What is strange is that, unlike the example of Furtseva, Khrushchev and many others, the language of this article and the level of discussion do not testify to the author's ignorance or vulgarity. Apparently, the feeling that many writers today call the 'strategy of hope' (applying the term to those days) was still strong at that time: the upsurge of hope in the period 1956-61 (despite the crushing of the uprisings in Eastern Europe and the warning to liberals at home) had not yet abated. Even the most perspicacious and decent people restrained themselves, waited and addressed themselves to what they regarded as useful, particular questions and 'small deeds'.

Thus, an article by A. Sharov, 'In Makarenko's path' was published in Literaturnaia gazeta, no. 46 (1959). Before discussing this article, I should like to make a brief digression: the Soviet tradition of mild opposition and legal criticism expressed in hidden meanings, in the choice of topic and in allusions intelligible only to the initiated, permits itself a slight, hardly perceptible confrontation with the authorities and always seeks the kind of heroes (in the Soviet period) who would permit the hope that decency and loyalty are compatible. For pedagogues (both academics and practical workers) A.S. Makarenko is one such hero. The educational colony which he established is portrayed as an island of true Communist education in an ocean of distortions of this principle brought into being by 'subjective', 'particular' and 'fortuitous' factors. Nobody took seriously Makarenko's pedagogical views, his legacy or the practicability of the children's institutions he directed. Nowadays Russian emigrants and Israeli repatriates have taken up this research. It is too soon to speak of results, but it can already be stated that they will not coincide with the official Soviet or generally accepted liberal versions.

Sharov writes about the relation between the Pioneer

detachment and the class: in the class children are of the same age; in the detachment there should be children of different ages so that distinct family detachments can be set up to promote the idea of caring for the younger children. He speaks of the need for continuity in school traditions, anniversaries, holidays and protests against the closing down of old schools and the establishment of new ones in their place, since this deprives the school of its traditions. Paying homage to the times, i.e. polytechnisation, he writes about the school enterprises that were being set up and about school groups that studied local lore and history. He defends the school administrator who shows initiative and originality and who, in his view, should not be tormented by endless inspection and petty surveillance. The article is written well, convincingly and emotionally, like everything that Sharov writes. But how could one speak of a sense of continuity in the schools when the Stalin school was being silently re-shaped into the Khrushchev school, without any explanation to pupils or teachers, or when there were tenth-graders who in the sixth grade had learnt countless odes to Stalin, or when there were older pupils whose parents had just heard Khrushchev's 'Secret Speech' and were discussing it at home? What can be the extent, depth or limit of the educator's initiative or originality against the background of the fierce attack on literary works at the end of 1956?

We are speaking here of a certain variation within a rigidly defined framework. Moreover, the ban imposed on society against investigating its own experience is most profoundly immoral. Sharov is compelled to remain _deliberately_ superficial and limited when discussing schools in his own country. The choice between remaining with the government or entering an uncensored spiritual world was becoming ever more inevitable for the teacher as well.

The press devoted more space to odes to labour than to any other topic: craftsmen, production brigades, work practice in factory shops and the fields and on construction projects. Grandiose figures were quoted: in the schools of the RSFSR there were 17 thousand pupils' production brigades, 60 million workdays were worked in 1958; 156 thousand head of cattle were being tended and raised by schoolchildren; ten million head of poultry were delivered by them; schoolchildren were building workshops, garages, greenhouses and had contributed millions of rubles to the economy. V. Eliseeva enthused in _Literaturnaia gazeta_:

'What truly miraculous changes the magician labour has brought into the life of schools!'; 'Not playing at labour, but real, productive labour!'[85]

As though learning were not work! As though the labour outside regular studies had improved the schools' professional work or enhanced the quality of education! As the director of a rural secondary school in those years, I can bear witness to the fact that, in the first place, most of the production brigades, poultry raised and calves fed by schoolchildren existed only on paper, and what was really accomplished, despite all the obstacles, was silently wound down over the next three or four years without any explanation to the pupils, just as the entire pro-Stalin school bombast of the previous 30 years had been stopped. It should be said that (except in very rare cases when really effective economic work was performed by the schools) teachers, parents, children and directors alike were not in the least enthusiastic about the 'magician labour', as it merely made their life more difficult.

*

In 1959 silence about past events had already been imposed not only on the schools but also on the whole of society and, first and foremost, on writers and teachers of literature. The authorities were not to blame if the silence was not total. Both Razgrom ('The rout') and Molodaia gvardiia ('The young guard') by Fadeev are studied in schools. An article on methods of teaching Fadeev's works recommended using materials of the writers' congresses. But Fadeev took to drink and committed suicide; he signed documents which sanctioned the agreement of the Union of Soviet Writers with the repressive measures taken against Soviet writers. More than 600 members of the Writers' Union alone had perished. Not only teachers, but also pupils listen to foreign Russian broadcasts and read memoirs that manage to be published - at one time Il'ia Ehrenburg's, at another, A. Dovzhenko's and others'. But when Fadeev is studied in school, the teacher is confronted with the categorical impossibility of making this a real lesson in native history, literature and morality.

Empty rhetoric floods the schools, which stand paralysed on the brink of the terrible revelations that were cut short.

Here is an example of the vocabulary used in articles about schools and Soviet youth from which it is recommended that pupils draw epigraphs for their essays (in these bright days of liberalisation):

> Now they can already work and live in a Communist way. And, after all, this means being happy. You see, if we were to transfer the beautiful word 'Communism' from the dictionary of social sciences to the dictionary of everyday usage, it would correspond to another simple and beautiful word - happiness.[86]

V. Kosolapov, who was to take over as editor of Novyi mir after the removal of Tvardovskii and his colleagues, exhorted school leavers - who have just left the schools which are so saturated with lies - that 'To the free all heights are accessible'.[87]

On the one hand, the literature of the Khrushchev school was somewhat freer and more varied than under Stalin. On the other hand, the lies of schools under Stalin were so all-encompassing and impenetrable that they created their own psuedo-reality which declared itself to be truer than real life. It invented (and still uses to this day) the opposition between the 'fact' - something particular, fortuitous, subjective - and the Truth, written then and now with a capital 'T': Truth, History, the Truth of the Party, the Truth of Marx/Engels/Lenin/the-present-General-Secretary (the first three names pattered off quickly and the last one ringing out grandly). In Stalin's times it had been possible to bury one's head in the rhetoric of pseudo-reality (the 'Truth') and live like that, declaring facts to be fortuitous or incorrectly understood and preserving a strained faith in the party and a kind of self-respect. But the 20th and 22nd Party Congresses, for a brief moment, had half-raised the painted back-drops of 'the Truth', and permitted society a peep into the abyss of what had been perpetrated. Then the hole in the canvas had been roughly patched up and the lying resumed as though nothing had happened. This was even more destructive in the moral and creative sense than when the party version of history and reality had been an all-encompassing armour. With every year - and sometimes month - that passed, loyalty to the lies that had been so swiftly revived became less and less compatible with personal honesty.

*

At the beginning of 1960 Literaturnaia gazeta organised a discussion on 'What disturbs the teacher' and invited teachers, workers in the field of education and literature and others connected with schools. The editor's summary of the topic was characteristically optimistic: '...never before has the school lived such a full life, with such interesting creative quests as today, when comrade Labour has stepped over its threshold!'.[88] However, the questions raised during the discussion, which remained essentially unanswered, went beyond the proposed bounds: Can productive labour be placed in the same category as socially useful labour and how can they be related to the life of the school?

- How can pupils' work practice in factories be organised in a tolerable and educationally effective way so that it does not turn into tedious and useless compulsory labour? 'Where are your generalisations, comrade scholars?'; 'Practical work in production ceases to be training or education'; 'The children have no time to comprehend the meaning of their labour, no time to study, to rest' (but, if we recall Furtseva, they have no need of that: let them become machine operators, who are needed more than intellectuals); 'Studies apart and labour apart' - all these are comments by teachers and school directors.
- 'How ... to reduce the overloading of schoolchildren and at the same time introduce productive labour?'
- '... The lesson often remains as it was before, with the traditions of many decades.' But new forms of lessons should relieve pupils of homework - not for rest, sport, art, social activities, but for productive labour.
- 'How should production training be designed to take account of the children's inclinations and aspirations?' For until then it had been designed according to the territorial principle: what kolkhozes and enterprises existed in the areas of the school.
- How the curricula in the various subjects should reflect the curriculum of polytechnical training. Etc. etc.

It should be noted that all these questions were raised at a time when the audience was not yet aware that the project, which had yet to be developed, was being cut back. In previous sections we analysed the laws and resolutions connected with the school reform and concluded that in

1959-60 they clearly testified to the state's economic impotence in the field of education. It knew that the expenditure needed to carry out the reform even partially was beyond its means. As early as 1959 the first appeals for the school's financial independence, for charity on the part of the kolkhozes, enterprises, organisations and institutions and for the schools to support themselves financially had been voiced. For this reason, the various points raised by the participants in the discussion - the need for additional paid posts to be established in enterprises for the instruction and training of schoolchildren; the need to speed up the construction of school, inter-school and inter-district subject rooms, workshops, greenhouses; the need to design new curricula, textbooks and educational aids; the need to organise entire schools to have an extended day with double the staff (for teaching and for extra-curricular education) - all these proposals were doomed to failure. What survived of them was only the extended-day groups and the workshops and subject rooms which school directors managed to organise with the help of sponsors without any state subsidy.

Purely academic questions relating to the life and work of schools were also raised in the newspaper. One central theme was the utter depersonalisation of the pupils both by the mass school curriculum and the content of the entrance examinations to institutions of higher education. 'Are we not losing Lomonosovs?' was the title of one article (by A.L. Rotar', in Literaturnaia gazeta, no. 77 (1960)) which complained about the lack of individuality in the examinations of institutions of higher education: the invariable essays, two or three sets of examinations (the humanities cycle, the chemistry and biology cycle which included all types of medical institutions of higher education, and the physics-mathematics-engineering cycle) without any attempt made to discover not only the students' knowledge but also their aptitudes. He noted that the introductory curricula of all institutions of higher education in the same cycle were identical and that everyone was treated alike. He also attacked (in those years this was still possible) the priority in admission enjoyed by production workers, rural residents and demobilised soliders and, most important, the illegal but most realistic privileges enjoyed by sportsmen who could bring their institute victories in students' competitions. All these he decisively called 'the pursuit of failure'.

Indeed, all these privileges recognise a priori, as it

were, the academic inferiority of the favoured groups of candidates for higher education. Instead of trying to improve their level of preparation either in school or in some kind of preparatory courses, they are helped to enter institutions of higher education with less knowledge than those who have been rejected. When in the second half of the 1960s state preparatory courses were set up in institutions of higher education for these privileged categories of candidates who were, and are, admitted on the recommendation of their kolkhoz, enterprise or institution, it was well known that the graduates of these courses would pass the very primitive examinations at the end of these year-long courses and would be enrolled in the institution of higher education without having to take the entrance examinations. Officially, the aim was to give rural and urban schoolchildren equal opportunities, to encourage work in production and army service after school. In reality, the aim was to reduce the educational opportunities of the children of the intelligentsia, to 'proletarise' and genealogically 'democratise' future specialists. Unable to compete with these 'non-competitive' students, the 'privileged' categories turned out to be only those who managed to bribe someone and - without any conditions - the children of highly-placed parents, people with contacts (who are ironically called '*vysshie pozvonochnye*', 'upper vertebrals', that is, those who are admitted to institutions of higher education when a bell is rung from above, *po zvonku svyshe*). The true academic and, later, professional opportunities of the candidates admitted regardless of their knowledge and abilities, were not enhanced by these practices. In the final account, the whole of society suffered and still suffers: Lomonosovs are undoubtedly being lost.

Rotar' pointed out very rightly that the overloaded, impersonal, universal curricula (combined, what is more, with production training) did not permit either the teacher to discover his pupils' vocations or the pupils to discern them in themselves and realise them. He also noted that most of the courses that prepared candidates for higher education were identical and had a disastrously low academic level.

Literaturnaia gazeta published many articles about the overloading of rural teachers, but did not touch upon the question of the colossal 'social' - i.e. state political - 'educational' and organisational - work that consumes the rural teacher's free time: wall newspapers in the kolkhozes and clubs; running political information sessions based on newspapers; informing the population of 'party and government' decisions; organising elections; lecturing according to a programme recommended by the party district authorities - all these activities are outside the discussion. However, the newspaper did write about the mountain of reports and school papers with which the teacher is burdened; about the lack of even the most basic food supplies, which obliges the teacher to have his own individual plot; about the cavalier way in which teachers, including women, are used simply as extra hands. One article, 'A mystery? No, a vocation!' (in no. 78, 1960) described now a sick woman teacher who did not participate in digging holes and erecting poles for the electricity supply to the kolkhoz had her electricity cut off and was ordered to pay 50 rubles (at that time the monthly starting salary for a teacher of grades one to four) for her failure to attend the subbotnik ('voluntary' unpaid work on free days). It described how teachers pay twice as much for electricity as the kolkhozniks (the same rate as non-workers).

When V. Kochetov was replaced as editor of Literaturnaia gazeta in March 1959, its pages became livelier. So-called 'problem' articles (i.e. those that discussed a particular problem) became more frequent and sometimes some interesting statistics would slip into print. Issue no. 79 (1960) contained a long article, 'A.S. Makarenko and the Soviet school', written collectively by a hero of socialist labour, the teacher N. Kirsanova, the teacher and writer N. Dolinina, the journalist S. Smolianitskii and the writer M. Tanich.

Before considering this article I should like to make a further digression about the constant interest in Makarenko's experiment shown by the Soviet school. It is apparently always overlooked that Makarenko did not work in ordinary schools but in a 'colony'. In the first place, his pupils did not have families and belonged entirely to the educational institution; secondly, these were not the typical school intake of relatively normal children, but waifs and juvenile delinquents (and older ones, since the pupils who were closest to Makarenko were kept in the colony until the age of 20-23, which can be easily ascertained from his books and from the preparatory drafts which are often more informative than the books). Moreover, Makarenko's work in his first colony took place at a very complex time. A close reading of his books by someone with a knowledge of children's homes and colonies will reveal shadows and phantoms of processes, phenomena and relations that Makarenko did not emphasise.

However, the Soviet teaching and scientific-pedagogical community insists on applying Makarenko's experiment to the ordinary day school with two shifts and, naturally, fails to work any wonders with his assistance. It is assumed that if Makarenko made such wonderful children out of homeless waifs and delinquents, then, if normal children can be improved correspondingly with his methods, they can be made into outright Wunderkinder and heroes. This, however, is not the case, not only because Makarenko worked out his tactics (which we shall not go into here) in special conditions and for a special kind of child, but also because all unique pedagogical systems and achievements are primarily fused with the personality of their creator - teacher or educator. Pedagogy is more of an art, a creative act, in perpetual development, than a science. Neither Korczak's children's home nor Makarenko's colony can be recreated from external evidence, if we consider that the latter really was like its description in the 'Pedagogical Poem': for that we would need Korczak and Makarenko.

Nonetheless, what does such an imposing group of authors write about Makarenko and the Soviet school? On the surface, there is nothing new: Makarenko 'fused living action with the dream', 'this is not the 1930s, but modern times'. But what action and what dream? - that is the question! Makarenko based his work on the teachings of Marxism-Leninism. What dream do the present-day admirers of Makarenko want to inspire in their pupils? The dream of Communism? But the pupils of the 1960s did not suffer from the idealism which would enable them to live this dream sincerely. Children do not want to prepare for life but to live it to the full, like any other group, say the authors of the article: 'The disease is described accurately by the words "divorce from life", against which the party, the Soviet State, have declared a resolute struggle'[89] - this is what the authors see as the meaning of what the Soviet teacher of the 1960s should learn from Makarenko. But if their pupils really plunge into life, will their educators and teachers be able to give their wards convincing and plausible answers to the questions that will inevitably arise? The authors of the article do not consider this, or at least not openly.

N. Dolinina has written many articles, plays and stories

in which she has apparently dealt with ethical and moral problems. These writings have certain features that are shared by all the most popular pedagogical writings of those years. Unlike Kabo in the 1950s and 1960s and Kuznetsov (despite the disputed and limited nature of their standpoint at that time), Dolinina contents herself with problems that do not go beyond the bounds of the classroom, the family, the arena of conflicts and relations of the individual and the group, but exclusively those problems of the child or adolescent. Moreover, both her young and adult heroes are unreservedly loyal to the official world view and stupendously blind to everything that at that time was shattering and shaking to its foundations the world view of their parents, teachers and real, living older pupils, not those cut out of poor newspaper. Like the article referred to above the attitudes of most of the child and adolescent moralists and psychologists of that time were profoundly immoral and succintly expressed in the words quoted above: '..."divorce from life", against which the party, the Soviet State, have declared a resolute struggle'.

After Khrushchev's almost inexplicable liberal impulse, which reached its height in spring 1956, the party and state began to wage a resolute struggle against the consequences of his incautious step, without actually making a declaration of war. This was also clearly felt by teachers of literature who had been raving about what Novyi mir had published in its autumn and winter issues of 1956 (Dudintsev, Granin, Kirsanov, Kabo, etc.), about the publications in Literaturnaia Moskva ('Literary Moscow') (Iashin) and other attempts by writers to overcome the 'divorce' between literature and schools and 'life'. Against the background of this main lie, which defines the above-mentioned article, all its remaining theses lose any realistic content.

A. Tvardovskii's speech to the 1960 Congress of Teachers was published in Literaturnaia gazeta, no. 81 (1960) under the title 'To teach literature is to create'. His speech about the joint creativity of the writer and the teacher of literature is profoundly true. It is also true that the teacher of literature is powerless if he does not possess a number of talents that are not commonly found: those of the researcher, orator, actor, pedagogue, etc. If pedagogy is always to a large extent an art that requires a gift, like any art, then the teaching of literature is perhaps primarily an art. Paradoxically, however, the more gifted the teacher, the less possible it is for him to teach literature creatively in Soviet schools. The syllabus strictly dictates which writers can be taught. Even in the so-called optional (extra-curricular) courses it is permitted to teach only a strictly limited 'set' of writers. The main elements of assessing these writers are irredeemably predetermined, and when the teacher studies poor or very variable works with his pupils, he is unable to change this assessment for fear (at best) of being dismissed and not allowed to teach in schools any more. There is a group of authors, a favourable reference to whom is equivalent to signing the order for one's own dismissal if one of the pupils should mention it or inform on the teacher, a possibility that can never be ruled out. Interpretation of the works studied can vary only within very limited boundaries. It is, of course, possible to display a certain 'originality' in interpreting Griboedev's Sof'ia Famusova or Anna Karenina; it is possible, at a certain risk, to introduce nuances that are not generally accepted into Gorky's Chelkash and Gavrila, Luka and Satin. But it is quite inconceivable (and this was true even in the most liberal years) to interpret Chernyshevskii's novel differently, to re-assess Goncharov, to ignore the proletarian primacy of Nil in Meshchane ('Landowners') or Pavel Vlasov in Mat' ('Mother'), to question the official interpretation of Fadeev's Rout and Young guard or, Heaven forbid, of Sholokhov's novels, etc., without endangering onself, one's pupils and one's school administration. The creative initiative of the Soviet teacher of literature, history, social science or the USSR constitution is therefore no broader than that of the economists: they are all doomed to variation within a principle that they know to be fallacious and a position that they know to be false.

At times I have been told by colleagues that 'soon' the humanities would follow the path taken by the natural and exact sciences: the latter were the first to escape from the dead scholasticism of Stalinism, and the former would follow them. I was told this for the last time six months before I left the USSR, by Iu. I. Sokolovskii, a man who was wholeheartedly devoted to the school and who was treading a very difficult path. We had once shared the illusions of the 'thaw' and had tried, by legal means ('together with everyone and at one with law and order', in the words of Pasternak) to revive the school, to rid it of lies - to do everything that should not be done. For the sake of this, Sokolovskii, a scholar and soldier, had left his prestigious and well-paid job and made a number of attempts to modernise school curricula and create an especially effective type of school. He had experienced high moments, hopes, disappointments, and nearly lost his son, who was convicted for defending the free-thinking teacher, but he still preferred to stick to the path of futile attempts to find a creative approach to schools organised on a totalitarian basis. At one time the graduates of my last school classes had listened enthusiastically to his wonderful lectures on the theory of relativity and non-Euclidean geometry as well as his wife's lectures on genetics, a subject which had only just been rehabilitated. One evening in the mid-1970s, in the flat of friends, some of my graduates, who by now were mothers and fathers but had maintained old contacts, listened with sorrow and pity as Sokolovskii clung on to the fragments of his illusions. His wife was no less distressed. Their son had spent nine months in a psychiatric ward and was now working as a postman and was seriously involved with Russian religious philosophy. Sokolovskii refused to hear about samizdat or tamizdat. He rejected outright all forms of secret or open confrontation with the authorities. He repeated over and over again: biology and physics had been emancipated - the humanities would also be emancipated. He broke off all relations with us and forbade his son to frequent our circle.

The comparison between these two branches of study was, however, quite false. First, the exact and natural sciences form the basis of technical development, while the humanities form the basis of man's knowledge of himself and society. No modern state can function without technology, especially a state with such a huge military-industrial complex and such international and internal policies as the USSR. Second, the humanities have not entered the phase of genuine official emancipation. The process of modernising and, to a certain extent, liberalising them has occured, and is occurring, despite official policies. The Soviet state has never permitted teachers or scholars in the humanities to step over the dangerous boundary of free analysis and generalisation. The state needs modern technology, but unfalsified knowledge of man and society about themselves is mortally dangerous to it. The state will never sanction freedom of knowledge in the humanities without ceasing to be itself. It expends huge efforts and funds on disinformation (not only inside the USSR but also beyond its borders) in the sphere of the humanities. Therefore all our fervent declarations (I also was involved in this in the period 1955-65) about the extremely primitive level not only of literature teaching in schools, especially rural ones, but also of the articles in the magazine *Literatura i shkola* ('Literature and the school') (see B. Sarnov's article 'Equivalent to losing happiness' in *Literaturnaia gazeta*, no. 117, 1960), about the low level of magazine articles on teaching methods, about the extremely poor quality of school essays, about the 'cramming' of pupils to pass the school-leaving or entrance examinations, instead of studying literature with them - all this was merely hot air. Anything else was impossible and was not expected of us, for it signified that same open or, for the time being, cautious confrontation with the authorities. Lies, or models instead of images, or the petty, narrow, sentimental quasi-psychologism - such was the state of official literature teaching. To adopt the opposite course meant taking risks every day for many years. Fortunate was the teacher whose own world view was no broader than the official limits.

Sometimes very instructive statistics would appear in newspapers, magazines or pamphlets. Thus, *Literaturnaia gazeta*, no. 6 (1962), published a long survey entitled 'They left school' about the failure to implement the law on universal compulsory education. The author, I. Metter, discussed the inaccuracy of statistics and illustrated his observations with a number of examples. It should be noted that in the period 1956-66 the liberalisation of the press was manifested in particular by an influx of statistics which was quite new for the USSR since the NEP period (this lasted until the end of the 1960s). An increase in the number of non-trivial statistical data in the press is always a sign of liberalisation. The two changes in leadership - Stalin -------> Khrushchev --------> Brezhnev (I omit the intermediary phases of 'collective' leadership) - bred a stream of statistical data that had been unprecedented in the previous 25 years: in official documents, in the press, in essays and memoirs which blended the artistic and documentary genres, in scientific and popular-scientific publications; even the pamphlets of the '*Znanie*' ('Knowledge') Society contained most valuable statistics (often in small print and sometimes scattered among statements that blatantly contradicted them). Even some party propagandists and lecturers of the '*Znanie*' Society used statistics which later formed the basis for a number of illegal works exposing the system.

Metter's article related that one of the heads of a city Department of Education had reported to a teachers' meeting that in grades one to eight, 17 children were not participating in any framework of study. His audience had reacted to this statement with much noisy agitation. After the facts had been checked, it was discovered that the 17 children were weak children who had not yet turned eight and whose mothers had not sent them to grade one but had delayed their starting school until the following year. However, it also became apparent that there were about 1000 children in grades one to eight, including these 17, who were not participating in any framework of study. Metter enumerates the ways in which statistics could be falsified:

(1) Not all children who should be in school are included in the list of universal education.
(2) False data are given about those who have left school: the class teachers who are responsible for the children who have left obtain false certificates from trade schools, evening schools for young people, house-management committees (that they have 'left town', etc.).

Metter, who is an observant and thoughtful writer, with a good knowledge of the problem, then analyses the reasons why children leave school:

(1) Needy families send their children to trade schools with short periods of instruction which do not require eight-year education and do not have their own regular schools.
(2) The author gives a very accurate analysis of the boarding-school venture, with certain inevitable shifts of emphasis:
Question: Why do such families not send their children to boarding schools?
Reply: 'As yet' there are not enough boarding schools (this was in 1962 when the boarding schools were already beginning to be curtailed, as we saw from the legislative acts. But either this trend had not yet been discerned or this was the usual homage to the censor). '...The cost of tuition in them is quite expensive' (of course: 25 per cent of the family's income, which barely provided the child with food and clothing and which did not include the days off and school and national holidays at home, pocket money or expenses on transport and recreation).

At this point a most interesting statistical detail is given which bears out what was said earlier - that the Soviet system was unable to cope with the boarding schools first and foremost economically: 'The construction and upkeep of boarding schools are extremely costly.' A boarding school costs several times more than an ordinary school and has several times fewer pupils than the latter.

(3) Metter notes the poor conditions in many schools and testifies that more children drop out of schools that have three shifts than from those with two shifts.

In short, the schools had not yet been brought to satisfactory standards of hygiene, so it was ridiculous even to talk of boarding schools on a mass scale.

(4) Schools try - by any means that are not criminally punishable - to get rid of pupils who repeat the same year many times, of backward, slow, difficult and troublesome children. They try to arrange for them to be admitted to trade schools which also provide secondary education or to evening schools and to find them jobs, but most of them end up on the street. Unfortunately, the author says little here about the success-rate pressure on schools which forces them to fear children who repeat the same grade or who are slow.

(5) In this survey I encountered for the first time a serious presentation of the problem of educating gypsy children (instead of the usual cinematically romantic and glibly optimistic treatment of the problem): the parents sell their children's uniforms and textbooks and forbid them to go to school. The author draws his examples from the experience of schools in the Gatchin District of the Leningrad Oblast.

Metter strongly disputes the expediency of removing children from normal families and sending them all to boarding schools. However, as we have seen, this policy was not a real threat to Soviet schoolchildren because of the state's economic impotence.

This article gave the attentive reader an accurate idea of the opportunities and the weaknesses of Soviet schools in the Khrushchev era. By contrast, another article by Dolinina, 'Why did the teachers keep silent?'[90] merely demonstrated the 'fighting potential' and the profound 'principled nature' of the law-abiding liberalism of those years. She begins with statements which echo the previous references to the CPSU's resolute intention to end the 'divorce from life': 'The XXII Congress of the CPSU ... has given us a lesson in the struggle to restore justice in any, even the most complicated circumstances ...'

Whenever I encounter such statements in the writings of people who are generally recognised as being neither ignorant nor stupid, I am always at a loss to decide whether this is mere hypocrisy and, if so, why. In those years, articles of a level such as Dolinina's had little trouble slipping past the censor without paying ritual homage to the sinister 'posthumous rehabilitation', and many did. Or was this an attempt to hypnotise the sinister 'liberators' by thrusting their own declarations in their face or teaching them a model of behaviour like children in the classroom? In any event, after recognising the 'fortitude' of the CPSU (in the 'struggle to restore justice in any, even the most complicated, circumstances'), a person is no longer eligible to moralise. Dolinina, however, does not stop moralising. In this article she fulminates against teachers who docilely accept the 'kul'tiki' ('mini-cults') of school administrators, and she defends an independent young teacher against the persecution organised by the director of her school and the collective of teachers intimidated by him. But her own, personal, writer's hypocrisy - her flattery of people who are far and away more criminal than the despotic director and ignorant teachers - cancels the emotional force of her article.

At the beginning of 1962 a series of ignominious responses appeared in the press to the unlawful trials of foreign currency speculators, in which draconian laws were retroactively applied. Against this background of new illegal death sentences (under laws introduced after the crime had been committed), a lengthy 'Conversation with colleagues' by L. Kovalev appeared in Literaturnaia gazeta, no. 61 (1962). Its epigraph, a quotation of N. Krupskaia, was extremely ominous: 'The school front is also a front of the struggle.' But against whom are this front and this struggle? Children do not like school, according to the article, because of bad, callous teachers who tend to be dictatorial and sanctimonious. They call the teachers' room a 'nest of gentlefolk'. The collective solidarity of the teachers compels them to cover up errors and keep silent about each other's shortcomings, to reject even the justified criticism of the children about them and their colleagues. Teachers persecute even the tiniest sign of freedom in dress or hairstyle, do not accept films about children's or young people's love, avoid sensitive issues, fear arguments, guard the myth of the teacher's infallibility and assume that literature and art should do the same. The author proposes a number of measures:

(1) to establish the true authority of the teacher which will be guaranteed by the high degree of integrity of the teacher himself and will not depend on the collective solidarity of teachers;
(2) to reject the power which routine views, methods, habits have over the teacher, including such habits as the use of pressure and compulsion instead of personal influence and persuasion;
(3) to reject formalism: the author gives the example of the school's wall newspaper which is boring and usually hated by the pupils. The author thinks that if formalism is rejected, it can be turned into a most interesting activity for the pupils.
(4) The author recommends most insistently that teachers deal 'percentage-mania' a final blow, as though it had begun to die instead of in fact continuing to flourish, as though its fate lay in the hands of the teachers and not of the state.
(5) (This is the author's main wish) to educate in children 'civic activity and civic courage' (Kovalev's emphasis). 'I fear indifferent people',[91] he concludes, ending the article with a reference to Janusz Korczak.

This reference and several other comments by the author indicate that he conceives of civic activity and civic courage as a development of the unmasking of events at the 20th Party Congress. He cannot discuss this directly and emphasise his personal attitude to the problem, so he uses a device which will soon come to characterise writing of a liberal inclination: the author tries to express himself in such a way that like-minded readers will understand him while people with different views and the censors will see their own ideas in his text. For example, he writes about the need to put an end to the myth of infallibility. To satisfy the censor, he adds the teacher's infallibility, which is permissible. But later he speaks of civic courage and civic activity. Are these virtues to stop at the school's threshold? The like-minded reader discerns that he is referring to further exposure of the myth of the party's infallibility exploded by the 20th Party Congress, to rejection of the possibility of anyone's infallibility, no matter whose. The only trouble is that the reader who is not so close to his way of thinking does not go further than the call to reject the infallibility of the teacher who, by the way, is oppressed and crushed and never regarded as infallible. Another example from the same article is the author's demand to deal 'percentage-mania' a final blow. The initiated reader knows that the pursuit of a high success rate is devouring the schools, that it is mighty and omnipotent, but the censor and reader who inculcate 'percentage-mania' have to be thrown a bribe: all right, damn you, I'll write 'deal the final blow' to create the impression that everyone is fighting it fiercely and that it's retiring into its hole all by itself.

This method seems to be tactically convenient: the public whom the author is addressing understands what he wants to write, while the persecutors (of both the writer and the reader) remain in safe ignorance. In practice, however, this is not so: the writer is understood only by the reader who shares approximately the same outlook as the writer and does not need his help. This reader is, of course, enriched by the information and gratified by the sense of identity, of thinking in the same way as the writer; but a reader who has not attained a similar level of knowledg and understanding of events will understand what is written in exactly the same way as the censor and the writer's supreme persecutor. Moreover, as the liberalisation waned, this device increasingly turned into a tactic of duplicity. Authors resorted to Aesopian language and began to work for both sides simultaneously. Samizdat came into being precisely because the Aesopian language of what could be published officially became clearly inadequate for communication between writers and readers. What is more, calls for civic courage made in an inevitably ambiguous manner, i.e. very uncourageously, negate the very message they are trying to convey.

The teacher found himself in exactly the same situation in the classroom. At the begining of the 1968/9 school year I was asked at my courses, which prepared school-leavers for the entrance examinations to institutions of higher education, what I thought about freedom of speech and the invasion of Czechoslovakia by Soviet troops. My courses were attended by candidates for institutions of higher education and faculties in the humanities in the town, including the law institute. Many of the latter's future students were already working in the large, grey building on Sovnarkom Street which housed the administrative offices of the Ministry of Internal Affairs, the KGB and the internal prison. With difficulty I mumbled that we were now studying Griboedev and that, as the question was not about our subject, I would only discuss it after the lectures.

Five years later, at the same courses, I was asked about my attitude to Sakharov and Solzhenitsyn. I replied that as I was not a physicist I was not familiar with the works of Academician Sakharov, while I did know Solzhenitsyn from the publications in Novyi mir and Roman-gazeta ('Novel-newspaper') and agreed with Tvardovskii's opinion of these works as expressed in his prefaces to the publications. But they persisted in trying to obtain from me an opinion of the works for which Solzhenitsyn was being criticised in the press. I replied that life had taught me not to have an opinion about books I had not read. This dialogue took place before an adult audience[92] which was listening with bated breath, and it ended in a startling manner. One of my students who often came to classes in the uniform of a KGB lieutenant (he was already working and after law school was preparing for admission to the law institute) turned to my naive tormentor (a lathe operator who had completed his army service and was preparing for admission to a teacher's institute) and exclaimed: 'Leave D.M. alone, won't you! Why are you putting her in an idiotic position?' On that note the dialogue ended - that time. However, my courses began to be visited too frequently by 'smokers' - that type of a man dressed in civilian clothes but with the ill-concealed bearing of an officer - who evidently gave the signal[93] that I spent too much time on the classics and too little on Soviet literature, and in spring 1970 I left the courses. But I shall speak about the first incident in more detail, for the boy who asked me about freedom of speech and the occupation of Czechoslovakia, Iurii Kovalev, a worker in one of the large plants in Kharkov, died a few years later of nephritis at the age of 21, so I can write about him without fear of harming him. The boy was 1.93 metres tall, looked like a Russian intellectual of the 1860s, with somewhat prominent cheek-bones and a face like Il'ia Nikolaevich Ul'ianov (without the beard). He came up to me after the lecture and we left the building together. He accompanied me to my home and came into our flat. After this conversation, as usually happened in such cases, I lay awake listening to the breathing of my sleeping family and wondered whether I had ruined them with my frankness with Iurii or whether, on the contrary, we had acquired another friend. Iurii believed in me during my lectures and placed me in a terrible dilemma (having served one sentence, I knew it was terrible): to instil in him the lies that were heard everywhere, sanctified by his trust and liking for a favourite teacher (a particularly hateful course) or to take the risk of exposing my family, friends, job and home (which was packed with evidence of my own and other people's sedition). I cannot say that the latter choice was always paramount: my personal feeling about the honesty of the person to whom I was talking, the state of family matters, the danger of the subject that I was working on at the time were also important. But it was inconceivable to lie to Iurii. I took the risk and won a friend, or rather friends, for after his death we remained friends with his unfortunate mother (her second son had blown himself up at the age of eleven while playing in a wood with a shell left over from the war). Iurii lived for three splendid years among a new circle of friends, reading, learning and trying to write, until the disease developed unnoticed with lightning speed and carried him off to his grave, tearing him away from the circle of friends that had become like a family.

I have provided these examples to offer the reader some notion of the everyday work of a Soviet teacher and the degree of risk and resourcefulness which 'civic activity and civic courage' demanded of him.[94]

One of the poorest institutions of Soviet secondary education is the evening and shift secondary schools for workers. Ostensibly, they should be a means of acquiring education for young people who deliberately choose this form of study and study of their own free will, with utmost diligence. This type of school cannot, of course, be as effective as normal secondary education, since it is very difficult to combine a job, usually an unskilled one or in industry, with studies and, frequently, a family and children. The curriculum is inevitably even more condensed than in the day schools, as there are fewer hours available: instead of the usual 34-36 hours a week (in the upper grades of the day schools), the evening and shift schools have four (sometimes five) workdays with four lessons per day, i.e 20-24 hours a week. Although they have an extra year of instruction (eleven grades), the evening schools have to a large extent turned into a means of dealing with the casualties of the law on compulsory universal education. First, the day schools use them as a means for ridding themselves of all the slow and difficult pupils, including those who repeat grades. Second, the staff in evening and shift schools are attached to the enterprises in their district and track down the youngsters who have not coped with the ordinary school framework, for whatever reason, and have stopped studying. With the help of the administration, these workers are persuaded and forced to attend an evening school with the threat of otherwise losing their jobs or, at any event, the possibility of promotion. Such pupils are poor students, or, more precisely, they continue not to study just as they did in the day schools. They are given 'satisfactory' marks, are transferred from grade to grade and graduated from school with a certificate saying that they have completed eight grades and sometimes even with a school-leaving certificate.[95] All this for having attended the school more or less regularly and for the sake of being able to keep such a pupil on the enrollment lists and, consequently, in the reports. It should be added that teachers' salaries are low, that there is a large surplus of teachers in the towns and that a teacher's work load depends on the number of classes in the school - hence the practice of semi-fictitious enrollment lists, of 'pupils' who put in an appearance in the class at least occasionally and enable the class to be preserved. Frequently only two or three pupils attend the classes in the evening schools and they leave with shockingly little knowledge.

As a teacher in the courses which prepared school leavers for the entrance examinations to institutions of higher education, I came across graduates from evening schools every year who had decided to continue their studies (after army service, already with families and with a strong desire to advance in their job or having found some professional vocation). They would make as many as 60 mistakes in the first dictations of 120-150 words, not to mention their essays - I did not manage to bring examples of the latter with me when I left the Soviet Union, but rarely have I seen documents which are as incriminating for the educational system as these feeble, illiterate efforts. But after two or three months it became obvious that they had been mostly written by intelligent, observant and thoughtful people with normal abilities. The graduates of rural schools and schools in remote districts were just as illiterate. Only a few individuals had managed to overcome the damage of evening school 'education'.

All these thoughts were expressed indistinctly, in a veiled and mild form, in the press and pedagogical journals. Thus, M. Tanich, in an article in Literaturnaia gazeta, no. 70 (1962), 'From 14 to 17', writes about the evening schools: '... the efficiency of the studies themselves is not always high' (it would have been more accurate to say 'always not', but that is inconceivable - it would not have been printed) 'the drop-out rate is high, discipline is poor.' Instead of the intended adult students 'there is a mass of youngsters from 14 to 17 years old' and a total lack of any educational work with them or, for that matter, of the possibility for such work; the 'voluntary-compulsory' recruiting of pupils in enterprises; the 'dead souls' who are listed on the class registers and who sometimes have never even put in one appearance in school. Of course, this article, which displays an excellent knowledge of the situation, gives absolutely no analysis of the true underlying causes.

*

Even the best pedagogue-writers tend to substitute superficial, secondary causes for the true roots of pedagogical problems. This is apparently the price they pay for being able to give at least an approximate description of the situation. The late Frida Vigdorova published an article in Literaturnaia gazeta, no 77 (1962), called 'The fresh water of philosophising' in which she attributed most of the defects in Soviet schooling to the glaring shortcomings of the pedagogy textbook of the former USSR Minister of Education, Kairov. It is, of course, always useful to discuss the defects of education, and Kairov's textbook is more than bad - I myself never managed to read it from beginning to end despite the innumerable examinations and courses for 'upgrading qualifications' based on this book. Clumsy writing, hackneyed party hypocrisy, ignorance, Marxist 'class' xenophobia, the author's utter lack of talent and intelligence - such were the shortcomings of what was for many years the compulsory textbook for everyone.

Vigdorova, however, had no choice but to single out in this orthodox Stalinist textbook defects which were far from its main ones and to substitute the deficiencies of a stupid and talentless teacher who is in the wrong job for the deficiencies of all practical pedagogy. Thus, even a person who is known to be honourable and talented, who in that same year had proved her civic courage by illegally recording in shorthand the trial of the poet Iosif Brodskii and distributing stenographic reports of it, is unable to write something that makes sense in a legal newspaper.

Here, in the author's opinion, are the main shortcomings of the textbook: '... deadness and boredom, discussion and not feeling ...' And here is the very root of the matter: 'It is a living person who sits behind the school desk, not a dummy. But not a single child looks at you from the pages of the textbook. Instead of living children there is a stereotype. A certain girl. A certain boy.' 'A textbook of pedagogy should not talk about a faceless "somebody".' But what about a textbook of medicine or physiology or psychology? Any textbook has to discuss the average and generalise the situation. The formalisation of pedagogical categories and how the practising teacher behaves towards the actual child are two different things. It is not formalisation, which cannot be avoided in any textbook, which is the main defect of Soviet textbooks on pedagogy, but the fallacious ideological and conceptual basis of that formalisation which the critic cannot legally question.

Here are some examples of the teacher's conversations with pupils and parents taken from Vigdorova's article:

The teacher visits the family of two alcoholic shop workers, a husband and wife, and tries to elicit from them a reply to: 'Well, are you still drinking? Are you still cheating the customers?' This is in the presence of the children whom the teacher invites to be witnesses, urging them to denounce their parents and confirm her accusations. Here it would have been appropriate to recall far deeper matters than a bad institute textbook: the teacher, after all, had been raised on the official glorification of children and adults who betrayed and killed their parents and loved ones (Pavlik Morozov in K. Trenev's Liubov' iarovaia ('Fierce love'); B. Lavrenev's Sorok pervyi ('Forty-first'); and later V. Kataev's Trava zabveniia ('The herb of oblivion'), etc.). It turns out, however, that it is the textbook of the loyal dimwit Kairov that is to blame for the teacher's moral and ethical blindness.

Or take the following dialogue:

Teacher: Why do you steal, Nikolai?

Pupil: I'm Boria.

Teacher: That's not important. The Motherland is raising you ... [etc. etc]. Think about what you're doing, Nikolai...

Pupil: I'm Boria...

Teacher: That is of no importance. Let it be Boria...

And so on, for four such exchanges in succession. Vigdorova thinks that the young teacher has 'learnt all the lofty words', that 'these words ... have their place', that she was taught 'words, not action or thought'. In the first place, she was not taught 'lofty' words but words that are hypocritical and ideological monstrosities, but which have entered the social usage and consciousness as being 'lofty'. Vigdorova shares this illusion to a certain extent (concealing the heart of the matter with phraseology), along with most of the dissident 'chartists' of the early 1960s. Second, what can be taught at all to the dimwit portrayed by Vigdorova who is incapable of remembering the name of the person to whom she is talking even after being reminded four times? At this point it would be appropriate to mention a problem which is common to the whole world: the methods of selecting candidates for teachers' institutes and the methods of awarding them professional testimonials on graduation. Such a discussion could include a description of the specific nature of the problem in a totalitarian society. But, once again, this would be to digress from our subject. However, even the renowned Polish pedagogue Jan Amos Kamenski could not have taught the person portrayed by Vigdorova anything: she has no memory.

The author is depressed by the situation of 'thinking students' being forced to use such a textbook. Thinking students, however, like the thinking teachers in the teachers' institutes and faculties, perceive Kairov's textbook as just another history of the CPSU or USSR, just another course in the 'Principles of Marxism-Leninism' or 'Scientific Communism' or 'philosophy', etc. The only trouble is that they have to take examinations in this course! Vigdorova is sorry for her heroine since '... the textbook teaches her that there are no misses'. 'The course of pedagogy prepares the student for cloudless weather', for pupils who are 'almost faultless'.[96] Is that the problem? Is that what it teaches? It teaches that 'our paralysis is the most progressive one', that's what!

Although the thinking student has at his service a vast amount of Russian pre-Revolutionary and translated classical pedagogical literature which has been preserved in the large libraries, it is not recommended or expounded to him. It is taught inadequately or distortedly and he often knows nothing about it and has to base his learning on (and later teach from) innumerable textbooks like Kairov's. Vigdorova herself notes that the 'textbook is very unfavourable towards researchers who say that the so-called crisis in the development of adolescents is unavoidable'. She writes: 'The textbook does not make the slightest attempt to analyse this idea, to think whether there is a grain of truth here, why it is wrong.'[97] The textbook recognises that such a crisis is possible in the West, but not here, not in Soviet boys and girls. But even Vigdorova does not place the epithet 'bourgeois', which she applies to Western scholars, in inverted commas, even though they are scholars and not members of the bourgeoisie! Moreover, she immediately doubts whether the 'bourgeois' researchers are correct to call adolescence a 'tragic' age: for her, the epithet 'complex' would more than suffice ('tragic is too much', it applies to 'there' but certainly not to our country). Nor does she touch upon the textbook's vicious attitude to any pedagogical idea other than the Marxist-Leninist one, which in principle is not a pedagogical idea but an ideological instrument.

Among Vigdorova's positive theses, intended to counterbalance her critical remarks in the eyes of the editor and the censor, is the very popular assertion that, for all its deficiencies, Soviet pedagogy is successful and remarkable for it brought the motherland victory in the Great Patriotic War and raised Iurii Gagarin and German Titov, the first Soviet astronauts. This article demonstrates the sheer impossibility (even at the beginning of the 1960s) of making professional reflections aloud, in print, without their being cut by the censor and self-censorship. Between the lines it is addressed to like-minded readers, but it merely reinforces the mythical conceptions of the uninitiated reader with the authority of a good person.

*

Meanwhile, Brodskii's trial was in progress, Pasternak was being stigmatised and hounded for Dr Zhivago; N. Aseev was having to defend the poet A. Voznesenskii against V. Nazarenko (in the magazine Zvezda ('Star'), no 7 (1962)) by proving that, contrary to what the latter said, his poems did not have a 'second meaning'. Brodskii was convicted and later emigrated. Pasternak was banished from the community of Soviet writers and uttered shortly before his death: 'I am alone. Everything is drowning in hypocrisy.' Voznesenskii was to betray the 'second meaning' of his poetry many times. But the Soviet school would not reflect any of these fateful events in its courses or optional subjects or try to fathom their meaning.

*

An article by K. Bukhtin, 'What lies behind the twos?' (Literaturnaia gazeta, no 101, 1962), referring to the failing mark of 2 out of 5) raised one of the central professional questions of any school. Let us see how the Soviet teacher answers it. The article noted the increase in the failure rate among pupils aged 11 to 14 (the middle, fifth to seventh grades: evidently they try to push all of them through the eighth grade). The pedagogical administration assumes that there is a concentration of 'teacher-bureaucrats' in these grades with a formalistic attitude to the pupils and their difficulties. The author suggests other, very realistic reasons:

(1) Poor rural primary schools: teachers in grades one to four (and certainly not only in rural schools, I would add) 'are just like nannies'.
(2) The teachers of grades one to four themselves complain that the individual approach to the children is lost in grades five to seven (where there really is no time for that, but nor is there in the first four grades).
(3) There are imperfections in the curricula and an abrupt switch in teaching methods between grades one to four and grades five to eight.
(4) The teachers are forced to manoeuvre between the Scylla of the teaching process and the Charybdis of unlearnt material. 'Everyone, of course, prefers to collide with Scylla.'

The metaphor in the last point is not very successful, as it is Scylla and Charybdis that collide while the teacher has to manage to slip through between them. However, it is the pupils' knowledge that is crushed in their inevitable collision. But the 'Scylla' of the school curricula (since we are already using mythological metaphors) merges with the Minotaur of 'percentage-mania'. In practice, it is unofficially prohibited to make pupils repeat a year in grades one to four (as director of a secondary school I fought against this unspoken prohibition for eight years). Since there are no examinations in grades one to three, and in the 1960s they were abolished in grade four as well, the teachers of the lower grades have complete control over the marks awarded their pupils. Desiring to avoid any unpleasantness, they promote all their pupils from grade three to grade four.

In 1955-9 I tried to obtain permission from the Zmiev District Department of Education of Kharkov Oblast for pupils in grades one to four to repeat a year for the following reasons and in the following way:

> (1) If a (mentally normal) pupil had failed to learn such a large proportion of the material that he could not make it up during the summer school holidays with the help of constant individual lessons in the school. We made it possible to conduct such lessons by the teachers' taking turns to interrupt their holiday which, as a matter of fact, they were not entitled to do. However, the teachers agreed to interrupt their holiday for 10-15 days and extend it accordingly afterwards until school recommenced. Soviet schools do not receive funds for supplementary lessons with backward pupils. We managed to extend the holiday because the school year never starts on 1 September, since all the pupils, even the youngest, are engaged in work on the kolkhoz. The young children help in the garden plots for about another month and the older ones in the fields, sometimes for another two to two and a half months.
> (2) A pupil (if, I repeat, he was mentally normal and could not make up the material he did not know during the summer) had to repeat the year in the grade where these gaps in his knowledge had begun. This meant that most of the pupils who repeated a year were to be in grades one to four.

Despite the resistance on the part of the District Department of Education, we managed to keep about two children down in each of the first four grades during two to three years. This greatly increased the real pass rate in the most pedagogically complex grades five to seven. But when I left the school because of my illness, this practice was stopped. Neither the administration nor the teachers of the first four grades, who have the lowest educational qualifications in the school and are therefore the most vulnerable, had the strength to continue the struggle.

The author of the article which we are analysing, K. Bukhtin, like the administration, also views the practice of keeping pupils down a year as an unconditional evil, as he approaches the matter in purely economic terms:

> The 29 thousand pupils who are repeating the same grade in Novosibirsk Oblast will cost the state two million rubles. These 29 thousand pupils will start work

> a year later. This means that the oblast will receive approximately 116 million rubles' less production.[98]

This approach is frequently found to this day on the pages of the Soviet press and in official speeches at teachers' conferences. 'Outstanding teachers' who contrive to avoid having pupils who repeat a year in their classes also often resort to this argument. Although it seems concrete and rigorous, in reality it is purely demagogical: who has measured (or can measure) the economic loss caused by pushing 29 thousand pupils - who have not mastered the curriculum but who have consumed the same funds as successful pupils - from grade to grade and graduating them from school at the same time as their classmates? Bukhtin touches upon another problem which has always been very popular in the pedagogical press and at teachers' conferences throughout the years: the psychological damage caused to pupils who repeat the same grade. Many such pupils do not return to school so as not to feel their own inadequacy in comparison with their younger classmates. At first sight this very widespread argument also seems convincing. But I had the occasion to express a different opinion, shared by many teachers, at teachers' conferences, in the Kharkov Oblast journal <u>Prapor</u> ('Flag') in 1964-5 and in the Institute for the Advanced Training of Teachers in 1958-9. If our aim is to spare the pride of pupils who fail year after year, then it would be better to issue them with a certificate that they have completed eight years of schooling at the outset and not waste on them funds, strength and nerves, theirs or the teachers'. But a <u>mentally normal</u> pupil[99] who repeats the same year suffers psychologically most of all from the fact that the previous gaps in his knowledge are not eliminated and that every day a new layer of uncomprehended material is added to them. The child, or adolescent, loses faith in himself, becomes bitter and enters into an active confrontation with the teachers, the class and sometimes even with society (not as a dissident - he has not reached that level of development - but as a hooligan or criminal). Moreover, being kept down a year at higher grades makes the pupil feel humiliated and even sinful. In grades one to four the children do not yet see it as a defeat, as a sign of inadequacy, and this is precisely the stage at which any shadow of disgrace or crime could be removed from repeating the year and the neglect and gaps in the child's knowledge could be overcome, his faith in his powers restored and his normal progress through school ensured. Typically, this point of view, for all its popularity, was not reflected in the central press.

This problem remains one of the major problems for schools and the individual to this day. The individual aspect of the problem is particularly acute since, on the one hand, the school is unable to cope with the problem and, on the other hand, the full burden - the humiliating situation, lack of respect, the sense of being an outcast by comparison with the successful pupils - falls on the pupil. The older he is or the more frequently he has to repeat a grade, the stronger is his sense of alienation from the good fortune of his classmates. Gradually, the only form of self-assertion accessible to him becomes hooliganism, violence, an attraction to the street and crime.

*

Mikhail Tsentsiper, one of the most famous teachers and administrators, a brilliant publicist and an active participant in all the school experiments of 1956-60, the director of Complete Secondary School of the City of Moscow No. 437, was a frequent contributor to the press. A long article by him, 'Yes, we must hurry', appeared in Literaturnaia gazeta, no. 107 (1962).

In this article Tsentsiper attacks the opinion which was popular at that time (and still is) among a considerable number of teachers and scholars in the field of pedagogy that the differentiation of instruction according to the pupils' interests would lower their overall level of development. He disputes the widespread conviction held by teachers in the late 1950s and early 1960s that the level of interest in studying was declining because of the 'polytechnisation' of the schools and the general orientation of the large majority of pupils not towards higher education but towards industry or the kolkhoz.

Since the number of students admitted to higher education had not declined, despite all the propaganda designed to direct the stream of pupils towards industry and the kolkhoz, the opinion of these teachers did not seem well-founded. The number of places in institutions of higher education and technicums had not been reduced. Whosoever wanted to continue studying had the same opportunities to do so as previously.

Tsentsiper considers that the curricula '"resound" to the development of science' and therefore become increasingly overloaded with more and more new material. He upholds the idea, shared by most of the best pedagogues, that all senior pupils should no longer be kept on 'absolutely identical educational rations'. He proposes reducing the volume of informational material compulsory for all pupils, dividing the pupils into speciality groups (profili), and increasing 'the proportion of classes in subjects where their hearts especially lie'. He is convinced that if this were done, the labour of study would become attractive because 'the most powerful motivating emotions would turn out to be attached to the category "ought" - the person would go to meet his own aptitudes and vocation'. He urges that the 'principles of science' be taught which stimulate the imagination and thought instead of trying to give pupils amorphous, infinitely expanding 'courses', not to cram the pupil's memory, but to enrich his memory with what is most important and essential. 'No, general education in schools will not "suffer" with differentiated instruction'. Quite the contrary: 'in such schools all the subjects will begin to sparkle,' he asserts.

He gives the examples of the Novosibirsk School of Physics and Mathematics, the Moscow School No. 425, and others: 'In recent years a variety of schools have appeared at last in our country: the boarding school and extended-day school, the 11-year school.' He insists that 'A vast country with its diverse and complex economy needs also good and varied schools. Including differentiated schools ...'[100]

Today, after the experience of many years, we can note: only a very few boarding schools have survived, mainly the specialised ones, for sick children, for gifted children (musicians, artists, dancers), in the north, in special climatic and demographic circumstances; there are no extended-day schools, only extended-day groups, mostly for children in grades one to six; the differentiation of instruction has virtually ceased: in the very large cities there are few schools with increased demands for foreign languages and few schools in speciality fields (in the physics-mathematics and biochemistry cycles) for the entire Soviet Union.

Does, however, the differentiation of instruction into several speciality groups solve the overall problem of raising the success rate of pupils? Differentiation is certainly necessary: it helps to eliminate the increasing overloading of curricula and increases the older pupils' interest in studying. But it does not eliminate or solve some problems and even compounds others. It has no effect on:

(1) the universal problem of discipline, order in the classroom, the organisation of the teaching process, relations between schools, pupils and parents;
(2) the Soviet problem of 'percentage-mania', i.e. the pursuit of a fictitious pass rate which exists only on paper. Most adolescents, and, even more so, children will not study seriously, no matter what the curriculum, unless their progress can be assessed with real marks.
It exacerbates:
(1) the problem of designing a curriculum of a high scientific level. It is very difficult, but absolutely essential for differentiated instruction, first to consider very carefully what is the main fund of indispensable knowledge which is needed by all pupils irrespective of the speciality area of the school which they will later attend. Second, it is essential to work out very seriously and scientifically the relation between the general subjects and those in the speciality group and the curriculum of each of them in a differentiated school.
(2) the problem of the teacher's qualifications in differentiated schools. The experience of Soviet 'profile' schools (I have knowledge of the Novosibirsk, Kharkov, Moscow and Petropavlovsk Tselinnokraiskii schools) has shown that differentiated schools need teachers of a far higher professional and cultural standard than do ordinary schools.

The problem of discipline is less acute in Soviet schools: there is a comparatively high degree of order in the pedagogical practice. On the other hand, the problems of a fictitious good pass rate and the low standard of teachers are very acute - so acute as to frustrate the efforts of the most active supporters of differentiated schools.

*

An article by S.N. Titov (a teacher and the father of astronaut German Titov) on 'Why we teach literature' provoked a discussion in Literaturnaia gazeta in 1962-3 in the section 'The school of 1962' and 'The school of 1963'. N. Dolinina responded in Literaturnaia gazeta, no. 139 (1962), with an article which described how she taught children Russian literature and how she thought it should be done. First of all, she weans the children from speaking in clichés. She writes clichés which she does not allow them to use in their essays on the blackboard. But how does she cope with ideas that are clichés, with ideas that in reality turn into their opposites, that are fictions?

She writes (and this is just before Solzhenitsyn's publications and after Pasternak's expulsion from the Soviet Writers' Union - and she is a fluent and well-read writer) that first and foremost the pupil has to be educated to be a 'real reader'. She writes:

> A real reader, I am convinced of it - is first of all an honest person. He is a citizen and a fighter, an intransigent, ironic, subtle adversary of sanctimoniousness and formalism, vulgarity and time-serving. Such a person cannot be educated by 'doing' character studies and [literary] figures. Many teachers realise this very well now ... And I work ... with the feeling of being on a tightrope: on the left are the syllabus and the examinations for the school-leaving certificate, on the right, what I see to be the children's needs.[101]

Is that all? A balancing act between the school-leaving certificate and her own understanding of a good book? But the heart of the matter lies elsewhere. Was N. Dolinina's literature syllabus so good that in 1962 she could, if she wanted, teach _Dr Zhivago_ instead of Ostrovskii's _Kak zakalialas' stal'_ ('How the steel was tempered') or Furmanov's _Chapaev_? (We had already read Pasternak's novel at that time and, knowing some of her friends of those years, I have no doubt that she had also read it.) Could she replace Sholokhov's _Virgin soil upturned_ with Vasilii Grossman's _Vse techet_ ('Everything flows'), which is also about collectivisation but a far better, more honest book, which had already appeared in _samizdat_ in the 1960s. Or could she read with her tenth grade, instead of Sholokhov's _Sud'ba cheloveka_ ('Destiny of a man'), _One day in the life of Ivan Denisovich_ which in 1963 was not even _samizdat_ but an official publication?

A certain Kiev journalist praised Dolinina to me at the end of the 1960s, saying (having read my notes on D. Granin which were published in the Israeli Russian-language journal _Vremia i my_ ('Time and we') only in 1978) that there was someone else who shared the opinions of myself and my colleagues. But in 1962-5 we were performing a balancing act not between the school-leaving certificate and our literary predilections, but between prison and repeating shameful lies to our pupils. The country was awakening in _Gosizdat_ (i.e. official publications), in _samizdat_ and in _tamizdat_ (illegal literature smuggled out of the USSR and published abroad) - Daniel and Siniavskii had 'broken a window' through to Europe - and in the cramped apartments of friends and in the classrooms of those who dared. But to make out that this balancing act between the abyss and lies (not only were we walking the tightrope, but we were also dragging our pupils, children and the future of the country, either towards the abyss or towards lies) was merely a matter of methods of teaching literature is downright wicked. Therefore, legal pedagogical writings were totally lacking in good faith when they discussed the fundamental questions of the life and future of schools.

Dolinina says that Soviet literature should be taught in grades seven and eight and the classics in grades nine to eleven. This is, of course, true: what can a 14- or 15-year-old see in Onegin, Tat'iana, Chatskii or Pechorin? But this is not the essence of the problem which *ostensibly* disturbs Dolinina most of all. What concerns her is the moral evaluation of literature teaching in Soviet schools. To teach Sholokhov, Ostrovskii, Furmanov, etc. in this way (and according to criteria that are known to be false) and not to teach the best Russian writers of the USSR and abroad of whom 99.9 per cent of the teachers are ignorant (Dolinina, though, is familiar with them, which is why her hypocrisy grates so much) is equally immoral and harmful no matter what the order in which they are taught - chronologically or according to increasing difficulty.

Dolinina proposes that the teacher study his favourite books with his pupils. She does not like Turgenev's *Fathers and sons* but likes his *Nest of gentlefolk* (I could not conceive of ignoring *Fathers and sons* and *On the eve*). This is a form of diversifying the syllabus which is still tolerable (even by the Ministry of Education). However, the majority of teachers, graduates from Soviet institutions of higher education, as well as abroad, may have bad taste. The literary, qualitative standard of what is taught has to be regulated in some way for the real, average teacher, not for the elite, refined ones like Dolinina. I favour some kind of choice from among a number of broad, diversified, tested syllabuses designed according to the criterion of quality. Otherwise, many Soviet teachers, given the choice between Pasternak and Eduard Asadov would opt for the latter. But Dolinina writes: 'I want trust. Elementary trust of the teacher and his work. And control can always be carried out.'[102] The payers of Soviet teachers' wages may well agree to this 'controlled' trust (very tightly controlled). But I, with hand on heart, am forced to admit that I would not have dared ask for their trust for myself or for many other teachers of literature. Given the slightest relaxation of control, the slightest relaxation of the authorities' vigilance, the teacher who really loved and knew literature and history (Anatolii Iakobson, for example, who trod this path) deceived his many-eyed Cerberi as best he could.

'Let them trust me to teach the children as I see fit, and then let them try me in earnest,' entreats Dolinina. She is evidently deeply convinced that she and her controllers share common goals of teaching. But Ivan Denisovich and Matrena's courtyard were just about to be published. What if she should suddenly take it into her head to study Novyi mir in an optional course? 'In your opinion, we should be some kind of encyclopedists,' one teacher said. 'Why encyclopedists? Just cultured and modern people,'[103] Dolinina preaches to Soviet teachers of language and literature.

Literature teachers have to be free people - honest, educated, but also with the opportunity and right to realise this education in the classroom. Nothing demonstrates so convincingly the lack of freedom of literature teachers in the period of the 'thaw', the impossibility of their realising their education, their dishonesty, as the very emotional and very nobly phrased and apparently very civic-spirited articles of the best teachers of those years.

*

Tvardovskii announced in Literaturnaia gazeta, no. 145 (1962), a new novel by Vladimir Dudintesev, Neizvestnyi soldat ('The unknown soldier') (which to this day has not been published and which may never have been completed) and praised One day in the life of Ivan Denisovich. Meanwhile, Dudintsev's novel Not by bread alone, re-issued in 1968, did not find its way into the schools.

*

At the beginning of 1963 the 'discussion' in Literaturnaia gazeta on Titov's article was concluded. His former teacher, A. Toporov, also replied to it. I place the word 'discussion' in inverted commas because really serious, profound questions were no longer raised in these discussions. Attention shifted to minor, purely methodological matters (how to teach children to read, to paraphrase a text, to express their feelings verbally, etc.). Titov himself was very satisfied with the 'discussion' his article had stimulated. The entire 'polemic' (nobody was in fact debating anything with anyone) boiled down to the style of the various pieces of advice proferred by recognised teachers and writers on how best to obtain from the pupil what the party and government ordered the teacher to obtain from him. A concluding article by Titov summed up the discussion:

(1) The discussion had become broader than he had thought and had drawn into the debate outstanding writers and educationalists.
(2) He considered that on average pupils had grown and become stronger and more developed than ten years before and wanted to study literature. (I myself think that a pupil in the first grade always wants to learn, and schools have to expend much effort to kill the child's interest in learning, if the parents have not already done so.)
(3) He noted that there were many extremes in the discussion. 'Is there any need at all for a textbook?' Some thought not.[104] Others assumed that literature lessons should educate readers, but not literary historians or critics. A third group (like Toporov) thought that literature lessons should educate the writer in the pupil, that every normal child had literary talent. Titov assumed that schools needed a literature textbook written by the best literary critics and writers.[105]

Commenting on Dolinina's proposal to make the choice of works studied in the syllabus more flexible, Titov wrote that a model syllabus was necessary as a kind of standard for the teacher. I agree with him in the sense that the syllabus should define a certain standard of compulsory knowledge which can be raised but not lowered.

Following Kabo, Titov considered that the history of Russia and the USSR should not be the end in itself of the school course in Russian literature, but that the historical approach should be intelligently combined with an aesthetic, literary approach. Indeed, the school literature course in the USSR tends to be merely a reflection of the Russian and Soviet history course (depending on the period studied). Although the course does contain elements of literary theory and psychological analysis, the aesthetic and theoretical factors are few and condensed, as the teacher's time is very limited, while the psychological elements are entirely subordinated to the ideological goals. The selection of authors and works is likewise subordinated to the historical and ideological goals.

In conclusion, commenting on the course of the entire discussion, Titov made the significant observation that the articles by rank-and-file teachers, especially those in rural schools, were more interesting and rich in content than those of, as he put it, the 'academics', i.e. scholars in the field of pedagogical sciences. He spoke at length about lightening the load of this largest category of teachers, those in rural schools, but, unfortunately, failed to analyse a more fundamental question - the problem of training rural teachers and of their progress and knowledge.

*

From 1963 the authorities addressed increasingly clear and harsh warnings to the intelligentsia from the pages of Literaturnaia gazeta. 1963 is usually regarded as still being the height of the 'thaw', but on 9 March 1963 the paper published a speech made by L.F. Il'ichev two days earlier at a meeting between party and government leaders and artists and writers. His 'criticism' was directed mainly against abstract painters. Among the numerous 'workers' letters' published by the paper on the same day were also letters from teachers in Lugansk (in the former and future Voroshilovgrad Oblast) protesting against 'pseudo-innovation' and asserting that part of the intelligentsia had 'lost its class feeling'. They defended socialist realism against the encroachments of 'socially irresponsible' artists. The teachers' letter was placed next to a letter from astronaut Iurii Gagarin against the same artists. Il'ichev calls the response of the Lugansk teachers 'apt and intelligent'. Indeed, the entire issue was reminiscent, on the one hand, of the newspaper campaigns in the era of 'Zhdanovism' and 'rootless cosmopolitanism' and, on the other, of the hounding of Pasternak, Dudintsev, Granin, Iashin,Kirsanov and Kabo under Khrushchev (1956-61). However, it was characteristic that, even though many well-known figures appeared in this context in the newspaper, including the ostensibly liberal poet Vladimir Soloukhin (no. 40, 1963), and although there was a ferocious attack on the last part of Il'ia Ehrenburg's memoirs, Marlen Khutsiev's film 'Il'ich's outpost' and against painters, well-known, active, major teachers did not lend their names to this campaign. They had to unearth 'teachers from Lugansk Oblast' and publish a letter from them in a central newspaper, the organ of the Union of Soviet Writers.

No literature teachers could, of course, speak out in defence of the abstract painters, Ehrenburg, Khutsiev or Evtushenko, even though the discussion on the goals of teaching literature, on the civic honesty of teachers and pupils had barely ended. This was the time when teachers and older pupils alike were engrossed in reading the last part of Ehrenburg's memoirs, while the Evtushenko of those years was their common idol. But everyone was forced to keep silent. Here indeed was a lesson in literature combined with a lesson in standing up for principles.

The polemical fervour of the articles on pedagogical subjects in newspapers and magazines was diminishing perceptibly. One example of this decline in the social involvement of such articles was an article in Literaturnaia gazeta, no. 28 (1963), 'Topics for school workers', on whether love should be discussed in schools.[106]

On 19 June 1963 Il'ichev's speech on schools to the Plenum of the Central Committee was published in Literaturnaia gazeta (no. 73) and all the pedagogical journals and newspapers. The fact that the reactionary Il'ichev, a man of Zhdanovite views, was the one to discuss this subject in the name of the party was also symptomatic of the 'swing to the right', the departure from the trends of the 'thaw' which had not yet had time to develop properly. Il'ichev quoted and praised a fable by Mikhalkov, which had not yet been published, 'The river and the bog', about a foreign ideological bog that resolved to poison the pure, swift-flowing Soviet river with its bacilli because it was powerless to stop its course. The standard of the fable, from the point of view of both literary value and content, is abysmal, but not a single one of the recently eloquent advocates of the teacher's literary erudition and freedom was given the opportunity or the right to publish a critique in response to this masterpiece and Il'ichev's insolent, ignorant and insultingly sermonising speech. One section of this speech proclaimed: 'To bring all forms of ideological weaponry into battle formation'; another was entitled: 'The Soviet school - an important stage in instruction and upbringing'. There were no responses to the speech by serious teachers, which meant that they had as yet managed to avoid being forced to laud it. However, an article by I. Moteshov called 'Truth and mini-truth', Literaturnaia gazeta, no. 80 (1963), compared, in the best pre-Khrushchev tradition, the 'large truth of Communism' which had to be 'revealed and taught to the youth and schoolchildren' with the small 'mini-truths' of negative 'details' which only obscure 'the large truth of Soviet life'.

Now, at last, followed responses from 'progressive' teachers: an article by a young woman teacher, 'Will you advise me where to work?', appeared in the following issue of the newspaper in which, in the best traditions of the superficial, narrow, petty, Soviet literary 'neo-sentimentalism' of those years, she described how she wanted to be not a teacher but a journalist. Dolinina replied with an article called 'For me there is only one answer' in which she noted that she had been teaching for 13 years and publishing regularly for eight years (since 1955) and advised the young teacher not to give up school and to draw material for literary creation from it. But in this article Dolinina, the author of essays, articles and plays about teachers' and pupils' honesty and devotion to their principles, about the culture of reading, the erudition of teachers, literary scrupulousness and taste, quotes from Khrushchev's and Il'ichev's speeches at that disgraceful meeting with intellectuals and refers to Il'ichev's speech on schools to the CC Plenum! Can the sincerity of these references be credited? But if they are sincere, so much the worse:

> That you still come across self-seekers, time-servers, etc. Yes, you do. We do not keep silent about that. Look at the content of the June Plenum of the CC CPSU - N.S. Khrushchev's speech, L.F Il'ichev's report. A harsh, merciless sentence is passed there on the kind of people who arouse your wrath. A relentless war is being waged against scroungers, parasites, self-seekers, time-servers. Everyone has to be a warrior. I, you - everyone![107]

It was explained to me that these respectful references to Khrushchev's and Il'ichev's speeches by such teachers was redeemed by what they did in the classroom, alone with their pupils. However, I do not agree. If their pupils have learnt to love and believe them in the classroom, then they will believe what they write as well, and the pathos of the article by the liberal, refined and erudite Dolinina is aimed at proving that Khrushchev's and Il'ichev's speeches direct us to fight against the vices of our society and not against the rebellious intelligentsia. She commands the young teacher and her colleagues to re-educate 'cowards, those who have taken the vow of silence, demagogues' <u>among the children,</u>

but does this herself according to the models of the anti-cultural, anti-intellectual, demagogic, deceitful speeches of Khrushchev and Il'ichev and proposes that they teach children, according to these same models, 'culture and good, honesty and truth, steadfastness and the ability to stand up for their convictions, to educate in them civic feelings'. All that was required of Dolinina was the courage not to quote the two supreme leaders of the party anti-culture, in her article, or not to publish her article in Literaturnaia gazeta but simply to send the young teacher a letter, visit her, invite her, risk being honest with her. This, of course, would entail certain dangers, but what is the alternative?

The talk about the reforms and radical changes in school structure, methodology and methods of education were inevitably reduced to mere problems of curricula concerning the volume of material and character and methods of teaching mathematics, physics, biology, chemistry or grammar. All the demands that were made on the schools became more and more directed at the teachers. As in Stalin's times, the slogan 'cadres solve everything' was heard, although formulated somewhat differently. Now everything depended on the quality of the teacher and therefore all the problems whose solution did not depend on the teacher (percentage-mania, pupils who repeated the year, the falsification of subjects in the humanities, ideological education, etc.) no longer arose, or lost their urgency. I. Ovchinnikova responded to an article by Kabo in an essay 'The teacher is what is most important' in Literaturnaia gazeta, no. 42 (1964). 'The teacher,' she wrote, 'is an actor who has to leave all his personal concerns behind the scenes when he goes on "stage", i.e. when he opens the classroom door.' Although such an approach totally excludes problems such as the teachers' excessive work load, difficult life and low pay, this idea does contain a large element of truth: the pupils are not responsible for the teachers' chaotic life or for their relations with the authorities. Ovchinnikova takes this thesis to its extreme by opposing it to the behaviour of teachers in the West, where prolonged strikes deprive innocent pupils of the possibility of studying. As usual, the truth lies somewhere in the middle: the trouble is that this impecunious, care-ridden and over-worked teacher, deprived of rights, cannot, day after day, act the happy, independent and cheerful spirit before his class, even if he wants to.

I recall that teachers were particularly hurt by what,

once again, as in the articles by Dolinina, Kabo and others, seemed to be the author's utter blindness or lack of sincerity. Or maybe this could be seen as a desire to prod the reader to thought, to make him feel how utopian the author's standpoint was. I do not know. When it is impossible to express one's thoughts directly, people sometimes resort to devices which they know to be futile.

Ovchinnikova stressed that 'the teacher's civic spirit, his uncompromising integrity' were absolutely essential traits of behaviour. She recommended that they should not avoid 'critical situations with which school life abounds (like, moreover, all life), but go to meet them, intervene actively and resolutely in everything.' She urged teachers 'never to evade a question outside the curriculum, however pointed it sounds' and asserted that 'the teacher is one who is always a militant optimist', while '... nothing is as dangerous as a teacher who know something from here to there'. This advice, which is perfectly valuable for a free teacher in a free school, sounded like either the apotheosis of blindness or hypocrisy or maybe an allusion to the unnatural circumstances at a time when the attack on writers who had taken the liberalisation seriously was in full swing. One day in the life of Ivan Denisovich had already become the topic of keen polemics between 'free-thinkers' and the 'orthodox': V. Lakshin, who supported the publication of Solzhenitsyn's stories in Novyi mir, was defending himself against Barabash, while my best pupils were pestering me with risky questions during the lessons. The teacher's job was either to risk his job or to avoid risk. But there was only one instance in which he could be urged to go to meet the pupils' questions boldly and openly: if he firmly shared the official viewpoint, in which case courage would mean the irreproachable defence of Suslov's views on literature and life, consistent support for what the best pupils, along with their most respected teachers, were ceasing to believe in.

The phraseology of the 'thaw', which was dying out in discussions on literary and social topics, was still being used in discussions in the press and journals on psychological and pedagogical themes in the second half of the 1960s. The 'right' (?) of adolescents to fall in love and the 'right' (?) of teachers to 'analyse' the notes of lovers out loud in the class were investigated. A teacher's ability to respect the semi-childish love of schoolchildren was presented in the press as free-thinking, as laudible audacity and courage. Sometimes tragic topics were discussed. N.Atarov related the suicide of a 14-year-old girl whose love notes had been read out to the class by the teacher (Literaturnaia gazeta, no. 107, 1964). The note was then given to the school director who summoned the girl with her mother and read out the note again before all the teachers. It was after this that the girl committed suicide. In an afterword 'from the editors' the word 'party' appeared in every possible context ('the party' teaches us to be sensitive, to be psychologists, etc., but we drove a girl to her death). Without this, evidently, this report of how a child was subjected to monstrous mockery would have been impossible.

The section in Literaturnaia gazeta called 'The school in the current year' disappeared in the second half of 1964. Only a few articles, some of which were interesting, by pedagogues were still published. Thus, in no. 143 M. Tsentsiper published his reflections on whether it was permissible to suspend 'bad' children from school: where did the 'bad' children come from, was there no other solution apart from expulsion or permissiveness, could 'bad children' be allowed to trample on the teacher's dignity? He did not offer a solution, but recommended reflection on the issues. This is a serious problem for all schools, even those in a free country. When a child reaches a mental, moral, ethical, etc. condition which prevents the teacher from being able to work with him with the normal methods used for a normal class, then supplementary methods of work should first be tried in the same school and the same class. Such children need extra attention from the school: supplementary lessons; psychological and medical examination; an informal, in-depth investigation of his family; the assignment of an individual teacher and educator to overcome his educational and moral deficiencies. This may be expensive, but a person who is crippled mentally and morally from childhood eventually costs society far more. Schools in the USSR are instructed to provide these individual forms of teaching, but without any payment, and what is more, the class teacher is obliged to do this work in his free time, the time he has for his family, since he is not released from any other school or social and ideological work for this sake. The result is that the work is simply not done, or only done as a formality.

Let us consider an ideal version of this problem. If all the attempts to involve the 'bad child' in the life of his class and the school have been made and have not produced any significant results and the child disturbs the work of the school, he can be transferred to another school (if he is still at an age when he is subject to compulsory education). But the school to which this 'bad', 'difficult' child is transferred should be better in all professional respects than the school which was unable to cope with him. It should have better teachers, richer resources, a longer school day (if it is not a boarding school) and a more complete and co-ordinated systemic approach to the child; it should have psychologists and other specialists. Re-education is immeasurably more difficult than education. But what happens in practice? In the USSR a child who cannot be dealt with in the framework of a normal school is transferred to an institution of education that is worse, poorer and harsher. There are three alternatives: (1) a school for mentally handicapped children; these institutions are usually, with few exceptions, of a very low standard and frequently have extremely meagre resources, but as these are medical institutions they do not concern us here; (2) a trade school or industrial school which, properly speaking, are not schools or educational institutions at all but a means of getting rid of difficult pupils by giving them some semi-skilled trade and adding them to the population of factory hooligans in outlying districts. Nobody in these institutions is concerned with moral education or - even less - with overcoming the deficiencies in the child's general or ethical education, and frequently these institutions are dominated by young criminals; (3) colonies for difficult children or juvenile delinquents, which are in fact prisons for juveniles. The problem of 'bad' children does not have a satisfactory solution either in the USSR or in Israel, or, judging from the limited data I have had access to, in the West. The solution as I see it, which could spare society many problems, could be summed up as 'for the most difficult children the best, specially organised schools'.

In the previous sections of this chapter, devoted to the legislative aspect of the educational reform of the 1950s and 1960s, we saw that the first signs that all the large-scale changes were being curtailed appeared in the legislation long before the groups connected with schools became aware of them. The public was still in the sway of the momentum of these changes, the momentum of the 'thaw' and reformism, while the state had begun to cut back everything that required major capital investment. Eventually, the public also became aware of the change in policy. Not long before the above article, Tsentsiper had described the growth in various forms of schools as a great achievement of Soviet secondary education of recent years and called the eleven-year secondary school one of the most brilliant testimonies to the growth of this symptom of progress. However, an article by him in Literaturnaia gazeta, no. 83 (1963), 'This should be thought about' questioned the expediency of eleven-year schooling. I do not mean to say that Tsentsiper was charged with the task of justifying the forthcoming abolition of the eleventh grade in day schools, although this possibility cannot be ruled out. However, the point is that, if he had previously had doubts about adding an extra year to the school course, he could not express those doubts in Literaturnaia gazeta until the authorities' policy of curtailing this experiment had been outlined, so he had praised the eleven-year school. But now he raised a multitude of objections to it:

(1) Pupils remain behind the school desk 'until their wedding'.
(2) Other ways of enriching the school course can be found.
(3) 'When you count the rubles and hours' it turns out to be too expensive a luxury for the country: every eleventh grade means large additional expenses, whereas this money could go to form a fund for improving school equipment. (As if the huge, rich country had no other resources.)

In this article, in which Tsentsiper quotes Il'ichev three or four times on the benefit of polytechnical training, he makes only a couple of mild allusions to the fact that the eleventh grade is superfluous in the context of this 'polytechnical' (i.e. superficially vocational, poor, narrowly industrial) training, but does not reveal the real reason why the extra year was not needed by the state or the school. This, however, was reiterated by teachers in all the teachers' rooms in those years: the eleventh grade had, in reality, been added not to satisfy the needs of education or the needs of the subject teachers but for labour training, which, as a rule, the pupils of the eleven-year school would not use on leaving the school. It was a sheer waste of money and time, and the state could not afford this extra expenditure on the eleventh grades, just as it could not afford boarding schools.

*

Articles in the press by teachers revealed ever more clearly how difficult it was becoming for writers who aspired to preserve the momentum of liberalisation to express themsleves at a time when policy had drastically changed. The open attack on Solzhenitsyn and all those who were trying to defend him (beginning with Tvardovskii) was about to be launched in Literaturnaia gazeta (Iurii Barabash's article 'What is justice?', in no. 105, 1963). A few issues later the newspaper published ferocious attacks on Iashin's Vologodskaia svad'ba ('Vologda wedding'), an irreproachably realistic story ('Truth without "embellishment"' by M. Sinel'nikov, no. 121). And the country's best teachers and teacher-writers, would be compelled, as always, to pay for every semi-truth in their articles with a lie that made nonsense of their efforts.

Liubov' Kabo published an article in Literaturnaia gazeta, no. 105 (1963), entitled 'Anything but "fish eyes"!' (i.e. 'indifference'), and another in no. 122, 'Litmus paper', subtitled 'What is modern philistinism'. Her first article begins sentimentally with how she taught a class to think. Then comes the romantic demand to open to children in school 'the expanses of Her Majesty Play'. Kabo is a gifted writer and she gives glaring examples of teachers' and school directors' insensitivity, pedantry, obtuseness and lack of understanding of the psychology and value system of children and adolescents. True, she does not avoid the obligatory kowtowing to the permanent victories and conquests sustained by Soviet schools under the party's leadership. For example: 'Was it so long ago that we were suffocating from "rhetoric" - from rhetorical instruction, from rhetorical education ... Was it so long ago that the remarkable school re-organisation was realised?' (What had been realised? It was just beginning to be curtailed! But it was impossible to publish anything without going through the necessary motions of etiquette.) Then, recalling that social studies were being introduced into the schools, Kabo asked a rhetorical question: 'What should be done so that this subject will educate citizens? So that the teaching of this subject will not become doctrinaire and dogmatic?' In her second article she wrote that whether a person was a philistine or not depended on 'the goal to which a person devotes his life'.

Kabo asserts that she has devoted her life to educating people who can think, and think 'in a non-doctrinaire and non-dogmatic fashion'. Nonetheless, like Dolinina and

Tsentsiper, she also wants to be published officially, and this is still possible for her because, although she criticises outstanding details, she accepts the main rules of the ideological game. The word is a powerful instrument of education - but only if it is truthful. Kabo's pupils, however, inevitably have to 'think' within the boundaries of the very dogma which the subject of social science, now being introduced as part of the school curriculum, is designed to inculcate into the pupils' minds! Kabo thinks that the only trouble with these dogma is the way they are taught: the teacher should present them in a skilful and original way, and the pupils should remain sincerely within their bounds (which is called 'thinking'). But what happens when Literaturnaia gazeta, the newspaper in which the teacher who teaches them to 'think', publishes her articles, begins to hound Solzhenitsyn and Iashin, and the teacher does not publish a word in their defence? Then the choice is either to teach the class not to think (or at least not to think things through) or to take the pupils who are emotionally and intellectaully strong by the hand and lead them into opposition, and the strongest ones into the underground. Or simply not to think at all.

*

It was precisely for this reason that the task of teaching to think, of utilising the information explosion of the 'thaw' and the overall relaxation of the regime (in the sense of educating civic-mindedness, historical perspective, independence - in the first place spiritual independence) was performed not by the famous teachers, but by the best ones, whom to this day I cannot name as that would be equivalent to denouncing them. Since the famous teacher participates in official public life and, therefore, bears a share of the responsibility for it, he is either compelled to live a double life, explaining at least to some of his closest pupils why he lies and what these lies are, or teaches his model of 'decency', the decency 'conforming to baseness' (both Saltykov-Shchedrin and A. Zinov'ev have brilliant examples of that type of 'decent person'). It seems inevitable that a teachers' underground will eventually come into being, analogous to literary samizdat. Samizdat and dissident activity could not exist even for a year were it not for the broad, elusive, obscure, widespread stratum of opposition which quietly disseminates their ideas, documents and books as a matter of course, day by day. From this stratum at times names emerge and become world famous, while at other times obscure victims disappear into the abyss of prisons, camps, exile, psychological torture chambers. And sometimes fame and disaster come at the same time.

*

Articles by mathematicians were the most well-defined and systematic of all the discussions published in the press. One example of the most interesting articles of this type was an article by G. Levitas, a teacher of mathematics. 'A person has come to learn' (Literaturnaia gazeta, no. 8, 1964). Levitas is a realist who thinks that only talented teachers can avoid having pupils who fail or repeat the year. (I am not convinced of this, as there are reasons for failure which are beyond the teacher's control.) He describes how mathematics can be taught better than is done on the average and considers the mathematics curricula (in 1964) to be boring, depressingly primitive and at the same time difficult, while all the problems and exercises are stereotyped. He gives a most interesting example of how the pupils' standardised way of thinking in mathematics makes them incapable of thinking in a non-stereotyped manner: an unusual kind of problem was presented to pupils - it was solved by almost all second-graders, by fewer pupils in grade three, and by none in grade four. The second-graders had not yet become accustomed to the stereotyped methods used to solve the usual types of problems, while the fourth-graders had been (subconsciously) preoccupied with defining the type of problem and seeking a stereotyped key to solving it. Levitas proposes a solution which was basically adopted at the end of the 1960s and the beginning of the 1970s because: (a) it was not ideological and did not trespass on any social problems; (b) it did not require additional major funds. He proposes experimental mathematics curricula which introduce the principles of algebra and inequality from grade one. He recommends improving the curricula in other subjects as well, referring to the primitive syllabuses of 'literary reading' in the first grades (these syllabuses were just as primitive in grades five to seven: in grade five advanced pupils who were reading Jack London, Dickens, Kuprin, Turgenev and Chekhov at home, 'studied' the fairy tale of 'Santa Claus' at school). Levitas suggests books that stimulate the desire to read. These books are indeed interesting, but to read them in the primary grades assumes that the children all come from educated families where books are an integral part of living. All such proposals and experiments are suggested by people who live in towns and for people who live in towns, moreover by the elite for elite pupils. However, the great majority of both pupils (in villages, outlying districts, from uncultured families) and teachers have sometimes not read the children's books that a child from a cultured, reading family will have read in grades one to five. The differentiation in the receptiveness and opportunities of pupils (and teachers) begins long before they encounter the school (as much in the USSR as in the rest of the world). Moreover, Levitas does not include in his proposals tales of fantasy, science fiction, detective and adventure stories and, what is most important, he does not touch on the problem of preparing children before school to love books.

*

If, in the case of Tsentsiper's article on the benefit of eleven-year schooling, there is still room to doubt whether it was 'ordered' by the editors or simply arrived at the right time, Kabo's article, 'Which way to go?' in Literaturnaia gazeta, no. 33 (1964) raised no such doubts. Throughout the world the periodical press occasionally orders articles from its regular writers, but the trouble in this case is that Kabo's client is always the same one and his demands concern not only the topic but also the concept, i.e. he determines not only the topic (the problem, question) but also the idea (the answer).

In almost every country the complete course of secondary schooling lasts twelve years, without polytechnisation. In this article Kabo asks how the ten-year course of schooling can be combined with polytechnisation. From among the measures that would really reform Soviet schools, she reiterates the proposal to differentiate the upper grades according to the three cycles - the humanities, physics and mathematics, and chemistry and biology. This measure was no novelty even in Tsarist Russia with its classical and non-classical Gymnasia and commercial schools with the complete Gymnasium course. It is practised in the upper grades of Western and Israeli schools (just as secondary schools are quite usual with production, or rather vocational training, which give their graduates a profession which they actually use). Kabo therefore proposes a measure which has long been the norm in other countries, but at the same time describes such specialisation as 'real' polytechnisation. Why? 'Poly' means 'many' while specialisation narrows the range of subjects studied. The reason has to be sought in ideology: Communist labour, in its original meaning, is labour that is liberated from narrow specialisation, from 'contradictions' caused by the division of labour. <u>Every</u> member of society has to become a poly-specialist capable of switching easily from task to task. But this utopian vision contradicts the reality of engineering, technology and the division of social labour in our times and the foreseeable future. Therefore the multiplicity of occupations is to be realised not within the framework of <u>every</u> pupil's life but within the boundaries of the <u>entire</u> educational system. With this approach, 'polytechnisation' does not contradict the differentiation of school courses. Nothing more is left of the original idea of polytechnisation than of the abolished eleventh grade, but the gain for the budget is enormous.

Kabo returns to the old dogma of Stalin's times that 'Cadres solve everything'. She discusses at length how, in the final account, the quality of teaching and education depends on the teacher, that a great deal depends on the general atmosphere in the schools and on the teacher as educator. She complains very timidly that the class teacher's work is still, in effect, practically unpaid and calculates that the class teacher is only paid an additional 7 rubles 50 kopecks a month, or 10.5 kopecks an hour for his work.

*

We have examined representative examples of pedagogical articles at the end of the 1950s and in the early 1960s in the most liberal publications of those years, <u>Novyi mir</u> and <u>Literaturnaia gazeta</u>. In these publications it is impossible to separate the authors' sincere convictions from statements influenced by opportunistic considerations or restricted by the awareness of inevitable censorship. On the other hand, they do give a complete picture of what teachers and other writers could say about such topics in the years of the 'thaw' and immediately afterwards. It can be stated with confidence that the picture of the state of schools, urban and rural, day and evening, depicted in these writings was fairly complete. But the analysis always stopped at the border beyond which lay an examination of fundamental problems concerning Soviet pedagogical goals, Soviet ideology and the Soviet system. Thus, when discussing polytechnical training, it was permitted to criticise shortcomings in the way it was being implemented and to suggest ways of correcting them, but it was absolutely impossible to write in the press that genuine <u>poly</u>technical education was impossible for modern man, that Marxism's basic concepts of the structure of social employment were not applicable to modern technology and the technology of the foreseeable future which do not enable the worker to be the universal polytechnician. In brief, no matter how absurd the policy of the authorities, its principles could not be scrutinised even though, in private conversations, teachers criticised them scathingly. When boarding schools began to be curtailed and the eleventh year of schooling was abolished, no one could investigate, in print, the economic reasons for the failure of the school reform which teachers were discussing among themselves quite confidently. No teacher could publish an article which would take the analysis of the crimes of the Stalin era - of which the people had been given a mere glimpse - a step further than the party organs had done. Pedagogical writings in the press had much to say about the mediocrity of ideological rhetoric in the schools, but the actual content of this rhetoric was never subjected to critical analysis. The appearance of samizdat and tamizdat and their infiltration among the most cultured teachers in the large cities - who in this sense were no different from the rest of the 'intelligent intelligentsia' (to use a phrase of G. Pomerants) - intensified even more the split between their private and public lives, the mutual antagonism of the two. In their own circles the most intellectual and civic-minded teachers shared the dissident moods and were involved in para-dissident activities: reading and disseminating samizdat and tamizdat. The most daring teachers sometimes included their closest pupils in their own circle, but any open act of dissidence deprived the teacher of his right to teach (at least), as happened to I. Gol'denberg and V. Pertsovskii in Novosibirsk. Solzhenitsyn, it may be recalled, was also a schoolteacher after his exile. I could name a number of other people, but I do not want to harm them.

NOTES

1. Narodnoe obrazovanie, p. 192.

2. Ibid. It should be recalled that Stalin ordered separate schools for boys and girls in 1943 which was an extremely difficult year with a desperate shortage of resources and premises. At that time hospitals had been set up in a number of schools. His yearning to restore imperial forms was so great, especially during the war, that he utterly ignored the economic aspect. In any case, the

priority of politics over economics is one of the fundamental principles of totalitarianism in general and Communism in particular.

3. In pre-reform money (before 1961).

4. When at the beginning of the 1970s, because of the rising cost of living in the USSR, stipends in technicums and institutions of higher education were increased - and at that time stipends were awarded to all successful students, while outstanding students received bonuses to their stipends - the overall size of the stipend fund was not increased. The teachers, as well as class representatives, Komsomol organisers and party group organisers among the students were demanded to reduce the number of students who received stipends. Stipends began to be taken away for missing lectures, for not doing 'voluntary' Saturday or Sunday work, for not going to work on a kolkhoz, for failure to attend a meeting, for passivity in social work, etc. Members of the students' organ of 'self-government' were also forced to participate in decisions on these matters.

5. Narodnoe obrazovanie, pp. 247-9.

6. D.M. Bardin, Proizvoditel'nost' truda i effektivnost' proizvodstva ('Labour productivity and the effectiveness of production') ('Znanie', Moscow, 1967), p. 33.

7. In the first case decisions are produced by a centre which stands above the whole of society, while in the second case - by an assembly of adult and competent (in the eyes of the particular society) members of the society.

8. See the above-mentioned Resolution of the CC CPSU and USSR Council of Ministers of 15 September 1956, Narodnoe obrazovanie, pp. 247-9.

9. The reformers envisaged that children would study in the boarding schools from the first to the last grade (eight or ten to eleven). Their number should therefore be correlated to the total number of schoolchildren and not only of those in the senior grades.

10. Narodnoe obrazovanie, pp. 247-9.

11. In 1955-62 I was the director of a rural secondary school with 600 pupils which served a district where there were several large villages. The school, which employed 45 people, was housed in the building of a former parish school with four relatively large classrooms (25-35 sq. m.), without a hall, laboratory or special subject rooms (kabinety) and in two village peasant houses with classrooms of 16.5-24 sq.m. Another small shack was occupied by the library. For years I tried in vain to obtain money for building the school. At the

beginning of the 1970s the situation had not changed. Approximately 1,800 ('new', 1961) rubles per year were allocated to capital repairs in our school and another 500 for current repairs. These sums were not even enough for the most urgent repairs or building on small extensions to the existing buildings.

12. Sponsors (shefy): in the USSR there are arrangements by which an organisation or enterprise takes a special interest in a priority construction project.

13. Data from reports of the Central Statistical Board published in the Soviet press. See Biudzhety SSSR ('USSR budgets'), 1960-70. 'Statistika', Moscow.

14. I assume that such a large increase in expenditure was a result of the increased number of pupils and the large increase in teachers' salaries in this period. Teachers of grades one to four received particularly large rises: the lowest rate, for teachers without experience and higher education, increased from 50-60 to 70-80 rubles a month (village, town).

15. In my paper 'My school. The experience of a Ukrainian rural school, 1943-63', published by the Center for Soviet and East European Research of the Hebrew University of Jerusalem (1979), and also in my essay 'My school' in the journal Vremia i my ('Time and we') (Tel Aviv), no. 34, pp. 161-99. I described one such attempt by a school to be self-supporting. The state stopped this attempt as soon as signs of genuine economic independence and the effectiveness arising out of this independence were manifested.

16. Narodnoe obrazovanie, p. 149.

17. Ibid., pp. 249-54.

18. In 1962-3 I was very ill and received a pension of 40 rubles a month according to disablement group II. At that time my daughter attended a boarding school. As I did not want to apply for a reduced rate and as I was hospitalised for a long time and fed free of charge, I paid the boarding school ten rubles a month for my daughter. My disablement pension, after 14 years of work in the educational system, was eleven rubles less than the minimum subsistence wage per person (according to official data, 51.4 rubles a month in 1967). My daughter did not have a father, but until I returned to work we were helped, and sometimes even kept, by my friends and my pensioner mother who, after working for 40 years, received a monthly pension of 47 rubles. Until I returned to work we were just as poor with or without the

ten rubles which I paid for my daughter. Our case is typical; my and my mother's pensions were average, not the minimum, at that time.

19. At the same time 1r. 30-1r. 80 a day was the charge for feeding a child in a children's tuberculosis santitorium with a school. In the general hospitals, clinical and surgical, this sum was 40-60 kopecks. The daily charge in special hospitals - tuberculosis, certain endocrinology departments - was 1r. 80. Patients in the closed hospitals (for the privileged), however, beginning with the oblast committee hospital, were fed like in expensive sanitoria.

20. The exceptions were the few boarding schools with good subsidiary farms and workshops which existed until 1964, and also the special boarding schools such as the university and academy schools for gifted children in Moscow, Leningrad and Novosibirsk. This did not extend to the music or art boarding schools.

21. The children's homes took complete care of orphans and children with only one parent without relying on the families for anything, while the boarding schools sent the child home on school holidays, weekends and national holidays.

22. In 1964-5 there was a famous trial in Kharkov of Chanyshev, the head of a furniture manufacturing complex. The trial involved boarding school No. 3 through whose workshop some of the illegal (black-market) jobs of the complex would pass.

23. A letter by a recidivist, Volobuev, who died of TB in a labour camp, gives a very realistic picture of life in a children's home - quoted in part 2 of Eduard Kuznetsov's memoirs in the journal 22 (Tel Aviv), no. 5 (1979) pp. 5-61, - as does the story by V. Pisarev, 'Kizilovoe derevo' (The cornel tree'), Novyi zhurnal (New York), nos. 149, 150, 151.

24. Pravda, 26 May 1959.

25. Ibid.

26. Ibid.

27. Unless the meagre level of the wages of workers and white-collar workers is considered as payment for these services.

28. Narodnoe obrazovanie, pp. 256-7 and Sbornik prikazov ('Collection of Orders'), no. 37 (1962), p. 14.

29. Ibid.

30. Ibid.

31. Ibid.

32. The appendix is not given in this collection of

documents, for the length of time for wearing clothing and footwear and also for using 'soft stock' (bed-linen, towels, etc.) was greatly increased which discriminated even more against the children who wore only state clothing.

33. The exemption of day-pupils (i.e. children who spent the night at home but used as much food and clothing as the full boarders) from only five per cent of the fee drastically reduced the chances that well-to-do families would want to send their children to boarding schools: the children in any case would have to be provided with additional food, clothing and amusement at home. Paragraph (e) made the situation of needy children much worse: without exemption from payment, such families preferred to send their children to children's homes, which did not charge a fee, or keep them at home. Everyone knows that it is easier to feed one person in a family out of the 'common pot' than to find money in the family budget to maintain him outside the home.

34. Narodnoe obrazovanie, pp. 257-8.

35. Ibid.

36. Ibid.

37. Ibid., p. 197.

38. Ibid., pp. 197-210.

39. Ibid., pp. 214-17.

40. Ibid., pp. 256-7.

41. Khrushchev's school reforms were, above all, very costly. I shall illustrate how reliable were the plans on whose basis the restructuring of Soviet education was to be financed: all the plans for reform in the 'superstructure' (education, culture, science, ideology, organisation and administration, etc.) depended on changes in the 'infrastructure', which were to consist of rapid planned growth of the productivity of the socialist economy. Let us compare some indices of plans for agriculture in the Khrushchev era with the corresponding indices of 1965:

Kinds of produce (in millions of tons)	Khrushchev's plan for 1965	Khrushchev's plan for 1972	Received in 1965	Kosygin's plan for 1970
Meat	16	25	4.8	5.9-6.2
Milk	100-105	135	11.5	16-17

As we can see, according to Khrushchev's plan, which until 1964 was vaunted to be the most scientific plan in Soviet history and was backed up by the titles of the most authoritative scholars and institutions, meat production was to increase more than four times and milk production more than eight times the figures given in Kosygin's equally 'scientific' plan that followed it. The actual figures for 1965 are over three times less than the target for meat production and almost ten times less than the target for milk production in Khrushchev's plan. What capital investments could be guaranteed and realised on the basis of such unsound and arbitrary planning? The data are taken from Soviet newspapers and directives of party congresses and plenums in 1961-5 which were published in huge quantities in the USSR.

42. 'Statute on the secondary general education labour polytechnical school with production training', 1959. Sbornik dokumentov narodnoe obrazovanie V. SSSR, (Pedgogika Publishers, Moscow, 1959), pp.203-10.

43. Resolution of the USSR Council of Ministers 'On improving the production and training of pupils in secondary general education schools' on May 30, 1961, quoted in Narodnoe obrazovanie v SSSR, sbornik dokumentov 1917-1973, (Pedagogika Publishers, Moscow, 1974), pp. 214-17.

44. Ibid.

45. In order to determine expenditure on labour at least a balance of such expenditure in preceding years is needed, but in the USSR this balance for 1960 was worked out only in 1962, while only in 1967 did the Central Statistical Board 'begin work on compiling the inter-branch balance of production and distribution in the USSR national economy for 1966'. See Bardin, Proizvoditel'nost' truda, p.12. An example of planned economic development...

46. In a number of countries, including the USSR, workers frequently earn more than qualified specialists, while workers in the service sectors in the USSR have a similar level of earnings (mainly illegal) as the party and administrative elite. But prestige remains prestige, and nowadays a degree to a large extent is a basis for a person's self-esteem, while most people have an increasing aversion to manual labour and aspire to something more than an unskilled physical job.

47. Obrazovatel'naia i sotsial'no-professional'naia struktura naseleniia SSSR ('The educational and socio-occupational structure of the USSR population'),

('Statistika', Moscow, 1975). Other sources are given in the text.

48. Ibid.

49. Ibid.

50. Ibid.

51. M. Lemeshev, Mezhotraslevye sviazy sel'skogo khoziaistva, voprosy analiza i planirovaniia (Inter-branch links of agriculture, problems of analysis and planning') ('Ekonomika', Moscow, 1968), p.11.

52. 'The elimination of classes is our main demand, without which the elimination of class dominion from the economic point of view is meaningless', wrote Engels in 1891 in his 'Critique of the draft of the social-democratic programme of 1891', in K. Marx and F. Engels, Sochineniia ('Works'), 2nd edition, (State Publishing House of Political Literature, Moscow, 1955) vol. 22, p. 235.

53. F. Engels, Critique of the social-democratic problem draft 1891 (Verlag Publishers, Berlin, 1963), p. 232.

54. F. Engels, The housing question, translated by E. Aveling (Kerr, Chicago, 1914), pp. 129-30.

55. F. Engels, The housing question (International Publishers, New York, 1935), p.30.

56. Ibid.

57. Quoted from the speech of Nikita Khrushchev 'For a stable peace in the name of the happiness and enlightened future of the people', at the All-Russian Congress of Teachers, Moscow, 6-9 July 1960, Stenographer's Report (Ministry of Education of the RFSR, Moscow, 1961), pp. 23-7.

58. Ibid.

59. Khrushchev is referring to the Riazan' Oblast whose oblast committee secretary committed suicide a few years later when it came to light that all the economic 'successes' which had made this oblast famous in the Khrushchev era had been faked.

60. 'Dozhila, v svinarki poshla' is said to this day of graduates from rural secondary schools unless, of course, they take extension-correspondence courses to progress from being pig tenders to livestock specialists or farm managers.

61. To be more exact: who had been prepared for the staged 'free chat' with ordinary kolkhozniks, team and brigade leaders who 'happened' to be in the vicinity.

62. On 13 January 1953 Pravda announced the arrest of a group of eminent Jewish doctors accused of plotting to cut

short the lives of Soviet leaders by means of medical treatment. After Stalin's death in March 1953 the accusations were withdrawn.

63. Streptomycin and other medicines for TB, which were new in those years, were issued free by special permits of the Town Health-care Committee or were sold (officially) at very high prices. They were also available, of course, on the black market (paramedical). One course of streptomycin cost 300 'old' rubles officially and 1000 rubles on the black market. Several such cycles were needed for a complete course of treatment. The same applied to penicillin in the 1940s. In the second half of the 1950s all medicines against TB also became free of charge.

64. Narodnoe obrazovanie, pp. 116-17.

65. Ibid., pp. 117-18.

66. Ibid., pp. 118-20.

67. This applies first of all to rural schools, then to schools located a long distance from large cities and districts, schools in the European and Asiatic Soviet Union, the Far East and Asian republics.

68. Ten rubles a month in the money of the 1960s and 1970s.

69. Later, more outspoken books would be published legally, but they would make their way past the censor at a time when samizdat already existed and after the publication of 'One day in the life of Ivan Denisovich' which substantially changed the whole situation.

70. E. Pomerantsova, 'The beginning of a great path' in 'Essays of our days' in Novyi mir, no. 7 (1956), pp. 3-15.

71. Ibid.

72. L. Aizerman, 'The living and the deadened' in 'Essays of our days' in Novyi mir, no. 7 (1956), pp. 16-30.

73. Ibid.

74. The last part of L. Kabo's story 'Na trudnom pokhode' was published in the same issue of Novyi mir. The almost simultaneous appearance of Kabo's, M. Bremener's and A. Kuznetsov's stories and the many articles about them is in itself proof of the attraction which the subject of schools held for writers and readers at the end of the 1950s.

75. E. Galperina, 'Vospitanie pravdoi' in Novyi mir, no. 12 (1956), pp. 262-5.

76. Liubov' Kabo, 'Ha trudnom pokhode' in Novyi mir, no. 11, pp. 105-206; and No. 12, pp. 82-189 (Moscow, 1956).

77. See L. Aizerman's article in Novyi mir, no. 1 (1959), pp. 206-11.

78. Ibid.

79. Ibid.

80. Ibid.

81. This is the same anti-semitic A. Markov who attacked Evtushenko in samizdat for 'Babii Iar' and of whom one samizdat poem says quite well:

> And to Markov the Third Markov the Second
> Cries from the grave: Thank you, hero!

Markov the Second was one of the most extreme anti-semites, a deputy in the last State Duma (from the Kursk Province, who was also called 'the nightingale of Kursk').

82. 'History is a great teacher' (no author cited) Literaturnaia gazeta, no. 85, (1959).

83. Semen Kirsanov, 'Sem' dnei ndeli', in Novyi mir, no. 9 (1956), pp. 16-32.

84. Vladimir Nemtsov, 'Ideas on education', in Literaturnaia gazeta, no. 27 (1959) and no. 31 (1959).

85. V. Eliseeva, 'In the name of Vadim's friends', in Literaturnaia gazeta, no. 30 (1959).

86. Vsevolod Voevodin, 'Communism is happiness', Literaturnaia gazeta, no. 135, (1959).

87. Ibid., no. 79 (1959).

88. 'What disturbs the teacher' (roundtable discussion with no author cited) in Literaturnaia gazeta, no. 2 (1960).

89. N. Kirsanova, N. Dolinina, S. Smolianitskii, M. Tanich, 'A.S. Makarenko and the Soviet school' in Literaturnaia gazeta, no. 79 (1960).

90. N. Dolinina, 'Why the teachers keep silent?' in Literaturnaia gazeta, no. 12 (1962).

91. L. Kovalev, 'A conversation with colleagues' in Literaturnaia gazeta, no. 61 (1962).

92. Not a servile, unthinking or compliant audience, as many people assume today, but an audience that thirstily drank in every living intonation, every non-trivial thought and discerned every allusion to the true meaning of events.

93. For the sake of justice I shall mention that the source of the 'signal' boycotted all my groups openly, outspokenly and indignantly.

94. A small detail can serve to illustrate just how little known the word samizdat was in 1962. Literaturnaia gazeta, no. 65 (1962), published an article by A. Alimzhanov and S. Nikitin called 'Samizdat', about the director of the Kazakh State Publishing House of Fiction, G. Samurzin, who abused

his official position to publish his own works. The newspaper would not have dared to give an article such a title nowadays.

95. The latter because universal secondary education is now interpreted in the USSR as being mostly universal secondary education for _working youth_.

96. Frida Vigdorova, 'The fresh water of philosophising' in _Literaturnaia gazeta_, no. 77 (1962).

97. Ibid.

98. K. Bukhtin, 'What lies behind the twos?' in _Literaturnaia gazeta_, no. 101 (1962).

99. I constantly emphasise 'mentally normal' because in Soviet schools, especially in rural areas (i.e. the ones that serve the masses of the population), it is incredibly difficult to get a mentally defective child recognised as ill and placed in a special _oblast_ school, to which there is always a huge waiting-list: because of the enormous number of alcoholic parents, the number of such children is increasing and, once again, especially in the villages, where there are far more families with a large number of children, than in the towns.

100. Mikhail Tsentsiper, 'Yes, we must hurry' in _Literaturnaia gazeta_, no. 107 (1962).

101. N. Dolinina, article in _Literaturnaia gazeta_, no. 139 (1962).

102. Ibid.

103. Ibid.

104. This is also a world-wide trend. I think that textbooks as well-designed educational aids and collections of exercises cannot be a hindrance even to a teacher of genius. Textbooks are an aid both to teacher and pupil.

105. One of the best literature and history textbooks in Soviet schools was (and is) the textbook for grade nine (the second half of the nineteenth century), edited by Professor Bursov. Its chapters are written by a number of eminent literary critics. Despite the inevitable homage paid to Soviet phraseology, ideology and literary and historical criteria, this is one of the most intelligent, emotionally rich and non-standard school textbooks. However, teachers in rural schools and many in urban schools criticised it: 'A textbook for intellectuals, for the elite. It's complicated, unintelligible, difficult...' (from a two year series of articles on 'Schools in 1962-3', in _Literaturnaia gazeta_, no. 139 (1962)). I constantly heard such comments, which said more for the level of the teachers than for the level of the

textbook (which is not difficult for a moderately well-read adolescent).

106. There was a well-known joke at this time about a sex education lesson. The teacher enters the classroom and announces that today there will be a lecture on love. 'But you all know about love between men and women. It is indecent to talk about homosexual love. So we shall talk about the love for our great Communist party!'

107. N. Dolinina, 'For me there is only one answer' in Literaturnaia gazeta, no. 81 (1963).

Chapter Five

THE DIFFERENTIATION OF OPPORTUNITIES IN SOVIET SECONDARY EDUCATION

I have had the occasion many times to hear from people who are familiar with Soviet schools, mostly from official Soviet scientific and statistical literature, that Soviet schools differ from those in a number of other countries in the equality of opportunity which they offer every child who crosses their threshold. This opinion is held by laymen, scholars, politicians and young people in various countries. This chapter examines to what extent it is founded.

It is known, of course, that there is no constitutional inequality of rights in Soviet education. However, as has frequently been noted, true inequality of rights often emerges most clearly when full equality of rights has been declared juridically, for a real right means a person's real, practical opportunity, and not merely legislation declared by the state. Modern Western democracy achieved juridical equality of rights for all its citizens long ago, but it nonetheless inevitably displays and frankly recognises (from a great variety of standpoints) the cultural inequality of various strata and groups of the population, their different educational standards, their different ethical systems, the different significance and prestige of various occupations, the different levels of income of various population groups and people with different occupations and qualifications, etc. Even if most of these inequalities could be excluded, the inequality of people's individual potentialities, which would inevitably lead them to having different social significance and roles, would manifest itself even more clearly.

Soviet society and, correspondingly, Soviet education, seem, on the outside, to be far more equable than Western society and Western education. The absence of private property and, consequently, of inherited wealth, the absence of private institutions of education, of highly prestigious fee-paying schools and colleges, etc. are viewed as the crucial factors here. However, one factor is overlooked about which emigrants from the USSR and former prisoners in Soviet and European concentration camps have written fairly extensively: when the overall level of rights and property is low, it is easier to create inequalities and privileges then when their level is high. Sometimes 200 grams of bread a day can make all the difference to a person's chances of survival. The level of education and, consequently, the chances of occupying a particular social position, may be determined by a distance of a few kilometers from a railway station.

The differences in the level of education received by Soviet children in practice, and not according to the Soviet Constitution, are so great that each level would require special investigation. I shall merely note some of these inequalities.

The first and main breach in pupils' educational opportunities occurs along the line dividing rural and urban schools. Soviet official publications constantly recognise that in order to enhance the quality of instruction in schools of general education and to reduce the number of pupils who drop out of school or have to repeat the year, it is necessary to overcome the gap between the teachers' level of education and qualifications and modern demands. Thus, in 1975, 27 per cent of mathematics and physics teachers and 23.1 per cent of biology, geography and chemistry teachers did not have higher pedagogical education. This shortage of teachers with higher education was particularly acute in rural areas where, in 1975, 55.5 per cent of school teachers did not have higher education. The situation is also bad in areas of Siberia and the Far East where, because of the frequently poor working and living conditions, the turnover rate of teachers is very high, as is the number of teachers who switch over to other branches of the economy.[1]

However, other data give an even more dismal picture of the educational level of rural teachers. In the 1970/1 school year, 266 thousand teachers (one in five) in rural schools had been working for 25 years or more, and less than one tenth of these older teachers had higher education. N. Khromenkov indicates a number of reasons for the low standard of educational and professional qualifications of rural teachers as a result of which the standard of graduates from rural schools is disastrously low.[2] I shall quote some of the most typical examples. First, rural schools, which comprised 81 per cent of all Soviet schools in the 1970s, are frequently extremely small, which makes them both very expensive and very poor: good resources (special subject rooms, laboratories, educational aids) cannot be established for these 'pygmy' schools; subject teachers cannot be provided with a satisfactory teaching load (there are not enough classes for them to receive full-time posts); it is impossible to build for such schools buildings according to model projects. '... A quarter of rural inhabited localities in the RSFSR have less than 25 residents. Moreover, the number of small inhabited localities has increased in a number of districts.'[3] Proper schools with all the facilities cannot be established in such localities. Meanwhile 'the standard of the study-educational process tells on the accomplishments of the pupils and their opportunity in the future to enter an institution of higher education or technicum. It is therefore understandable why many rural teachers, dissatisfied with the state of school education, try to change their place of residence.'[4]

A kind of vicious circle is set up: the decline in population cripples the schools, while the low standard of education contributes to the migration of population which, of course, also has other demographic causes (the lack of jobs, the attraction of the towns, the low standard of living and cultural amenities, etc.).

Teachers rarely remain in rural schools unless they themselves are natives of those villages and received their education in the same poor schools and completed it by correspondence course. Such teachers simply cannot work in the large urban and central district schools. The author of the article we are quoting from, Khromenkov, who has just sorrowfully established that there are disastrously few teachers in the villages with higher education and that their qualifications are low, concludes that, in order to rectify the situation(!), 'teachers' without any special education should be sent to the villages (only such teachers could stay there, others would run away): 'The small size of classes in schools in rural areas has a detrimental effect on the pedagogical and economic effectiveness of general education.'[5] A Resolution of the CC CPSU and the Council of Ministers on the rural school noted directly that 'the level of study-educational work of rural general education schools lags behind modern demands and in many cases the graduates of rural schools are inferior in their accomplishments to graduates of urban schools'.[6] As a rule, the 'pygmy' schools in the villages have fewer teachers, fewer educational and visual aids and lag behind in the development of their material base. Their overheads are exceptionally high. If in the country as a whole the cost per pupil is 140 rubles a year, in a large school with three parallel classes in every year it is 50 rubles a year, while in a 'pygmy' school with 6-18 pupils it exceeds 540 rubles.[7]

In a secondary school with ten classes, i.e. without parallel classes, teachers in a number of subjects cannot be given a full teaching load. In such schools, a teacher of physics and astronomy will have 17 hours of classes a week, a teacher of geography 13, of biology eleven, of chemistry ten, of drawing and draughtsmanship six, of singing and music four. As a result, teachers are forced to teach several subjects, which has a detrimental effect on the quality of the teaching. The more difficult work conditions of teachers in rural schools by comparison with their urban colleagues (the need to teach several subjects, the large amount of preparation, the lack of libraries and centres of teaching methodology, the shortage of educational aids, etc.), the lack of prospects of development of many rural schools and the inadequate housing and living conditions, all contribute to the high turnover rate of rural school teachers.

One solution proposed was to assign to rural schools young teachers who originated from the villages and therefore 'adapt to rural conditions far more easily'.[8] Thus, the former rural schoolchildren are to teach in inferior schools where they have no one to learn from, as most of the older teachers do not have higher education. They will acquire their degrees by correspondence course (i.e. they will merely go through the formalities of gaining a degree) and graduate from institutions of higher pedagogical education in the same remote areas of the country where they work. These institutions of higher education in remote, outlying provinces are known to be inferior to those in the central areas of the vast country. Moreover, the quality of these correspondence courses is always very low because, except for the two months a year when the students go to sit examinations (two weeks in January, ten days in March and the whole of July), they live in desolate places where there are no libraries of the necessary standard, have a heavy load of work both in and outside the school (the 'social' work) and live in conditions more difficult than a European, American or Israeli could conceive of. The distance between the cultural level of the average rural teacher with many years' teaching experience and that of a graduate from a good urban secondary school is insuperable. I came to teach Russian language and literature after two years of university education, after a five-year break in my studies and without any experience, not in the remote northern, eastern or Siberian backwoods but in one of the small rural schools in the densely populated Kharkov Oblast. My colleagues were conscientious and diligent, but the gap between their general cultural level and that of my classmates in my final years at school was appalling. I do not want to be misunderstood: I am not talking about their ethical standards or maturity and wisdom, nor about their experience of life (in these respects much could and should be learnt from them), but only about their disastrously low level of book-learning and professional skill. The materials which I quoted concerning the situation in the 1970s show that there has been some improvement: at that time only 55 per cent of teachers in rural schools in the USSR were without higher education (as compared with 80 per cent in the earlier period). However, this figure is still high and, as it is only an average, it does not describe specific districts: it is the inequality of opportunity of specific, real children and population groups that we are discussing here, and not of the abstract, 'statistically average' child.

Newspapers, magazines and the professional teachers' press occasionally make timid comments on the serious inequality in the standard of education received by rural and urban pupils and, consequently, in their future opportunities. They note the following reasons for this inequality:

(1) the tiny, dying villages where the living conditions are not even barely adequate, where there is no cultural life and where there are no full-time positions for the teachers of specific subjects (in grades five to ten);
(2) the lack of roads, the extent of which is inconceiveable not only to a Westerner but even to a Soviet town-dweller who has not visited his country's backwoods;
(3) the intolerable climatic conditions in certain areas of the country;
(4) the lack of funds, or rather the reluctance to spend the huge amounts of money necessary to build

> and maintain large schools of a high standard in peripheral areas (which would be central to these areas).

The government has chosen another way of dealing with the problem which seems cheaper but which in fact is disastrously 'costly' for society, as it causes irreparable damage. Rural school-leavers, who are known to be poorly prepared, are given priority in admission to institutions of higher education without having to succeed in the competitive entrance examinations. For example, Kharkov University sends its employees as 'recruiters' to the villages in the spring of every year who promise rural school-leavers admission either to the preparatory course, after which entrance to the university is almost automatic (the 'graduation examinations' of these courses are a formality and extremely basic) or to the first year of the university course, without having to take the entrance examinations.

In addition to the professional and cultural level of rural teachers, that of the heads and inspectors of the peripheral Departments of Education is also extremely low. V. Rusakov, an inspector in the Tambov Oblast Department of Education and a specialist in Russian language and literature, made an interesting remark in an article, 'On some methods of inspection', in the journal Narodnoe obrazovanie .

> In our opinion it is very important for the inspector to have a library containing methodological aids, dictionaries, the journals Kommunist, Russkii iazyk v shkole [Russian language in the school], Literatura v shkole ['Literature in the school'], to subscribe to Uchitel'skaia gazeta ['Teachers' newspaper'], Literaturnaia gazeta and the oblast newspaper, which should become a habit for the inspector.[9]

When reading the official Soviet press it is essential to understand its language, formulae and hidden meanings: 'which should become a habit for the inspector' means that the situation in reality is quite the opposite. Usually the 'inspectors' attend a few lessons, hold a few discussions on these lessons (at best with the pedagogical council), glance over a few curricula and conclude their work with a heavy drinking bout in the director's home. There are exceptions. Table 5.1 gives some idea of the educational level of school administrators in certain areas of the USSR at the end of the 1950s:[10]

Table 5.1: Percentage of school administrators without appropriate education

Area of USSR	% of total no. of school administrators
Karel ASSR, Khabarovsk Krai, Kemerovo, Ul'ianovsk, Chitin and other Oblasts	10-26
Altai Krai	82
Bashkir ASSR	83
Dagestan ASSR	79
Udmurtsk ASSR	73
Primorsk Krai	70

The author concludes these examples with 'etc.' (i.e. similar data from numerous other areas could be quoted). There is no breakdown, however, of the uneducated administrators by district within these huge areas, whether they are concentrated in the towns or the villages, but it seems likely that they are mostly in the latter. In this article the author also touches upon the educational level of teachers in various areas of the USSR. Although his analysis is far from complete, it reveals the interesting fact that there are far more teachers than school administrators with appropriate educational qualifications. In other words, the teachers have a higher educational level than their administrators. Evidently this is because the posts of school director and deputy director in the peripheral areas are party appointments (belong to the nomenklatura) in which party and ideological criteria and not educational qualifications are paramount. The same author's data on the education of teachers are given in Table 5.2 (the table relates to the lack of appropriate education: i.e., for grades one to four specialised secondary education; for grades five to seven incomplete higher education; for grades eight to ten higher education).

Table 5.2: Educational qualifications of teachers

Area of the country	% total without appropriate education	% of teachers with inadequate education		
		grade		
		4	5-7	8-10
1957/8 school year in entire country	17.5	no separate figures available		
1958/9 school year in entire country	12.5			
By areas of the country				
Tuvin Oblast		34.4	2-0.77	26
Dagestan		20	29	14
Bashkiria		no data	20	19.9
Moscow Oblast		7.3		8.7

And the results? Magazines and newspapers overflowed with data at the end of the 1950s and the beginning of the 1960s that showed that whenever the oblast Departments of Education carried out direct checks on rural schools, they discovered that the actual success rate of pupils was much lower than that reported to them.

It is important to note that the examples which I took from Narodnoe obrazovanie on the low educational level of school administrators related mainly to Asian national republics, krais and oblasts. The European part of the USSR, including the Ukraine, presented a completely different picture at the beginning of the 1970s. V. Chernysheva, a researcher in the laboratory of social psychology in the Uk.SSR Scientific Research Institute of Psychology, gives the following data:

> A thousand school directors from 25 oblasts of the Ukraine were covered by the questionnaire. We broke down the data into five groups according to the length of time the school directors had been working in their

> administrative capacity: up to five years, from five to ten years, from ten to 20 years and over 25 years, i.e. we divided the school directors into those with little experience, moderate experience and long experience. Among the research sample were 597 directors of rural schools, 403 of urban schools, of whom 822 were men and 178 women ... Half were directors of primary and eight-year schools, a third of ordinary secondary schools and one sixth of large schools in oblast centres and major cities. Of the thousand school directors, 997 have higher education and only three primary school directors have incomplete higher or specialised secondary education.[11]

Although almost half of the research sample worked in towns and not villages, the percentage among them with higher education was still extremely high.

A. Polisan, in an article in Narodnoe obrazovanie, no. 3 (1958), 'On cadres for the schools of Siberia and the Far East', wrote that the 27 pedagogical institutes and 47 pedagogical colleges in these gigantic territories satisfied only 40 per cent of the demand for teachers. Nonetheless, in 1956-7 the number of candidates seeking admission to pedagogical institutes declined by approximately 30 per cent. The author did not offer an explanation for this unfortunate fact. We may recall that these were the years when Khrushchev's school reforms were beginning and when funds were being feverishly sought to bring about the transformation in secondary schools. Polisan also noted that 50-60 per cent of the teachers 'imported' to these areas returned home to the European part of the USSR within two or three years. He noted that teachers in Siberia and the Far East were provided with no accommodation and minimal amenities and that the cultural life to which urban residents were accustomed was absent in these areas. The entire teaching staff in Khabarovsk Krai and Irkutsk Oblast was renewed every two to three years.

Polisan proposed, first, employing only graduates of Siberian and Far Eastern pedagogical institutions of higher education and colleges in schools in these areas in the hope that they would be willing to return to their native 'pygmy' schools, to the backwoods from which they had fled to institutions of higher education, and would reconcile themselves to the low standard of the candidates and their own graduates. Second, he demanded that rural (i.e. the least prepared) school-leavers be given priority in admission to institutions of higher education, noting that although rural schools comprised 80 per cent of schools in Siberia and the Far East, only 10-12 per cent of the total number of students in pedagogical institutions of higher education and colleges in these areas came from the villages.[12] The author did not take into account the small number of pupils in this 80 per cent of 'pygmy' schools as compared with the 20 per cent of urban, i.e. large schools. To fill the institutions of higher education with school-leavers who came mainly from the villages and then to send the young specialists back to the villages meant perpetuating the vicious process of recycling ignorance in the remote rural schools. In other words, Polisan's article was recommending that 80 per cent of the schools in two vast areas of the USSR - Siberia and the Far East - be discriminated against with regard to the quality of education received by their pupils.

In the period 1956-70 another form of discrimination against rural schools was discussed in the press more and more frequently: the transfer of the expense of building and repairing rural schools from the state to the kolkhozniks. P. Isaenko wrote in an article 'Peeping into the future' that the 23 kolkhozes in one of the districts of Voronezh Oblast had built eleven schools in 1958 and systematically carried out repairs on the schools in the district at their own expense.[13] The author ostensibly supports the 'initiative' of the kolkhozes (i.e. the behaviour of the oblast party and Soviet leadership, which burdens the kolkhozniks with the expenditure on 'free' Soviet education), but immediately afterwards he reminds the reader that until 1958 (he is writing in January 1959) the schools were constructed 'without plans' and without receiving for this purpose the necessary building materials (allocated according to the legal centralised distribution system). In 1959 the kolkhozes of the district would begin to produce bricks and mortar by themselves, out of their own 'local' funds and 'then it will become easier'. In the towns schools are built only according to model designs and in a centralised way. Those who pay the most tax and are the most exploited - the kolkhozes - are in effect deprived of the right to 'free' education from the funds created by the taxes which are levied on them and have to bear the additional cost of their children's education in the form of building and repairing schools.[14] Isaenko writes:

> The kolkhozniks regard highly the construction of schools and children's institutions with the manpower and funds of the kolkhozes. However, there are also difficulties in this matter. There is a shortage of plaster and paint, as a result of which the finish is poor. We consider that stove heating should not be used in schools as it is expensive and unhygienic, but it is very difficult to obtain radiators and pipes for water heating. There is a grave need for lathing, nails, window-glass and cement. If the kolkhozes could be assisted to obtain these materials, then within three or four years all rural schools could be fully equipped...

I left a rural school in an area neighbouring on the Voronezh Kharkov Oblast four years after the events described by Isaenko in his article and I can testify that no assistance was given to the kolkhozes to build and repair state schools at their own expense, not in 'three or four years' (1962-3) and not in 20-25 years (the 1980s).

The norms of hygiene were never observed in rural school buildings, which were mostly not standard buildings but which had been built or added to at random. In the years 1949-53 I worked in rural schools which had kerosene lighting, and in 1953-63 electric lighting. In the first case several kerosene lamps (without which it was impossible to work in winter in the first two lessons of the first shift, the last three of the second shift and all four lessons of the third, evening shift) went out for lack of oxygen in the classrooms. In the second case, when I was already director of a secondary school, I read thoroughly the handbooks on school hygiene and brought the classroom lighting to the required level by hanging four to six bulbs above the desks instead of one 100-watt bulb above the teacher's table. At the end of the year I had to battle with the kolkhoz which sold the school electricity: the funds allocated for lighting in rural schools were several times less than what was required according to the norms of hygiene and which were allocated to urban schools without any trouble. In my case, the school worked off its debt to the kolkhoz in the fields, and that was how we henceforth provided the school with lighting: the pupils paid for adequate lighting with their labour.

A section in Narodnoe obrazovanie, no. 10 (1960), entitled 'In the CC CPSU and the USSR Council of Ministers' and subtitled 'On school construction and the measures to improve the resources of schools', informed readers that the plan for putting new schools into operation had been fulfilled in 1959 by 80 per cent in the country as a whole, by 57 per cent in Azerbaidzhan, by 49 per cent in Kirgizia, by 51 per cent in Turkmenia, by 62 per cent in the Uzbek SSR and by 65 per cent in the Kazakh SSR. The plan for putting boarding schools into operation (the epicentre of Khrushchev's explosion of school reforms) had been fulfilled in 1959 by 69 per cent in the country as a whole. In the first quarter of 1960 all these indices had declined (it was not stated to what extent). What was being proposed as the solution to this situation? To transfer the burden of accelerating the completion of new 'free' schools to those same kolkhozes (and according to market prices, i.e. prices that have been bolstered), out of the modest funds previously destined for the use of individuals who were building their own homes: 'it is proposed to allocate building materials and articles (timber, roofing, glass, cement, piping and sanitary and electrical equipment etc.) to schools which are being constructed at the expense of the kolkhozes'. .. 'out of the market funds in the necessary quantities'.[15] We shall return to the situation in the schools of the 1980s in Chapter 7.

*

It is widely thought that inequality of opportunities on a national basis in the sphere of secondary education is non-existent in the USSR. The decline in the number of Ukrainian, Belorussian or Moldavian, etc. schools by comparison with the number of Russian schools is usually attributed to the desires of the pupils or their parents themselves. The local language is still studied in Russian-language schools in non-Russian areas of the USSR (although in some cases it is not compulsory but depends on the pupils' wishes), while a good knowledge of Russian and the study of the general educational subjects in Russian gives the school-leaver far more extensive opportunities than a good knowledge of his native language. Russian is the language used by the peoples of the USSR to communicate with each other, the language of the government, army and most institutions of higher education. There are national languages such as Hebrew or Yiddish whose study is not even optional (even if the pupils and their families want them to be taught) anywhere in the USSR. However, the Jewish problem is a special one and does not concern us here, as it would require special research. In any event, the disappearance of Jewish schools and the fact that neither Jewish language can be found on the curriculum of any school in the USSR no longer surprises anyone. According to Narodnoe obrazovanie, in the RSFSR there are non-Russian schools in 15 autonomous republics, five autonomous okrugs (regions), ten national okrugs, 27 krais and oblasts of the gigantic Russian Federation. National-minority parents try to send their children to Russian-language schools, and most teachers and parents agree that 'Russification' should begin earlier in the national schools. In Tataria and Bashkiria, for example, where instruction in the national schools is carried out in the native languages up to the school-leaving certificate and Russian is taught as just one of the subjects, the doors of institutions of higher education are virtually closed to the graduates of these schools, even in their own republics. These institutions are mostly Russified in the Tatar and Bashkir ASSR, except for the native-language faculties and pedagogical technicums and faculties (though not all). However, within the republic the range of institutions of higher education is narrow (they offer few specialities which interest the modern school-leaver), and graduates from the national schools of these republics cannot enter institutions of higher education, the entrance examinations to which are in Russian, since they do not know Russian. The teachers propose quite openly a complete switch to Russian in the national schools (some from grade three, others from grade five and others from grade eight).

An article by two school inspectors in the RSFSR Ministry of Education, 'In Perm Oblast non-Russian schools are badly managed' described how there were few groups of teachers of the Komi-Permian nationalities in the pedagogical institutes and technicums, and the number of such graduates was not large enough to provide instruction in the Komi language even at the primary level, not to mention the senior grades. Not all children were in school, presumably (the inspectors do not write about this) because children in some families, especially in the villages, speak their native language and cannot go to a Russian-language school. The drop-out rate from the seven-year schools in a number of districts of Perm Oblast (with a Komi-Permian population) was as high as 40 per cent. The inspectors themselves wrote:

> A large proportion of non-Russian schools in the oblast are in a state of neglect; many school buildings are in

> need of major repairs, the schools are inadequately equipped, the sports and geography areas are poorly equipped. The school buildings are badly constructed. Despite the poor conditions in which non-Russian schools are accommodated, their construction is not planned in a centralised way and in most cases is financed by voluntary rate payments.
>
> One of the reasons for the low success rate of the pupils and the high drop-out rate from schools is the inadequate number of dormitory facilities as well as the poor condition of these facilities.[16]

Later they wrote that the number of boarding schools in the Komi-Permian National Okrug was small and that this number was hardly increasing while 'their state is not improving'. Secondary School No. 8 in the town of Kudymkaraia was attended by children from 28 settlements situated 20 kilometers and more from the school, 'but the school has no boarding facilities'.[17] It was hardly surprising that the drop-out rate was 40 per cent, for the situation meant that only children whose parents in distant villages could afford to pay for their food and lodgings outside home could go to school. The construction of boarding facilities, however, was financed by 'voluntary rate payments' and consequently, the pupils' villages (kolkhoz) would not spend their meagre funds on building boarding facilities in the town's school, while the tiny central town of the district was similarly unwilling to do this for pupils from the villages. We should bear in mind that even in 1959 it was difficult for such an article to be published and that if it actually was published after the inevitable struggle, the situation must have been even worse than the published part of the article described.

Many school directors did not have higher education and, the inspectors wrote, nor did ' a considerable number of teachers of grades five to ten'. 'In the twelve secondary schools of the national okrug there are only ten teachers of the native nationality in grades eight to ten' and of these 'only four have higher education'. However, it was not only the Komi-Permians who suffered. 'Tatar and Mari teachers have a poor knowledge of Russian' but taught it in the rural national schools (moreover, in the primary schools, where the foundations of linguistic habits are laid). The authors wrote that there were not even enough primers in the native language in Tatar and Udmurt schools nor enough Russian primary and national-language textbooks, Native speech. In 1959 children were learning from tattered primers and textbooks published in 1953, 1954 and 1955 and handed down from class to class - and this, I may add, in a country where millions of tons of unsold official publications are sent every year straight from the storehouses and shops to the paper dumps, as the press reported many times in the years 1956-68. The inspectors also reported that children finished the eight-year (previously seven-year) national schools at such a poor standard that they were subsequently unable to go on to secondary schools. The drop-out rate from secondary schools among children of the national minorities was 16 out of 20. 'The success rate in Russian, the native language and mathematics is particularly low.' And they emphasised once again that the teachers were very poor.[18]

Another article in Narodnoe obrazovanie, 'Universal education in districts of the extreme north-east', reported that in the 1950/1 school year 225 pupils had been admitted to the first grades in the Koriatsk National Okrug; of these, 37 had completed seven classes in the 1956/7 school year.[19] The situation was serious not only in the national schools, but in all the schools in remote (rural) districts. V. Evdokimov, head of the Alekseev District Department of Education of the Stalingrad (Volgograd) Oblast, reported in the same journal, in an article titled 'From small to amalgamated schools', that 'reports on the unsatisfactory situation of instruction and education in most primary schools of the district' were so frequent that pupils from small rural schools who were admitted to grade five of the amalgamated school had to be sent back to grade four. He proposed uniting and amalgamating schools, but did not know how or who was to finance this.[20] A school director would have to display great persistence and courage to send pupils back to the previous class. Such a step is severely discouraged in the USSR, as it doubles the expenditure on a pupil's instruction in that class. However, a pupil with a good knowledge of Russian can in some cases change his school (and his family - their place of residence) and thus escape from the blind alley of the remote peripheries of the country. A child of the national minorities is doomed to cultural degeneration by the poor quality of the non-Russian schools in the USSR.

The opportunities of children of the national minorities[21] increase as one comes closer to the west of the country and the republic and oblast urban centres, and decrease as one moves towards the north, east (north-east, south-east) and the rural periphery. I am not discussing here the profound problem of preserving native languages or the degree to which the USSR needs a language for communication among the different nationalities. I shall merely say that so long as the USSR exists as a multi-national, multi-tribal state (which it is today), its peoples need a language of inter-national communication and none of them should be discriminated against in this way. There is, however, very obvious discrimination which deprives vast numbers of the national minority populations of the opportunity of competing with those who have a good knowledge of Russian after they complete primary or eight-year schools.

The preservation of national languages is, however, a complex historical process and is an independent subject outside the scope of the problems studied in the present work. I shall merely offer the opinion that this matter should be left entirely to each people and each individual to decide. The <u>opportunity</u> to learn the native language and culture of one's people should be granted to <u>every</u> individual and <u>every</u> people. In the USSR these opportunities are distributed very unevenly and fluctuate between the prohibition or total impossibility of learning one's language and culture and the preferential propagation of the Russian language in colossal non-Russian territories inside the USSR and even in countries outside its borders.

Let us return, however, to the reality of education. Russian is, therefore, essential for a citizen of the USSR and without it the opportunities of schoolchildren, school-leavers and students are severely reduced. We have already indicated that the national minorities who reside in the peripheral regions of the USSR are taught Russian poorly. Let us now proceed to the western republics of the USSR. An article entitled "Russian teaching in schools with the Latvian language of instruction' described how Russian was taught in these schools from the second half of the first year. Tests revealed that the pupils had a good knowledge of spoken Russian and were able to conduct conversations freely, that they mostly spoke with the correct intonation and could construct complex sentences. Most of the pupils were fluent in reading and the teachers made sure that they read correctly and expressively and helped them to understand what they were reading. An analysis of the tests written by the pupils showed that those in both urban and rural schools had thoroughly mastered grammatical written

Russian:

> ... Serious attention is paid in the curricula of courses in the IUU [Institute for the Advanced Training of Teachers] to pressing questions of teaching methods. Questions of work in Russian are given special consideration. Every district has long-term five year plans to upgrade the qualifications in each school and in the district as a whole in 1971-5, which propose to incorporate 100 per cent of school directors and 85-95 per cent of the teachers. Card indexes are kept in the teaching-methods rooms on the attendance at courses of school directors and teachers.
>
> Considerable work on teaching methods is being conducted in the republic with teachers of Russian language and literature.
>
> ... Over the past 15 years the composition of the Russian teaching profession has changed considerably. The number of teachers with higher specialised education has increased from 28 per cent in the 1956/7 school year to 63 per cent in 1971/2. Their training was carried out in the Department of Russian Language and Literature in the Faculty of Languages and Literature of the P. Stuchka Latvian State University and in the Faculty of Languages and Literature of the Daugavpils Pedagogical Institute where work on the vocational guidance of student youth is constantly being carried out.[22]

What does this have in common with the situation in the schools of Tataria, the Komi-Permian National Okrug or the north-east of the country which we discussed above? Only one thing:

> However, there are many shortcomings in this matter which influence the composition of the student body. Thus, out of 663 students of Russian language and literature, only 30.8 per cent are graduates of rural schools; in both institutions of higher education only 65 of the students (10.2 per cent) are men.
>
> The graduates are allocated work mainly in urban and rural schools with Latvian as the language of instruction.[23]

Here too rural schools are in a worse situation than urban ones. It is endlessly reiterated in the press that:

> All nations and nationalities of the USSR have voluntarily chosen Russian as the common language of inter-national communication and co-operation. It has become a mighty instrument of mutual communication and cohesion of the Soviet peoples, a means of joining in the best achievements of culture of the fatherland and the world.[24]

The article from which I took this particular quotation also stated:

> One of the tasks of the Departments of Education is to ensure that the elementary military training of pupils is carried out in Russian. It is very important for the intake of young people into the Soviet Army to have a good knowledge of Russian, the language of inter-national communication, in which their army service is conducted.[25]

In my experience as a teacher, deputy director and director of a Soviet school, I can testify that this injunction is <u>never</u> violated. Military training is strictly conducted only in Russian and never in the national language.

The situation of Russian teaching in the Ukraine is as good as (and probably even better than) in the Baltics. The degree of effort expended by the government on Russifying the various peoples depends not only on their distance from the centre or the lack of major settlements in the territory where a particular national minority resides, but also on the potential danger posed by a particular people as a separatist force. In this sense the Baltics and the Ukraine occupy one of the first places. There is also growing danger from the Central Asian Muslim republics where until now the teaching of Russian has been of a far lower standard and not as widespread as in the non-Russian European republics. I shall not be surprised if, along with the creation of the Afghan barrier, there will be increased pressure on the education organisations of the Central Asian and Caucasian republics to Russify these areas.

L. Tychina, a specialist in teaching methods in the republic laboratory of educational methodology on technical methods of instruction of the Ukrainian Ministry of

Education, wrote:

> The most favourable conditions for conducting lessons in Russian language and literature on a high technical level have been created by the collectives of the schools: No. 19 in Sevastopol, No. 36 in Kherson, Nos. 18 and 57 in Kharkov, Nos. 45, 78, 171, 190 in Kiev.
>
> Each of the above schools has two to three laboratories (kabinety) for Russian language and literature, pleasantly decorated, equipped with technical resources and with a sufficient quantity of educational visual aids, both manufactured in factories and made by themselves.
>
> It is only in the laboratory that it has became possible for the pupils to work independently with the aid of screen and sound while preparing their homework (listening to recordings of artistic recitals, viewing slide-shows and slides in conjunction with the laboratory's materials).
>
> The rich literary material on various subjects which has been collected in the laboratory does not lie idle but is needed and used for work.
>
> When working in the laboratory, the teacher is able to improve the content and methods of homework while actively including audio-visual aids in his work. For example, the following is suggested as one of the individual assignments for able pupils: 'To prepare an article "Gorky in the Ukraine" as a teaching aid in literature, basing it on the material in the film of the same name. Which were the most significant frames that you used to illustrate the article? Explain your choice.'[26]

It is typical that not a single rural school is among those named in this lengthy article by the ministry's specialist in teaching methodology. Nor are any schools in the Western Ukraine given as examples of successful, well-organised Russification, as that area is doing its utmost to resist this process. Can the cultural and educational discrimination practised against the national minorities be seen as a manifestation of the Russian national character, of general Russian great-power chauvinism? I think not, because of two primary factors (among a number of secondary ones):

(1) The Russian rural 'backwoods', the northern,

eastern and north-eastern peripheries of Russia as well as urban schools in outlying districts of Russia also suffer from discrimination in the fields of education and culture.

(2) Soviet education is totally controlled by the state, and the Russian population - Russian in the ethnic sense of the word - have just as little influence on government policy in this field as other peoples of the USSR (except for those peoples which for a certain period or in general are particularly discriminated against by the government).

The Soviet government's school policy is as paradoxical as other aspects of its national policy: there are peoples who suffer from discrimination, but there are no privileged, 'ruling' peoples. The USSR is a rigidly centralised empire, and, through the course of history, the central, European part of Russia has become the centre of that empire. Therefore the preference given to Russian - as the language of the empire's administration which penetrates its every pore, the language of the army and of inter-national communication - is inevitable as long as this imperial structure is preserved.

*

There are also profound differences in the conditions in individual schools, even in the towns, which are influenced by many factors: the area in which the school is located, who the parents of the pupils are, the school's relations with the higher organisations of education. Schools in the capital and in the major cities of the RSFSR establish contacts with scientific-research institutes and major enterprises in order to set up special rooms for all the subjects which (from the point of view of the rural, outlying or north-eastern schools, for example) are fantastically well equipped. Thus, B. Krasnik, an Honoured Schoolteacher of the RSFSR and director of Leningrad School No. 534, described how a 'problem laboratory' had been organised in the school in the 1967/8 school year by the Institute of Schools of the RSFSR Ministry of Education:

> The scholars in this laboratory - Candidate of Pedagogical Sciences M.A. Bantova, Candidate of Pedagogical Sciences T.G. Ramzaeva and other researchers led by Professor A.A. Liublinskaia, continued their research on the development of

> curricula and textbooks and on elucidating the extremely important question of the relation between the standard of knowledge and the standard of accomplishments of the pupils.
>
> Everyone understands how much more complex it is for the teacher to give lessons if they are attended by researchers. However, the joint work with major specialists, consultations with them and their advice and help, greatly enriched the teachers' experience. It was precisely this circumstance that permitted us, on the basis of the first experimental classes, to teach what comprises the new foundation of future didactics for secondary school teachers.[27]

An article 'On measures on the further improvement of the work of the rural general education school' in the same journal, Narodnoe obrazovanie, later that year admitted, however, that '... the organisation of school education in the village has grave shortcomings. The level of teaching and educational work in some rural schools of general education lags behind the requirements of modern times'. The author recognised the need to 'carry out in rural areas an extensive programme of construction of new school buildings, of adding classrooms, subject rooms and other educational premises to the existing school buildings, as well as boarding facilities for the pupils and residential blocks for the teachers'.[28] We described earlier how this construction was carried out, and what is more, it is not even set the same goals as in the large cities.

Even in the largest cities, however, the funds allocated by the state to the education organisations are not sufficient even to modernise the best central schools attended by children of the most influential residents of that particular city. Officially, no such schools exist, but in reality influential people live in the best parts of the cities and their children are automatically concentrated in the two to three best schools of these areas. Both the lower-ranking urban elite and the most educated parents use every legitimate or illegitimate means to 'arrange' for their children to attend these schools. In Kharkov these are schools Nos. 1, 5, 36 and others (in the 1960s there was also the School of Physics and Mathematics No. 27, but by the mid-1970s it had become an ordinary school). In these schools the highly-placed parents of pupils organise the special subject rooms, technical aids, means of delivery, including even motor vehicles, repairs, assistance in construction and obtaining scarce materials, all in the guise of the school's 'sponsorship' by the enterprises, organisations and institutions subordinate to the parents. The sponsors supply equipment, scarce materials and manpower and also frequently pay for various acquisitions which the schools make in excess of the budget: books, apparatus, pictures, etc. In this way central schools come into being, richly endowed with all the trimmings that the teaching being practised in them could possibly require.

In a country the size of the USA or the USSR no centre is able to extend its control equally to the entire school system. The diversity of ethnic, cultural, territorial, geographical, economic and historical factors; the conflicting local interests of numerous peoples; the very number of schools, pupils and institutions and professional people connected with them - all these render centralised influence in many cases ineffective, not in all respects necessary and unable to produce equal results in every case. How do both giants solve this problem? In the USA the federal government is only responsible for devising the most general statutes. School matters are mainly within the control of the states which, in turn, give extensive freedom to the community and the forms of education which it devises. In this case, the inequality of opportunity which exists for various groups of pupils is not juridical inequality but inequality that is the result of historical and social circumstances. However, it undoubtedly exists and attracts the attention of society and the state. The problem is not hushed up, ignored or denied, and various efforts are being made to solve it, while serious public and state activity and conflict develop around it.

In the USSR, by contrast, the state authority refuses to relinquish even the tiniest crumb of initiative in the field of school (and all other forms of) education. The state's governing influence, however, is unable to take in the entire huge system. It therefore selects, as in all other fields of government, two or three questions which are vitally important to it (i.e. to <u>the state</u>) and concentrates its regulating influence in these directions. This category includes:

(1) The exclusive control by the state over ideology: here standardisation is most complete.

(2) The Russification of all military training - no

deviations are possible here either - and the Russification of instruction as such in general which has become increasingly forceful in recent years.

(3) The duration and budgets of schooling: the only deviations from the state budget which are possible are those that economise on state funds through the aid of kolkhozes and enterprises.

(4) The reservation of higher educational opportunities for the children of the 'elite' and of the strata of the population which serve it directly.

(5) The official standardisation of the school curricula. I say 'official' because all the respective types of schools (primary, incomplete secondary, secondary, certain types of specialised schools) are issued with identical state curricula in all subjects and identical topics for 'cultural-educational' work.

It is this standardisation of <u>documents</u> (pieces of paper) that the uninitiated observer sees as equality of opportunity. Nonetheless, some children are taught by illiterate teachers from tattered twenty-year-old books, while others are educated by scholars with the help of modern technology, visual aids, punch-cards and programmed, 'modernist' textbooks. The most important point, however, is that the problem of educational inequality is hushed up. Only a few, mild, semi-allegorical signals that not all is in order filter through into the press (from 1964/5 ever more rarely). The republics, krais, oblasts have no independent opportunities to influence the process.

The main problem is that the inequality which begins in secondary school extends to the pupil's entire future life, while both the state and society pretend that this problem does not exist.

*

I shall conclude this discussion of the inequality of opportunity in Soviet secondary education with a few general remarks. Schools in every society are a phenomenon which cannot be analysed in sufficient depth without qualitative analysis. Such analysis necessitates a practical knowledge of the character of the main processes, links and inter-dependencies summed up in the word 'education'. The ratio between the formal level of education in a country and its economy is certainly not direct. Academician P.L. Kapitsa has written that the number of academics (not schoolchildren, from whom academics have yet to grow) per

1000 of the population is approximately the same in the USSR as in the USA. The productivity of their work, however, according to his calculations, is half that in the USA.[29] The data presented by a witness of such standing cannot be doubted, especially as they could only have been made less harsh for official publication. An article in Literaturnaia gazeta, reported that:

> Calculations based on data in statistical publications permit us to state that in 1966 every milliard rubles of the gross output of all enterprises in our country corresponded to the work of 4.3 thousand engineers employed in industry, its scientific-research institutions and design and planning institutions. In American industry, however, 1.2 thousand engineers are needed for the same magnitude of value (milliard rubles' output). In other words, the 'output' of engineers in the USA is 3.6 times greater than ours.[30]

I have quoted these data to emphasise that for an evaluation of complex, comprehensive, multi-faceted social processes even the most skilled qualitative analysis has to be corroborated by statistics. But nor are statistics adequate without a qualitative investigation.

I shall give one small example: when speaking about Soviet secondary education, it is not sufficient to rely on such indices as the number of schools. Official data of the Central Statistical Board (in the book SSSR i SShA ('The USSR and the USA')) revealed that the number of general education schools in the USSR had grown from 124 thousand in the 1914/15 school year to 221 thousand in 1959/60. In the USA however, the number had declined - from 272.5 thousand schools in 1921/2 to 137 thousand in 1958/9. These data suggested the quantitative conclusion that while the number of schools had increased in the USSR, in the USA it had declined. Moreover, in the USSR the number of pupils had increased by 350 per cent over this period, while in the USA by only 190 per cent. Some authors see this as a sign of the rapid growth of the Soviet educational system, a view which is also shared by commentators in UNESCO. However, different data give a different picture: the total number of pupils in the 1959/60 school year in the USA was 33.9 million, and in the USSR (whose population is considerably larger than that of the USA) 33.4 million (data of the Central Statistical Board).[31] Hence, the number of pupils was almost the same in the two countries (somewhat larger in the USA), while the number of schools in the USA was far smaller. To someone with a knowledge of the real situation of Soviet secondary education the explanation for this is obvious: the USSR has a disastrously large number of 'pygmy' schools in dying villages that give their pupils a second-rate education. Another source gives the following data:

> An analysis of the existing school network which was conducted in a number of areas of the country revealed its irrationality as a result of the underestimation in the past of a number of demographic factors. For example, in the Serebriano-Prud District of Moscow Oblast with a population of 21 thousand and slightly over four thousand pupils, in the 1971/2 school year there were 25 primary, nine eight-year and three secondary schools. The investigation revealed that of the primary schools five with two classes in each year, three with one and a half classes in each year, 16 with one class in each year and four of the eight-year schools were wrongly located on the territory of their districts, as it turned out that many pupils lived a long way from the schools. Despite the large number of schools and the density of their distribution (one per 2.3 square km.), it was still necessary to transport 985 pupils of grades one to ten and assign 339 to the boarding facilities, which necessitated additional state expenditure (more than 150 thousand rubles a year). The existence of a large number of schools determined the small number of pupils in them: from six to 70 pupils in the primary schools, from 89 to 154 in the eight-year schools; because of this the cost of instruction per pupil in the district fluctuates between 93 and 543 rubles in the primary schools, between 126 and 262 rubles in the eight-year schools, and around 160 rubles in the secondary schools. Calculations show that in order to incorporate all children in secondary education it is enough to have in the district by 1980 eight schools (four secondary and four eight-year schools) which would allow a saving of 285 thousand rubles.[32]

These data pertain not to Siberia or the Far North but to districts near Moscow.[33]

A researcher who intends to base his work on quantitative indices when analysing the real Soviet situation has to study newspaper articles, journals and books on subjects which are apparently unrelated to the topic of his research. There are many specialists and writers in the USSR who have a profound knowledge of their field and the circumstances connected with it and desire to inform the reader of them. Because of tactical considerations, however, the most important and accurate information often has to be reported in passing, to be sprinkled inconspicuously through the text or set in small print. There is another difficulty in understanding the Soviet education system: it is well known that the road from society's expenditure on education to its receipt of economic outputs from education is extremely long and complex and that it is difficult to take all the factors which determine both the expenditure and the outputs into consideration. This is a highly complex task for schools in all countries, for today, throughout the world, school time is crammed with information, and is very expensive. Imagine, however, in addition to these general difficulties, schools in which the humanities, literature, native, Russian and foreign history, social science, the fundamentals of law, economic geography, all repeat over and over again the same ideological pattern prescribed by the official ideology and give the pupils false notions of the past, present and future of their country and the world. Add to these subjects the compulsory hours of political education, 'Lenin lessons' and tests all devoted to the same task. Subtract from the free time of the already over-loaded pupils the compulsory hours of Pioneer and Komsomol assignments devoted to the same task of forming the prescribed world view and add the fact that the entire aesthetic education given by the school is yoked to the same task, etc., etc.

I would like to forestall the objection that it is inappropriate to include ideological problems in an analysis of secondary education, destined for people who are relatively well informed about the general situation in the USSR in this respect. However, I am discussing not so much the ideology *per se* as the purely economic effectiveness of Soviet secondary education. It can be demonstrated by taking the topics of the courses in the humanities and economic humanities as well as the hours spent on purely political and social education, that, regardless of the extreme overloading of the curricula, Soviet schools duplicate a considerable proportion of their courses many times over. The reason is that the same dogmas and interpretations, directives and concepts - the fallaciousness and social danger of which I am not discussing here - are included compulsorily in all courses and all 'educational measures'. Only a detailed analysis of the compulsory six-monthly, termly and daily lesson plans of Soviet teachers (all plans are subject to the approval of the teaching department of the school) would reveal in purely economic terms the cost of repeating the same ideologised and outright ideological sections of all the courses in every subject (not to mention the special 'educational' hours).

Even the reader who is well informed about the Soviet system as a whole must conceive of the Soviet school not only as some special cultural and pedagogical phenomenon but also as the most important part of the Soviet social structure. In order to understand the school, a number of links between this part and the whole must be isolated and interpreted. The school cannot be examined otherwise than as a sub-system of the system 'society', and a sub-system cannot be examined without locating its place within the system or without analysing its functions within the system. If there are no links between the part and the whole, the sub-system as such disappears: what remains is some independent phenomenon, which actually does not exist in society. Therefore, the point here is not the 'ideologisation' of the scientific material nor propagandist tendentiousness, but the observation of scientific accuracy and minimal approximation to the truth.

NOTES

1. See Obshcheobrazovatel'naia i sotsial'naia struktura naseleniia SSSR ('The general educational and social structure of the USSR population') in the series Narodonaselenie ('Population') ((Statistika', Moscow, 1975).
2. Obshcheobrazovatel'naia i sotsial'no-professional'naia struktura naseleniia SSSR ('The general educational and socio-occupational structure of the USSR population') in the above series.
3. The article 'Universal secondary education and demographic processes' in ibid.
4. Ibid.
5. Ibid.

6. From 'On measures to further improve the working conditions in rural general education schools', published in Pravda on 6 July 1973.

7. Ibid.

8. Article referred to in note 3 above.

9. V. Rusakov, 'On some methods of inspection' in Narodnoe obrazovanie, no. 1 (1959), pp. 31-7.

10. F. Maksimenko, Deputy Minister of Education of the RSFSR, 'Work with pedagogical cadres is a most important matter', Narodnoe obrazovanie, no. 5 (1959), pp. 14-19.

11. V. Chernyshova, 'The difficulties of the activities of school directors' in Narodnoe obrazovanie, no. 2 (1972), pp. 72-4.

12. A. Polisan, ibid. no. 3 (1958), pp. 8-11.

13. Ibid., no. 1 (1959), pp. 24-5.

14. As a person who worked in and directed a rural school for many years, I can testify that the construction of 'non-model' schools by kolkhozes means adding on or erecting some primitive rural-type premises which the kolkhozes undertake only in extreme cases when the schools are literally suffocating from overcrowding and lack of air.

15. 'In the CC CPSU and the USSR Council of Ministers' in Narodnoe obrazovanie, no. 10 (1960), pp. 18-19.

16. D. Korzh and P. Ivantsova in Narodnoe obrazovanie, no. 7 (1959), pp. 40-3.

17. Ibid.

18. Ibid.

19. G. Sevilgaiva, 'Universal education in districts of the extreme north east', Narodnoe obrazovanie, no. 11 (1961), pp. 27-32.

20. V. Evdokimov, 'From small to amalgamated schools' in Narodnoe obrazovanie, no. 11 (1961), pp. 33-5.

21. I emphasise except for the Jews, who are considered to be a national minority only in instances, and for purposes, of discrimination. The Crimean-Tatar people is in a similar position today, completely ignored as an ethnos. The gypsy language is also not studied anywhere. However, a discussion of these problems would lead us too far away from our topic.

22. From the editorial 'Russian teaching in schools with the Latvian language of instruction', Narodnoe obrazovanie, no. 12 (1972), pp. 116-17.

23. Russian-language schools are usually allocated teachers who have graduated from institutions of higher education in the RSFSR. This is part of the general policy of

Russification in the Baltic republics to which specialists and workers from the RSFSR are sent on any pretext.

24. From the CC CPSU Resolution 'On the preparations for the 50th anniversary of the formation of the Union of Soviet Socialist Republics'.

25. 'To improve the teaching of Russian in schools in every possible way', Narodnoe obrazovanie, no. 6 (1972), pp. 2-4.

26. 'Russian language and literature rooms (kabinety) in Ukrainian schools', ibid., no. 1 (1973).

27. 'In co-operation with scholars', ibid., no. 1 (1973), pp. 76-9.

28. Editorial in Narodnoe obrazovanie, no. 9 (1973), pp. 2-4.

29. P.L. Kapitsa, Teoriia, eksperiment, praktika ('Theory, experiment, practice') ('Znanie', Moscow, 1966), pp. 2-4.

30. 'Third question - what is an engineer's output?'.

31. Obshcheobrazovatel'naia i sotsial'no-professional'naia struktura naseleniia SSSR ('The general educational and socio-occupational structure of the USSR population') in the series Narodonaselenie ('Population'), ('Statistika', Moscow, 1975), pp. 30-1.

32. See Narodnoe obrazovanie, no. 4 (1973), p. 10.

33. To corroborate my observations on the disappearance, the waning of villages and the survival in them of unviable schools, I quote the following table of the distribution of the population in rural areas of the USSR taken from Sovetskaia pedagogika ('Soviet pedagogy'), no. 6 (1973), p. 93:

The proportion of small inhabited localities in rural areas (in % of their total number)

RSFSR and economic districts	Inhabited localities with a number of residents			
	up to 25	26-50	up to 25	26-50
	1959		1970	
RSFSR total	26.9	15.6	25.1	15.7
North-west	31.8	26.2	40.2	23.9

Central	23.0	19.8	28.2	21.6
Volga-Viatskii	25.6	18.7	27.9	16.8
Central-Chernozemnyi	17.7	6.6	13.9	7.4
Povolzhskii	38.9	10.6	15.5	6.1
North-Caucasian	34.9	7.4	6.9	5.0

Chapter Six

SOME TRENDS IN THE DEVELOPMENT OF THE SCHOOL IN THE 1970S

I do not intend here to give a complete analysis of the state of Soviet secondary schools in the 1970s and the trends in their development. I shall merely note some trends which I observed, not from inside a school but somewhat from the side-lines, first as the director and teacher of courses for candidates seeking admission to institutions of higher education in the Kharkov Oblast's Teacher's House and later only as a teacher in them. I worked in these courses from 1968 to 1976. Their aim was to prepare secondary school graduates for admission to institutions of higher education and university faculties in the field of the humanities. In this capacity I had the opportunity to observe the level of secondary school graduates every year in the period 1968-76, in particular in the humanities. The courses taught Russian language and literature, German, English, French and Polish languages. On the basis of these observations as well as my constant perusal of the Soviet periodical, in particular pedagogical, press, I shall express some thoughts about the Soviet school in the 1970s.

The ideological control of the authorities over the schools and the work of teachers intensified considerably in the 1970s as compared with the period from 1956 to the end of the 1960s. Critical articles and discussions on schools and pedagogical themes in general virtually disappeared from the non-pedagogical press (Literaturnaia gazeta, Novyi mir, etc.), while the pedagogical press (Uchitel'skaia gazeta, Narodnoe obrazovanie, etc.) devoted far more space to articles containing directives from the authorities, by school directors, inspectors, administrators, which were concerned primarily with the schools' ideological tasks. Here are some typical excerpts from Narodnoe obrazovanie in the early

1970s. L. Kudriavtseva, head of the Minsk City Department of Education, wrote in an article 'To improve inner-school control', about the work being done in the best schools in Minsk:

> The Communist upbringing of pupils is assigned a special place in the system of instruction for leading cadres. Every year the study of topical themes of the ideological and political upbringing of pupils is concluded with conferences and seminars: 'The ideological-political upbringing of pupils during lessons and in extra-curricular work', 'Teaching in the party spirit -the most important demand of the modern lesson', 'V.I. Lenin and the Communist upbringing of youth', 'The role of organisers of the extra-curricular and school educational work and ideological-political upbringing of pupils', 'Educating the Communist awareness and political activity of pupils in a process of extra-curricular and out-of-school work'; seminars on 'The organisation of work in the school on raising the ideological, scientific-theoretical and methodological training of cadres in the light of the decisions of the XXIV Congress of the CPSU', 'On measures to improve extra-curricular and out-of-school work with pupils', etc. Reports are made to the conferences and seminars by leaders and party workers of the city, representatives of the republic's Ministry of Education and departments of education.[1]

The pedagogical periodical press contained a vast quantity of such articles in these years.[2] The contributions in these periodicals by teachers are no longer marked by the spirit of criticism or even limited civic-minded ideals which we saw in the previous period. Teachers write articles (or rather the editors order articles from teachers) on narrowly professional, methodological and political-ideological topics, while the number of well-known literary names which appear in these publications has declined sharply. Writers have apparently become convinced that they are powerless to bring about a radical improvement in the moral and civic atmosphere of the schools and have abandoned this theme.

The military training of pupils was also given greater attention in the 1970s after the relaxation of the first years of Khrushchev's school reforms. Thus, the last issue of <u>Narodnoe obrazovanie</u> in 1973 concluded with a long section containing several articles under the general heading 'To improve military-patriotic upbringing'. Eighteen months previously (in no. 6, 1971) the journal had published the following piece under the heading 'On elementary military training':

> The Collegium of the USSR Ministry of Education has adopted a Resolution 'On the state of elementary military training in secondary schools, pedagogical schools and the measures to develop it further in 1971'. The Collegium noted that the work on the military instruction and military-patriotic upbringing of pupils has become considerably more active, more concrete and purposeful.
>
> Elementary military training has been introduced in 7,765 secondary schools and pedagogical colleges (involving about a million pupils, including 450 thousand boys of pre-conscription age).
>
> Military instructors are selected in all the republics, over 70 per cent of them are reserve officers and about 45 per cent have higher education. In most republics and oblasts a definite system for upgrading the qualifications of military instructors has been established...
>
> It is proposed that the Ministries of Education of the union republics should take measures to eliminate the shortcomings and introduce elementary military training in 1971 in schools with the largest numbers of grades nine and ten; propagandise the experience of the work of the best military instructors in the periodical press, at meetings and conferences on public education; study and generalise, jointly with the republics' scientific research institutes on pedagogy and institutes for the advanced training of teachers, the best experience of schools in elementary military training and organise its dissemination; provide schools and pedagogical colleges in good time with the obligatory practice weaponry, instruments and military technical equipment; study and check the quality of the pupils' instruction and accomplishments in elementary military training; recommend the construction of shooting-ranges on a shared basis with other departments and also with the help of pupils, enterprises, kolkhozes and sovkhozes.

The aim was therefore to intensify the military and ideological upbringing of schoolchildren who would comprise the most active age group of the Soviet population in the 1980s. This, I think was very telling. This trend was combined with a growing effort, in the sphere of foreign policy, to feed the sense of an external military threat. A vast amount of propaganda material intended for schoolchildren was concerned with the direct military threat to the USSR posed by 'world capitalism' and 'international Zionism'.

The 1968-70 school years were marked by the preparations in schools for the hundredth anniversary of Lenin's birth and then by the celebrations of that event. The entire educational, instructional, extra-curricular and aesthetic work of the schools was imbued with the subject of Lenin. This was so artificial that it gave rise to a number of jokes as well as creating a profound aversion on the part of pupils to the three years of 'Lenin lessons', 'Lenin assignments' and albums, excursions, concerts, shows, all modifications on the same, never-changing theme. The pupils became markedly less enthusiastic about school, which was increasingly imbued with the banalities of official rhetoric that was supplanting the barely revived humanitarian interests of the 1960s. The pupils' active intellectual life took place more and more in a context outside the school's field of vision.

The schools of the 1970s, however, did have one positive task: to replace the obsolete curricula and textbooks with new, methodically modernised ones. This restructuring also affected primary schools: for the first time in the history of the Soviet school the curricula in grammar, mathematics and natural sciences began to be constructed not in the cycles which I described earlier, but sequentially, extending and deepening the pupils' knowledge from grade one to grade ten. As it is beyond the scope of this survey to describe specific changes in specific curricula, I shall merely outline certain features of this re-structuring. It is important to note first of all that the ideological elements of the curricula were not altered and that for this reason the history, social sciences and literature courses remained basically unchanged. The literature course was somewhat extended to include Dostoevskii, who had been 'rehabilitated', and surveys of several other subjects and optional subjects, but the general ideological aims and principles governing the choice of writers studied did not change.

A number of other curricula in grammar and mathematics (and partly in the natural sciences) were, however, considerably improved by the abolition of the cyclical structure. Now the material was to be studied sequentially, and more thoroughly, guided by the logic of each particular subject, progressing from the simple to the complex. These curricula were also re-designed to exploit the intellectual potential of the children more fully and at an earlier age.

At first the new curricula were introduced into the so-called 'base' (model) schools, experimental schools (those attached to the scientific institutions of both the Ministry of Education and the Ministry of Higher Education) and the specialised schools (schools of physics and mathematics, etc.), and then they gradually began to be introduced into all the schools. At this point, however, a very grave difficulty was encountered: the introduction of the new curricula in the schools in the large cities (the central day schools and specialised schools - either the experimental ones or those specialising in a particular subject) had brought about a marked improvement in the pupils' accomplishments, while the large majority of school-leavers - those from rural and district schools in the outlying districts, from the schools for rural and working youth and from extension-correspondence secondary schools - completed their secondary education knowing as little as before. I had the opportunity to observe this phenomenon during my work in the courses which prepared candidates for the entrance examinations to institutions of higher education right up to the end of the 1975/6 school year, when all the senior pupils had been taught according to the new curricula, some of them since grade five. The level of literacy of the majority of students (except for those from the best schools mentioned above) in the elementary sense of spelling and punctuation, continued to decline. Throughout these years (1968-76) I continued to maintain my contacts with my former colleagues, teachers in rural, district and ordinary schools. I also met and had professional contact with specialists in teaching methods at the Institute for the Advanced Training of Teachers and had the opportunity to become familiar with the work of both the Novosibirsk and Petropavlovsk-Tselinokraiskii Schools of Physics and Mathematics, whose teachers and scientific-educational heads were conducting educational work among teachers in their oblasts. These enthusiasts had set themsleves a specific goal: to introduce the mass of teachers to the new language, mathematics and biology curricula (the latter had been profoundly re-structured after Lysenkoism and the rehabilitation of genetics). The difficulty of their task was compounded because the re-organisation had started in the primary schools: abstract grammatical categories and the most simple equations were introduced from grade two, but the teachers of the lower grades of ordinary rural and urban schools are the most numerous and least well educated of the Soviet teaching community.

There were enormous difficulties in mastering the new curricula, especially in the rural schools where the teachers of the lower grades had been working for decades, had long since lost the habit of assimilating new knowledge and acquiring new skills and usually had received their secondary pedagogical education by correspondence courses. The new curricula, textbooks and mathematical problem books presented well-nigh insuperable difficulties to the large numbers of teachers in the villages and outlying areas. Their level of teaching became even lower than when they had followed the previous, very imperfect curricula, whereas it was precisely in these schools, where the children usually have a far lower level of general cultural development than in urban schools, that the teachers should have a particularly high level of knowledge and professional skill in order to overcome this difference.

The Minister of Education, M. Prokof'ev, wrote that the training of most teachers in all subjects that were taught in primary, eight-year and secondary schools was not sufficient to enable them to master the new curricula ('The main task of the school', *Narodnoe obrazovanie*, no. 9, 1969). Contributions from the provinces and articles by educational leaders also continued to appear in the pedagogical press in following years that testified to the inability of a considerable proportion of teachers to cope with the difficulties they (the teachers, not the pupils) had in mastering the new curricula.[3]

Narodnoe obrazovanie in the 1970s published much valuable material on teaching methods in the various subjects. The contributions from different parts of the country presented progressive methods of teaching specific subjects and the experience of the best teachers and gave serious didactic recommendations. In general, much space in these years was occupied by teaching methods and the organisation of the educational process as well as problems of teachers' self-education and of upgrading their qualifications. Only ideological themes and articles containing directives, which never have to compete, received more space.

Despite this, the difference in quality between graduates from schools in the centre and those in the outlying regions was not reduced, because the professional and general cultural preparation of the large majority of teachers who were already working could not be improved. What is more, the teachers were as over-loaded as before with political-propaganda work inside and outside the school. They had no time to work seriously on raising their professional standards.

The chapter on the school reforms of the end of the 1950s and the beginning of the 1960s described how the construction of boarding schools was halted and the transition to a boarding system of secondary school education rejected. Meanwhile, the problem of finding premises for schools in the rural periphery and outlying districts of the USSR remained extremely acute in the 1970s. As before, other problems - economic and demographic - affected this problem: the dying out of small and medium-sized rural settlements; the lack of roads, a problem which starts within a few hundred metres of the railway lines, rivers and large motorways; the lack of means for transporting pupils and of funds for either maintaining the very small, dying schools or renewing the construction of boarding schools. The teachers' press abounds in evidence of all this in the 1970s.

*

Thus, the development of secondary general education in the USSR in the 1970s was characterised by the following trends:

(1) The decline in pedagogical discussions in the press on matters of principle which had arisen from the revival of public life at the end of the 1950s and the beginning of the 1960s. The interest in social matters of teachers and the most advanced senior pupils in urban schools, especially in the capitals (like that of the entire intelligentsia which inclined to an individual view of events), virtually disappeared from official school life and the pedagogical periodical press.

(2) The introduction of the new curricula and the consequent changing demands made on teachers and the

inability of the majority of rank-and-file teachers in the villages and the outlying districts to cope with the new pedagogical tasks. The abundance of articles in the periodical press connected with the introduction of the new curricula.

(3) The sharp increase in party and government ideological control over the schools and the military training of senior pupils.

(4) Continuing difficulties in the distribution of the schools and the size of schools as a result of general economic and demographic processes occurring outside the towns of the USSR, i.e. directly affecting approximately 40 per cent of its population.

NOTES

1. L. Kudriavtseva, 'To improve inner school control' in Narodnoe obrazovanie, no. 8 (1973), pp. 17-20.

2. See for example A. Pashchenko, Secretary of the Dnepropetrovsk Oblast Committee of the Communist Party of the Ukraine, 'An important means of ideological education of pupils', Narodnoe obrazovanie, no. 1 (1973), pp. 50-1. Here are some titles of the innumerable articles on political education in Narodnoe obrazovanie in the 1971/2 school year:

Year		No.	Page
1971	L.I. Brezhnev: The formation of the new man is one of the main tasks of the party in the construction of communism (from the report of the CC CPSU to the XXIV Congress of the CPSU)	5	2
	Editorials		
	We are led by the party of Lenin!	3	2
	To lead public education in the spirit of Lenin	2	22
	The decisions of the XXIV CPSU Congress - our fighting programme	6	22
	To realise the decisions of the XXIV CPSU Congress	7	2
	Problems of the Organisation of Education		
	M. Prokof'ev: To realise the decisions		

Year		No.	Page
	of the XXIV CPSU Congress	7	2
	Directives of the XXIV CPSU Congress in action (in the Ministry of Education of the Kazakh SSR)	8	11
	V. Kobzar: Party organisation and the school	3	6
	A. Mel'nik: The experience of the party organisations of the schools of Moldavia	3	11
	A. Mogilevskii: District party meetings of Communist teachers	7	16
	S. Shermukhamedov: The concern of the Party organisations of Uzbekistan for education	5	5
	School matters are a party matter (conversation with leading party workers of Smolensk area)	3	16
	<u>The School and Life</u>		
	G. Volovnikova: The heroic-patriotic theme of All-Union essays by schoolchildren	3	50
	O. Volodin: On the path indicated by the party	1	2
	E. Zil'berman: Senior pupils study Lenin's legacy	7	96
	P. Pshebil'skii: Lenin halls and museums in schools	4	33
	R. Rogova: Bringing up senior pupils on Lenin's behests	4	26
	V. Ul'ianov: N.K. Krupskaia in the hearts of our schoolchildren	2	93
	G. Mikaberidze: Who receives education in the USA?	3	100
1972	<u>Editorials</u>		
	To educate Communist conviction	3	2
	<u>School - Family - Community</u>		
	L. Aizenberg: V.I. Lenin on self-education	1	8
	A. Arsen'eva and F. Korolev: Methodological problems of Marxist-Leninist pedagogy	4	6
	M. Kondakov: Decisions of the XXIV CPSU Congress and the tasks of the district Departments of Education	2	2

Year		No.	Page
	T. Kutsenko: To improve the leadership of school Komsomol organisations, to increase their role in the Communist upbringing of the workers	9	4
	A. Fedulova: Fifty years of the Lenin All-Union Pioneer Organisation	5	7
	Decisions of the XXIV Congress of the CPSU in action (on the conference of heads of rural district Departments of Education)	3	24

And so forth, in the same spirit and style.

3. See, for example:

S. Gromtseva, specialist in teaching methods and inspector in the RSFSR Ministry of Education, 'The study of literature according to the new curricula', Narodnoe obrazovanie, no. 8 (1969), pp. 55-8; I. Borisov and V. Viviurskii, 'Physics in grades eight and nine', ibid., no. 8 (1971), pp. 120-1, and 'To improve the teaching of chemistry', ibid., pp. 121-3; 'In the USSR Ministry of Education', and 'Russian language in grade six', ibid., no. 9 (1973) pp. 109 and 111; 'Self-education - the way to increase expertise', subtitled 'The self-education of teachers and school directors (a letter on methodology)', ibid., no. 10 (1973), pp. 118-26; P. Semakin, 'Natural history and geography', ibid., pp. 124-5; 'In the USSR Ministry of Education. To improve the teaching of mathematics according to the new curricula', ibid., no. 11 (1973) pp. 124-5; and so forth.

Chapter Seven

THE SOVIET SCHOOL IN THE EARLY 1980S AND THE FORTHCOMING REFORM

Soviet schools today are once again on the threshold of radical reforms. The value of these changes and the extent to which they can be implemented cannot be forecast without taking another look at the entire situation of schools. This survey will also enable us to trace how the trends in Soviet secondary education noted in the previous chapter were resolved in the 1980s. Certain repetition is inevitable, but I shall resort to it only in order to complete the picture and reveal the dynamics of the processes presented in this book.

1. DID THE NEED FOR UNIVERSAL SECONDARY EDUCATION EMERGE IN THE SOVIET UNION IN THE 1980s?

The postulate adopted under Khrushchev, that all young people in the USSR should be enrolled in some form of secondary education (day, evening, extension-correspondence schools, etc.) remains in force in the school reform of 1984. At the same time, the term 'young people' is being given a very broad interpretation if we can judge by the recruiting, virtually 'mobilising' functions with which the evening and multi-shift schools of working and rural youth (ShRM) are being charged. Even people of thirty years of age or more, who are already parents, are being urged to attend these schools, sometimes against their will. We shall consider how well they study in these circumstances below. Let us leave aside for the time being the subjective motives of adolescents when deciding whether to complete their general or specialised secondary education or not. Soviet society functions according to centralised planning and the needs of the state take priority over the individual's freedom of choice (openly or not). The question is to what extent the Soviet state needs all its citizens to have such a high standard of education, not from the point of view of propaganda or ideology (every citizen in a developed socialist society should have complete secondary education) but from a realistic, social and economic point of view.

The answer to this question appears to be the same today as in the 1940s-1970s. The New York Russian-language newspaper Novoe Russkoe slovo ('The new Russian word', the oldest Russian-language newspaper in existence today, dating from 1910) published an article by Professor Iudovich in its 24 March 1984 issue, entitled 'Immortal manual labour'. On 7 April 1984 V. Golovskoi responded in the same newspaper to this article and an article by two well-known Soviet economists that appeared at almost the same time in Literaturnaia gazeta:

> Candidates of Economic Sciences, A. Shokhin (head of a laboratory in the Central Economics-Mathematics Institute) and E. Feoktistova (a researcher in the Labour Institute), present a number of surprises in their article.
>
> The first is the precise figures on the use of manual labour. Prof. L. Iudovich informs us that 40 million of the 112.5 million workers in the national economy use manual labour in their work. But the Soviet authors make a significant correction: there are not 40 but 50 million 'ruchniki' (as those who still work in eighteenth-century conditions are affectionately called).
>
> This, moreover, is the result of 'the greatest' progress, since over the past 25 years the number of people 'engaged in manual labour' in the national economy has declined from 54 to 37 per cent in industry and from 78 to 58 per cent in construction. Amazing achievements! But at the same time, the authors of the article note, the total number of workers engaged in manual labour has grown by 25 per cent in industry and even new manual labour occupations have emerged!
>
> But what about construction and the auxiliary industries where there is not even a trace of mechanisation?!
>
> If that is not enough, the authors, like true Marxist

> economists, look ahead and assert that at the beginning of the third millenium (!) the number of those employed in manual labour in industry in the USSR may constitute 25 per cent, and in construction 40 per cent!
>
> The article in Literaturnaia gazeta gives us a glimpse of a truly unresolved problem confronting the Soviet economy: the level of mechanisation and automation in most fields of the economy is so low that there is not even the hope of getting rid of spades, hammers, planes, scythes, axes and rakes. On the other hand, the older workers are leaving and the more educated young people do not want to engage in 'dirty' manual labour, even if it pays more than mechanised work.[1]

This is a generalised picture, with the writer viewing it somewhat from the side-lines. The following quotation, however, is a painting from life, not from an émigré newspaper using Soviet sources, but directly out of Pravda itself, from a report by the paper's correspondent in the Tadzhik SSR after a visit to one of the republic's best cotton farms:

> In 1983 the Lenin Kolkhoz in Gissar District sold the state 5,398 tons of raw cotton. Of this, only 345 tons were picked by machine. The kolkhozniks with the help of workers and employees [picked] 2,677 tons and senior pupils and students of the SPTU* the rest, that is 44 per cent of the harvest. The Secretary of the Party Committee, P. Pulodov, relates that in favourable years half the crop is, however, picked by combines. But that happens rarely. And even where the proportion of machine-harvesting is growing, the work-load on schoolchildren and students is increasing. They follow the machines, picking up the segments of raw cotton that have been dislodged, of which 300-400 kilos per hectare are collected, and clean the fields of the last bolls. This is uneconomical, but the special instruments available are imperfect and there are extremely few of them.[2]

---

* Srednee professional'no-tekhnicheskoe uchilishche = 'secondary vocational-technical school'.

I omit the correspondent's complaints about employing schoolchildren in unsuitable work and the poor progress of pupils who work for months every year picking the cotton by hand.

The situation is not only not improving but deteriorating. On 6 March 1985 Pravda published an article 'The cotton season is not for schoolchildren' (the article demonstrates the reverse), describing the situation in Uzbekistan:

> The kolkhozes and sovkhozes of the republic have 35 thousand cotton-picking machines and much other productive machinery. With their help virtually the entire harvest can be picked quite quickly. At least, several years ago more than three and a half million tons of raw cotton (almost two thirds of the total) were brought in by machine.
>
> The picture is quite different in recent years. Last autumn only about one and a half million tons of cotton were picked by machine. The machine-harvesting assignment was fulfilled by only 44 per cent. This was in the republic as a whole. Many kolkhozes and sovkhozes managed only 5-20 per cent.
>
> ... It is paradoxical, but a fact: powerful machines stand on the edge of the road, while many hundreds of thousands of boys and girls work in the plantations.

In some districts machines were almost not used at all.

In circumstances in which about half of the workers are engaged in manual labour and in which it is foreseen that the situation will remain approximately the same until 'the beginning of the third millenium(!)', is there an objective need for all citizens to receive complete secondary education? Whatever this education is like, it leads to a certain ambitiousness: firstly, the person who has achieved it wants to use it; secondly, he does not want to wield a spade when he has a school-leaving certificate or degree. On the other hand, people do not need a certificate, and even less so a degree, if they are to pick cotton bolls or perform many other useful but routine, unskilled jobs, even if they are mechanised. Today heretical opinions that universal complete secondary education is a superfluous extravagance for the Soviet state and society do occasionally make their way into the Soviet pedagogical press, which is usually very loyal and optimistic. Professor M. Zakiev, the rector of the Kazan Pedagogical Institute, wrote in Uchitel'skaia gazeta on 1 March 1984, in an article entitled 'Labour is joyful': 'It seems to me that compulsory full-time schooling should end in grade nine and only those who desire to study should enter grades ten and eleven of general education schools and vocational-technical schools'. But what about the others? Surely a developed socialist society cannot take a step backwards and reject universal secondary education? The author suggests that those who do not wish to remain in school should go to work and until a certain age 'let us say until the age of 20-25, receive compulsory secondary education in evening or correspondence-extension vocational-technical schools. This should be established by legislation.' Realising that workers and people with families have little motivation to continue their studies, Zakiev advises establishing 'a fixed scale of wages not only for those who have higher education but also for those with secondary education. This will stimulate the desire to receive an education while still continuing to work.'[3] This would indeed be an incentive if the pay increment for those with secondary education was significant, to which a state that has no technological need for this is not likely to agree.

Working youth, however, are usually not eager to upgrade their educational qualifications without any specific need. An article in the same paper on 6 December 1983, 'The collective sends in its resignation', gives evidence of the lack of interest of young workers and their immediate superiors in universal secondary education. It describes the disastrous situation in the Egorshin evening school (in the RSFSR): 'ghost' students, false records in class registers on pupils' attendance of lessons, fake marks, fictitious certificates. On 19 January 1984 the paper published an avalanche of teachers' responses to this article which demonstrated just how common such practices are in the ShRM. Here is an example:

> Certificate or Learning
>
> We, teachers at an evening school, are tired of making deals with our conscience. Often instead of pupils we create a 'fake'. We master the 'science' of forging documents. It's disgusting ...
>
> The time has passed when graduates of the ShRM used to make intelligent replies during examinations. Now cribbing is the best hope. And we are obliged to reconcile ourselves to this. Can a pupil who has

> appeared in school intermittently, as a 'favour' to us, know much?
>
> Modern production needs educated workers and the aim should be that young people go to the ShRM of their own accord. Not for a certificate, but for learning.
>
> Why are many enterprises forced to violate laws in order to pay their workers fully for the privileged day of study? Is it not time to solve this problem on a nation-wide scale? Let the brigade workers fulfil the quota fixed for that day for their comrade.
>
> ... And another thing. The number of hours allotted to individual consultations and receiving tests should be drastically reduced. It is truly shameful to receive this unearned money: almost none of the students attend them. You calm yourself with the thought that this is pay for our hardships, for going the rounds of the addresses of those on the class register.
>
> I have been thinking about this letter for a long time. But now I am afraid - what if my superiors find out about it. Surely this is not a normal phenomenon? This is why I am not signing my name.
>
> Teacher in an evening school, Moscow.

<u>Uchitel'skaia gazeta</u> reported on 2 April 1983 that 'According to data of the Central Statistical Board at the end of 1980, 77 per cent of young people without secondary education in the Tadzhik SSR' were not in school, the figure in rural areas being as low as 16.5 per cent. It noted that the situation was also 'disturbing in a number of other republics'.

Readers of <u>Literaturnaia gazeta</u> asked in the issue of 1 November 1984 'Why are evening schools not mentioned in the draft of the CC CPSU?' (referring to the draft of the school reform). This question was justified. Evening schools are one of the most unsuccessful sectors of secondary education and if the authors of the draft of the school reform had been really concerned with improving general secondary education they could not have ignored them. The newspaper, having consulted specialists on this question, made the vague assumption that the reform could not but have a positive effect on the quality of the work in the evening schools as well, but in passing noted the following:

> Evening and extension-correspondence schools are attended by people who already have a profession. Therefore, all the clauses of the draft concerning the labour education and vocational training of pupils in schools of general education do not apply to them.[4]

This is the crux of the matter. The goal of the reform was to draw pupils as early as possible into the system of productive labour and to provide the vast majority of young people with the most common rural and urban skills. The poor secondary education of those who already have and use such skills did not, therefore, concern its authors. Evening students will perhaps be afforded some relief by the fact that, according to fleeting illusions in the text of the 'Basic trends of the reform', secondary education will be essentially unified, simplified and reduced in scope (contrary to the trends of the 1970s).

2. THE REFORM AND SECONDARY EDUCATION

The reform of general secondary and vocational education, the draft of which was published in January and the final text in March 1984, and the cycle of special Resolutions elaborating it steadfastly ignore the two self-evident facts that approximately 44.6 per cent of Soviet workers are engaged in manual labour that does not require secondary education and that people who receive secondary education do not and will not want to do unskilled work, and the better their general education schooling, the less they will want such work and the higher their individual demands will be. The point is not so much the physical difficulty or lack of prestige of unskilled, mechanised or manual labour, which is often paid relatively well, as its routine nature and its complete unrelatedness to the intellectual potential of the worker with secondary education. The reform aims at giving every boy and girl complete secondary education by the age of 17 while ensuring that the vast majority of graduates from schools and PTU (Professional'no-tekhnicheskie uchilishcha, 'vocational-technical schools') that give secondary education (SPTU) be trained in the most common construction, industrial and agricultural skills which they will be obliged to use in the jobs to which they are allocated. The latter is the main goal of the reform and recurs time and again in its text and the texts of the special Resolutions which elaborate it.

According to data of Soviet demographers, Soviet industry employed 20 million new workers in the 1970s. Not more than ten million were envisaged for the 1980s, hence one of the basic theses of the reform promised: 'Taking into consideration the wishes of the youth, the community of parents and the workers' collectives, to study properly the possibility of lowering the age limit in a number of occupations.'[5] Such age limits have been fought for by the progressive public throughout the world for two centuries, including in pre-Revolutionary Russia, and until now they had been considered in the USSR as one of the main conquests of socialism. The country's demographic balance, however, necessitated a review of these assumptions that protected young people from premature excessive workloads, and production from inferior workers.

The reform is planned to take five or ten years and, therefore, to be completed in the mid-1990s. Its goal is defined in the preamble: to introduce into institutions of secondary education of all kinds (for all ages) 'labour education ... as the most important factor in personality formation and as a means of satisfying the needs of the national economy for labour resources'.[6] The 'ideological-political education of the youth, the formation of a Marxist-Leninist world view' comes next in all sections of the reform, and finally, the last aim of the reform, is 'to increase the quality of education and upbringing', and to provide a 'firm grounding in the principles of science'.[7] Schooling is to last eleven years, as at the time of Khrushchev's innovations in the field of education, but this extension of the school course is to be implemented gradually by lowering the age at which children start school to six years, and not by adding another senior grade.

The expediency of sending six-year-olds to school is very debatable. Although this is the practice in many Western countries, it is combined with twelve years of schooling, so that girls and boys finish school at the age of 18. Moreover, the achievements of this year of schooling are very debatable. The designers of the school reform in the USSR, however, planned that most young people by the age of 17 would be working in areas necessary to the state. Their goal, in the words of <u>Uchitel'skaia gazeta</u>, was from the age of 17 'to bind together the young person's "I want" and "I can" with our "must"'.[8] This was why the extra year was added not at the end of the school course, where it would have been most academically effective, but at the beginning. The transition is to take place gradually, to encompass an ever-expanding circle of schools. This gradualness is also perplexing. The reform states that some six-year-olds will do the same course in the kindergartens, but does not explain whether they will subsequently start school in grade one (that is, start all over again) or in grade two, along with other seven-year-olds who have started school at the age of six. Nor does it consider children who do not attend kindergarten, who, according to data of the Ministry of Education, constitute about 50 per cent of children in the country (when rural areas are counted). Surely it would be more expedient first to thoroughly prepare all schools for admitting six-year-olds and then introduce schooling for such children everywhere simultaneously?

I. Zver'ev, Vice-President of the USSR Academy of Pedagogical Sciences, was gravely concerned with the problem of having six-year-olds in school and especially with the health of children who would be burdened with a large additional work-load. In an article in Uchitel'skaia gazeta, 31 March and 3 April 1984, he wrote: 'It is known that even now a considerable number of children come to school in poor health and even with chronic illnesses ...' He feared that reducing to six the age at which children started school would increase the probability of 'nervous breakdowns in young children'. 'Unfortunately', he wrote, 'these are observed in a number of cases, so that the general task of the school, kindergarten and family is to avoid stressful situations of high tension', which are not infrequently seen in seven-year-olds when they start school, not to mention six-year-olds. He was also concerned about young children's need for sleep during the day:

> It has been established that the need for sleep during the day gradually disappears by the age of seven. It is not so easy to create conditions for six-year-olds to sleep during the day. Even now this is not provided in many schools and kindergartens.[9]

Meanwhile, he added, experiments on lowering the age at which children start school to six revealed:

> ... unfavourable indicators of the state of health of six-year-olds: frequently their deportment deteriorates,

> shortsightedness occurs, there is a loss of weight, a decrease in the haemoglobin level in the blood, headaches, sluggishness or increased irritability appear, the ability to work declines.[10]

If this was the case, was it worth introducing this measure, and if it were not introduced, how could seventeen-year-olds be sent to work, which was the main goal of the reform? Zver'ev did not favour giving kindergartens the task of instructing six-year-olds, as he assumed that this was the function of schools, and called upon schools, pedagogical science and health care agencies to study the problem of six-year-olds, which would demand 'enormous efforts'. Experiments had shown that:

> Some six-year-olds do not master the curriculum. The family and school have to pay special attention to solving the problem of the necessity of making a backward child repeat the first year of schooling. Experience shows: it is better to 'delay' a weak [pupil] at the beginning of schooling than to transfer him automatically to the next grade.[11]

In this case, however, he would complete his eleven years of school at the age of 18 and the aim of sending him to school a year earlier would be frustrated. It is doubtful, therefore, that such a practice will be encouraged.

Finally, Zver'ev reminded the reader, the need to teach Russian to six-year-olds in non-Russian kindergartens should not be forgotten: that is, in effect, to teach them two lanugages, which also greatly increases their work-load. Indeed, the reform pays much attention to the teaching of Russian in non-Russian schools, comparable only to the attention devoted to labour and ideological and military-patriotic upbringing (with the latter particularly stressed).

With children starting school at the age of six, primary school again lasts four years, as it did until the 1970s, although at that time it was the seven- to eleven-year-olds who attended primary schools, whereas now these are the six- to ten-year-olds. Grades five to nine are to cover the course of the incomplete secondary schools (until now grades four to eight).

In the years prior to the reform there had been a struggle to send 40 per cent of children after incomplete secondary education to the PTU (a small proportion to the technicums) and to leave 60 per cent in grades nine and ten of the schools. Now, as a result of the reform, it is planned to double the number of pupils in grade nine who go to the PTU and to leave not more than 20 per cent of ninth-graders in grades ten and eleven. What will be the juridical principles and criteria of this selection?

When the draft of the reform was being discussed, many proposals were put forward to admit candidates to the senior grades by competitive examinations according to the number of places planned, as in a number of Western countries; but far-reaching apprehensions were also voiced about this measure. Some people were disturbed by the following prospect:

> If the number of ninth-graders directed to the PTU is to be double the number today, then COMPETITION to enter the senior grades will arise by itself. We all know from experience what a painful phenomenon competition is for young people, especially if we are speaking of comparing abilities. Inaccurate marks, a low opinion, even a conflict between a teacher and a pupil can all influence a schoolchild's fate and bar his way to an ordinary school ... An unhealthy hullabaloo may arise ... around the limited number of places in the senior grades. Great care must be taken ... to avoid creating the ground for such hullabaloo and the 'parental competition' which takes place during admission to certain institutions of higher education.
>
> Iu. Kaminskii, engineer.
>
> Moscow.[12]

The expression 'certain institutions of higher education' was undoubtedly used to mitigate what was being said since this 'parental competition' exists in all institutions of higher education, except in very rare, untypical cases. In a society riddled with a mass of unofficial 'ranks' and contacts, it is difficult, if not impossible, to avoid such abuses. Nonetheless, what, apart from entrance examinations, can provide a legal and - ideally - fair basis for selecting the 20 per cent of pupils to be left in the schools? (Both children and parents have an aversion to the PTU.) True, in the same issue of Literaturnaia gazeta, an optimistic reader, I. Malenkov, teacher (master) of industrial training from Sverdlovsk, wrote that:

> The PTU cannot remain in the form that frequently depresses schoolchildren today. These will be real 'CENTRES OF CHILDREN'S VOCATIONAL TRAINING' built with consideration for the psychology of adolescents, that is, a complex of factory shops, workshops and lecture halls filled with modern technology, electronic computers, etc.[13]

But when is this to be and where are the funds for this to be found today when, as the newspapers constantly report, even the most indispensable school and pre-school construction and repair drags on for years, even in emergency cases? Meanwhile, as D. Dekkhanov of Tashkent wrote in Uchitel'skaia gazeta, 7 February 1984, parents try by fair means or foul to extract their children's documents from the PTU to which the schools send them. (Section 4 of this chapter discusses the actual situation in the PTU.)

Let us recall what happened forty or so years ago when the trade schools and the factory-plant schools were set up and youngsters were put on trial for running away from them because of the excessive work-load and difficult living conditions. Today there are no trials as yet, but Dekkhanov suggested 'regulating' the transfer of adolescents from the schools to the PTU, while not explaining how this is to be done.

Geidar Aliev, however, member of the Politburo of the CC of the CPSU and first deputy chairman of the USSR Council of Ministers - who in the past was a regular worker of the notorious 'security organs' - considered such an approach to be insufficiently liberal. In a speech to a session of the USSR Supreme Soviet on 12 April 1984 he argued that:

> ... all graduates of grade nine should have equal opportunities to complete secondary education ... Let the pupil make the choice himself, taking into consideration both his inclinations and aptitudes and the needs of society. And his parents and teachers are called upon to help him make the right choice.[14]

But what if his choice, inclinations and aptitudes do not accord with the needs of society? Uchitel'skaia gazeta, 8 May 1984, published under the heading 'Business-like planning session':

> Last year the director of Ashkhabad Secondary School No 6 received a quota of 23 graduates from grade eight to be assigned to the PTU. But only three expressed the desire... At present the Ashkhabad Secondary School No. 6 has not yet received the quota of those to study in the PTU. But the results of a questionnaire are already known. Only one pupil in grade eight has decided to go to a PTU. And there are about 60 of them. As for the tenth-graders, they all want to go to institutions of higher education.

Further testimony is provided by an article by N. Anisin of Kaluga, 'Plan and recruitment', Uchitel'skaia gazeta, 19 April 1984, who met a class teacher at a rally on vocational guidance. She had 42 pupils in her eighth grade, of whom she had to assign 25 to a PTU according to the plan. After prolonged and, for her, painful efforts at persuasion, only 15 pupils had agreed to go to a PTU 'and only to those that give non-dusty trades - microchip assembler, radio tuner, computer operator'. The main need for workers is, however, precisely in the most common 'dusty' trades, so what can be done? The teacher had a ready answer: 'Our director will select the "superflous" ones, the pupils who are somewhat weaker, and will refuse to admit them to the ninth grade... He'll win round the parents: "I'm fulfilling the plan. Go and complain about me."' The correspondent was still not satisfied: 'But let us put ourselves in the parents' place: our child has the right to study wherever he wants.'

The reform is called upon to unite two contradictions: freedom of choice and the state's planned disposal of the fate of young people. By rejecting the only sensible solution - competitive entrance examinations to the senior grades - the authors of the reform undoubtedly prefer compulsion. The very text of the 'Basic trends of the reform' contains that contradication: 'the needs of the national economy', placed first, are combined with 'the inclinations and aptitudes of the pupils' and the parents' wishes',[15] although it does not explain how all these are to be united in practice. However, on 4 May 1984 a Special Resolution of the CC CPSU and the USSR Council of Ministers on the production training and vocational guidance of school-children, stated outright, without reserve: 'To regulate the planned allocation of graduates of nine-year and secondary schools in different directions for further instruction and job placement.'[16] This is reiterated in Section 38 of the 'Basic trends of the reform' which proposes setting up special 'inter-departmental commissions in the centre and locally: from the USSR Council of Ministers to the executive committees of the town and district Soviets of People's Commissars. To charge them with ... allocating the streams of young people who continue their studies after finishing incomplete secondary and secondary schools...'[17] The only way in which such commissions could regulate this allocation would be through quotas which would be binding upon both the schools and the school-leavers. In this case the rejection of competitive entrance examinations into the senior grades and the few prestigious PTU on the grounds that examinations limit the freedom of choice of pupils and their parents hardly seems appropriate. Even without examinations, no choice is offered!

The reform eventually plans to unify the senior grades of schools and secondary vocational-technical schools (SPTU), that is in effect to deprive schools of the senior grades and to complete non-vocational general education in nine years of schooling. When and how this will happen ('over a period of five to ten years') is not stated. During the coming years, however, it is already planned to introduce instruction in the most common production trades into the tenth and eleventh grades of all secondary schools (at present this exists in approximately 30 per cent of senior grades). The initiators of the reform are not at all pleased with the fact that only an insignificant proportion of school-leavers work or study after school in the particular trade which they learnt at school and usually do not work in it for a long period. The schools are urged to educate school-leavers to go to the kolkhozes, sovkhozes, factories and construction projects, but are given no indication of how they are to achieve this, as nobody knows.

Teachers have been complaining for many years that they do not have enough time to teach the basic subjects of the school course, particularly in the SPTU where the general subjects have on the one hand become a semi-formal 'makeweight' to vocational training and on the other hand take time away from the specialised disciplines. They fear that general secondary education in a large proportion of the SPTU will be as much of a formality and as low in quality as in many of the schools for working youth today. This is because, in the first place, the schools will continue to send to the SPTU all those who cannot or do not want to attend a regular school and, secondly, the teachers in the SPTU will choose to ignore general secondary education. Uchitel'skaia gazeta reported on 7 February 1984:

> Iu. Peretokin from the town of Rudnoi in Kustanai Oblast notes the shortcomings in the vocational training of pupils in the PTU. The reasons, in his view, are that the general subjects have 'cramped' the specialised disciplines. The solution which he proposes is to teach in the PTU only the future trade and those sciences that are indispensable for training a highly skilled worker.

The editors did not agree with him, arguing that this would limit the worker. However, in the vast majority of cases, nine years of general education or merely a few of the subjects taught in the senior grades are indeed all that the worker needs for his job, so why overburden the PTU students? Consequently, the SPTU curriculum should contain only those general subjects that the pupils will need in their trades when they finish the course. If they should desire afterwards to enter an institution of higher education, they should be entitled and enabled to take examinations in the subjects that they lack, in extension courses or in schools of working youth. This is possible in many countries today, even years after leaving school, and in some countries there are narrowly specialised institutions of higher education which admit students on the basis of incomplete or specialised school-leaving certificates.

Another complaint constantly heard from teachers in the USSR is that they do not have enough time to teach the material, although they usually fail to mention the excessive amount of material in the curriculum noted by the authors of the reform. On the contrary, the best teachers even consider the amount of material studied to be inadequate. But the lack of time leads to an intolerably excessive work-load for the pupils. Thus, Doctor of Pedagogical Sciences N. Dairi described the over-loading of school curricula and textbooks in history in Uchitel'skaia gazeta, 18 February 1984. This is a subject whose ideological importance is considered paramount and in which the amount of material is constantly growing: 'Were I Il'ia Muromets himself in teaching, I could never cope - the textbooks are so over-loaded.'

An exaggeration? Unfortunately not.

> An extensive course in modern history, a course in the history of the USSR in the 1960s-1980s has been added, the study of local history has been introduced, and in the union republics courses in the history of the republics. All this is important and necessary.
>
> But how much time has been added? None has been added, but subtracted - ten hours a week instead of the previous twelve. And the time for the courses in the ancient world and the middle ages which prepare schoolchildren for understanding the more complex courses that follow has been cut by a third![18]

Lawyers are making increasing claims on the time of schoolchildren and PTU students. When discussing the draft reform, an inter-departmental co-ordinating-methodological council on legal propaganda in the USSR Ministry of Justice proposed introducing a number of courses into the school and PTU curricula to ensure the law-abiding conduct of the future adult citizens. A. Orleanskii wrote about this in Uchitel'skaia gazeta, 25 February 1984:

> The main point of the proposals providing for the improvement of the system of the moral-legal upbringing of pupils is that it be carried out consistently from the first to the last grade, in all courses of the PTU ...
>
> It is clear that additional lessons will be needed in order to implement the lawyers' proposals. This is not a simple problem. At present the pupils are manifestly over-loaded with class hours. But ... it is worth revising the history course ... 'to free in this way 'hours' for ... lessons that are more necessary to the modern adolescent, aimed at radically improving moral and legal upbringing and the learning of Soviet legislation.

He also complained about the lack of hours devoted to mathematics.

What do the teachers suggest and request? First, they hoped that the additional year of schooling would be allotted to alleviating the situation in the general disciplines, whereas in fact it is to be devoted to productive work and vocational training. Second, as in previous years, insistent demands were voiced to divide general secondary education into speciality areas: the humanities, physics and mathematics, and chemistry and biology. Another solution would have been to reduce drastically the ideological instruction and guidance and transfer the hours wasted on it to teaching the general subjects, but this of course is impracticable in the USSR.

The authors of the reform did not take the path of dividing general secondary education into 'specialisms' by setting up schools or classes in speciality areas. Instead they propose revising the curricula of all the general subjects so as to exclude secondary and excessively complex material, that is, the trend is to reduce and simplify them. All the publications devoted to the reform reveal this same trend of de-academisation, unification and simplification of the courses in the general subjects, which at the end of the twentieth century is a barely comprehensible anachronism. Where will competent teachers for the institutions of higher education come from? It is clear that a modern industrial state, in particular one that lays claim to world leadership, cannot function properly without higher education of a high quality.

On 30 April 1984 Uchitel'skaia gazeta published material which elaborated the general text of the 'Basic trends' of the school reform and shed light on some of the questions we have raised. The following weekly hours of instruction are planned for pupils: grade one, 20 hours; grade two, 22 hours; grades three and four, 24 hours; grades five to eight, 30 hours; grades nine to eleven (or twelve), 31 hours. In addition, 'for pupils desiring to deepen their knowledge in certain subjects of the physics-mathematics, chemistry-biology, social-humanities and technical cycles' two hours in grades seven to nine and four hours in grades ten and eleven are being introduced 'over and above the standard curriculum'. The word 'desire' does not make it clear whether these extra classes will be compulsory and the choice limited to the cycle desired, or whether pupils will be able to limit themselves to the general, simplified course of all subjects if they so desire without deepening their knowledge of a particular group of subjects (outside the compulsory school timetable). The 'differentiation of certificates', announced in the same Resolution is evidently connected with these extra specialised subjects. The latter are to contain, in addition to the usual mark for conduct, marks for the pupil's diligence in study and socially useful labour.

The number of school hours quoted above is increased not only by extra courses. In the national schools an extra two or three hours per week are allocated in grades ten and eleven to the study of Russian (in addition to the hours included in the timetable); as it is not specified whether these additional school hours depend on the desire of the pupil or not, they are evidently compulsory. Socially useful productive labour (not to be confused with vocational production training, which is allocated special time) is also given extra time: in grades two to four, one hour per week; in grades five to seven, two hours; in grades eight to nine, three hours; and in grades ten and eleven, four hours. In addition to these weekly hours of labour, annual practical labour is introduced (productive labour in the economy of the town and country): in grades five to seven, ten days; in grades eight and nine, 16 days, in grades ten and eleven, 20 days. For this purpose the school year is extended and the summer holidays shortened by the corresponding number of days. We should remember that after children start going to school at the age of six, they will be only eleven years old in grade five. During the school year it is forbidden to use pupils for agricultural and other jobs other than in the time indicated above, but this practice is so deeply rooted in the life of rural schools and their relations with the kolkhozes and sovkhozes that it is hard to imagine how it can really be stopped.

The demand to intensify and improve the military-patriotic training of schoolchildren - a form of education quite unknown in Western schools - is specially emphasised (and reiterated many times).

The reform does promise one very valuable change that teachers have long hoped for: a reduction in the size of classes: from grade one to nine, up to 30 pupils, and in grades ten and eleven, up to 25, which also applies to general boarding schools (in children's homes and boarding schools for orphans it is proposed to have 20-25 children per group). These improved quotas, however (which are still too large in grades one to four in the view of many top specialists) are to be implemented 'consecutively', from grade one over a period of eleven years, starting in 1986. As for reducing the number of children in extended-day groups to 20-30, it is stated: 'These norms of class size will be introduced from 1990.'[19]

3. LABOUR INSTRUCTION IN SCHOOL

On 4 May 1984 a Resolution of the CC CPSU and the USSR Council of Ministers which elaborated the general text of the reform was published in the press: 'On improving the labour upbringing and vocational guidance of schoolchildren, and the organisation of their socially useful, productive labour'.[20] This Resolution allotted three hours in grades two to four, four hours in grades five to seven, six hours in grades eight and nine and eight hours in grades ten and eleven to the pupils' labour instruction and socially useful, productive labour. Unlike in the article of 30 April 1984 quoted above (p. 243), this Resolution did not stipulate that the hours set aside for socially useful labour would be outside the regular timetable, in the pupils' free time. It can only be assumed that the time devoted to production training proper, and not just to labour (in grades two to four, two hours per week; in grades five to seven, two hours; in grades eight and nine, three hours; in grades ten and eleven, four hours) will be included in the regular timetable to the detriment of general secondary education. What is more, a new subject is being introduced: 'The fundamentals of production. Choice of occupation',[21] but it is not specified from what grade or how many hours are to be devoted to it. It is proposed to publish an 'Encyclopedia of occupations for youth' for this course. Thus the general course has to be constricted to make room for another subject as well as labour instruction.

The Resolution silently assumes that as a result of these measures, the majority of schoolchildren will go on to practise the trades acquired in school after grade ten (from the age of 16). It is proposed that the USSR State Committee on Labour and Social Questions, the USSR Ministry of Education, the USSR State Committee on Vocational-Technical Education, the USSR Ministry of Health and the All-Union Central Trade Union Council, 'jointly with the departments concerned', review by 1 January 1985 the reduction of age limits in order to allow young people to work independently in a number of trades including, from the age of 16, as combine operators and tractor drivers. It is proposed to reduce the output quotas for them in the first three months 'after starting regular work' by 40 per cent, and in the second three months by 20 per cent, after which they will have to fulfil the quota of an adult in the same job.

At present 30 per cent of schoolchildren are given training in production skills, but usually they cannot be compelled to use these skills when they leave school. Moreover, the state often derives no significant economic benefit from the millions of schoolchildren who are already engaged today in productive labour, for part of their school and holiday time. Will the introduction of vocational training resolve the cadres problem (i.e. the need for skilled workers), which is the main problem for the Soviet leadership? Only if 17-year-olds can be compelled to work in the trades in which they have been trained in school. But how can this be done?

The USSR Minister of Education, M. Prokof'ev, writing in Narodnoe obrazovanie, no. 9 (1982), stated that despite the attention given this problem by the Komsomol, party, government, Ministry of Education and all rural schools, only 30 per cent of school-leavers remained in the villages in 1981. Follow-ups that were carried out two or three years after they had left school revealed that during this period most of those who had remained earlier had now managed to migrate to the towns. The problem of 'attaching' (zakreplenie) rural school-leavers to kolkhozes and sovkhozes remained unresolved. Indeed, how could this be otherwise when the urban construction organisations and factories wait for the rural school-leavers and offer them jobs and hostels, for it is they who make up the main labour reserve in the most common trades in construction and industry, as they are too poorly educated to enter institutions of higher education. The village does not attract them even as future qualified specialists: the minister noted sorrowfully that only twelve per cent of rural school-leavers went on to study the trade that they had been taught in their school labour agricultural training. This situation does not apply only to the villages: Uchitel'skaia gazeta wrote in an editorial on 26 November 1983:

> The number of school-leavers who go directly to production or continue their training in accordance with the type of labour training in school or the UPK* ... is

---

* UPK = Uchebno-proizvodstvennyi kombinat ('educational-production complex') which provides facilities such as workshops and equipment for production training for several schools in one area.

> on the whole still far from adequate. In Belorussia, Moldavia, the Ukraine and Estonia this figure is, for example, 27-29 per cent, and in Georgia and Armenia, only six or seven per cent.

V. Arsenov, head of the education section of the USSR State Planning Committee, wrote in the same paper on 24 February 1983 that 'In the past school year only 65.4 per cent of schoolchildren among those who received production training passed qualifying examinations in base enterprises. Of these only 11.6 per cent work in the national economy.' He concluded that the time had come to begin counting the costs of these programmes. On 14 November 1982 Uchitel'skaia gazeta sounded the alarm: schoolchildren who finished UPK did not subsequently use the skills they had learnt:

> In the last school year over a thousand pupils graduated from the Ashkhabad UPK - of which there are two in the city. Only 15 per cent of them, having begun independent life, are working today in enterprises in the capital of Turkmenia in the trades whose rudiments they acquired in the educational-production complex.

Production training, we should note, costs a considerable amount of money.

While teachers and the general public were still only surmising about the future reform (after Andropov announced it at the June 1983 Plenum of the CC CPSU), Literaturnaia gazeta wrote on 12 October of that year that the UPK were under fierce attack, the main grievance against them being that most of the pupils did not go to work in the trade which they had been taught there. This situation makes nonsense of the reform: there is no guarantee that after vocational training has been made universal (as opposed to the 30 per cent of children it covers now) school-leavers will head for jobs in production, which is what teachers and educators are being called upon to achieve.

A mass of published material testifies that an early familiarity with production, with the actual practice of its most common trades, not only does not attract schoolchildren to it, but repels them. In any society where people are employed in difficult manual labour or in routine, mechanised tasks on a scale such as in the USSR, the more educated the majority of the citizens, the harder it becomes to find people to perform these tasks. The Soviet state intends to solve this problem through planning the use of its young people for these tasks. But how can a person who has a school-leaving certificate and a common skill in production be forced to put the former aside for an indefinite period of time and practise the latter? Here too, as with the problem of allocating the ninth-graders to the different kinds of schools, some forms of compulsion will evidently be indispensable.

Candidate of Economic Sciences, K. Subbotina proposed using financial pressure on schools to force them to recruit school-leavers to work in production and to use the production-technical schools more effectively. She suggested that when funds are allocated to schools 'data on the job placement of school-leavers and the continuation of their studies ... according to the type of labour instruction in the school ... the assignment of graduates of the school to jobs ... the participation of the schoolchildren in creating products needed by society'[22] should be taken into consideration. In her opinion, the ruble should be used as a means of punishing schools which do not succeed in these respects. If her proposal were adopted, schools, that is teachers, would be laden with yet another heavy burden of responsibility: they would have to supervise the destinies of their school-leavers and wield some kind of influence over them wherever they lived, and if the latter's conduct failed to satisfy the agencies controlling the schools, then the schools budgets should be cut, which would affect not the pupils who had already left but the quite blameless pupils still in school. The folly of using such a measure to influence the administration of schools is self-evident.

On the other hand, 20-25 per cent of school-leavers today are absorbed by institutions of higher education, and some by the technicums. The authors of the reform plan to leave approximately this proportion of pupils in the senior grades. Does this mean that schools will mostly prepare candidates for institutions of higher and secondary specialised institutions of education, and if this is the case, why do the pupils need the mass production skills which cost the state so much money? What is the point of unifying and constricting general secondary education for the sake of teaching these skills? And why build the costly inter-school educational-production complexes?

The authors of the reform expect that society will

receive a considerable economic return on the socially useful labour of schoolchildren, but in the meantime an increasing number of alarming articles are appearing in the pedagogical press on the economic and educational ineffectiveness of this productive labour. V. Zaitsev, head of the Traktorzavodskii District Department of Education in Cheliabinsk wrote in Uchitel'skaia gazeta on 12 September 1983:

> In our district there are 17-and-a-half thousand pupils. Last year they manufactured 14.5 thousand rubles' worth of products in school workshops, on orders received from industrial enterprises. 82 kopecks per person! What productive labour, what economic education can be seriously talked of!

A. Zalutskii of Frunze echoed him in the same paper on 17 November 1983:

> Once a rural teacher boasted that in one month her class had earned 34 rubles from harvesting...
> 'But let's calculate how much each of your pupils earned a day.'
> They did. It turned out to be approximately three kopecks. Enough for a glass of soda water. This is incredible!

However, the return on the work of schoolchildren is not so ludicrous everywhere. Frequently, especially in the villages, it is a very serious matter. On 27 August 1983 Uchitel'skaia gazeta published a remarkable article, 'Union with production', by L. Gordin, a professor, doctor of pedagogical sciences, one of the leading members of the Scientific Research Institute of General Problems of Upbringing of the USSR Academy of Pedagogical Sciences. The impression created by this article was that the aim of the school reform was to make schoolchildren shoulder a considerable proportion of the costs of their education, for which they were to pay with economically effective labour. This idea was being discussed sympathetically on the pages of the mass press and, according to Gordin, some writers depicted 'the unification of schooling and productive labour as something that promises really fantastic profits'. They proposed 'to make the entire educational system pay its way' by means of this labour. He considered this utopian, reminding the reader that 'the classics of Marxism-Leninism always indicated that the expenditure on education and raising children can be only partially covered by means of their labour'.

Until now education in the Soviet Union has been considered to be free, even though it is paid for out of the taxes levied on the workers. I wonder whether it will still be considered free when it begins to be tangibly covered by the labour of schoolchildren?

According to data of the Central Statistical Board, the state spends over 17 milliard rubles annually on educating children and adolescents, while the return on the labour of schoolchildren in the 1982/3 school year was only half a milliard rubles. Even if this figure increases very soon, as Gordin hoped, to one milliard rubles a year, there will still be a long way to go until schools pay their own way. Nonetheless, he prophesies, this milliard will be a steady contribution to the state budget and then 'hundreds of additional schools, kindergartens, pioneer camps, courses for young technicians' will be established from the earnings of pupils. The Academy of Pedagogical Sciences considered it necessary to designate these funds precisely for this special purpose. Thus, the children would not be paid wages, even with tax deductions like the wages of other workers, but would directly finance their studies with their labour.

It is becoming increasingly clear, however, that the effective employment of children, apart from detracting considerable time from their studies and rest, will demand huge capital investment: specialised workshops, training factory shops, well-equipped educational-production complexes, special machine tools and equipment adapted to the age of schoolchildren in the various grades are needed as well as qualified teachers who combine labour skills with technical and pedagogical education. All this comes down to problems of time, funds, materials and specialists, without which all the talk about the effective labour and serious vocational training of schoolchildren will remain talk. Finally, it is necessary to double the number of SPTU and dramatically improve their quality which today is usually low.

The leadership is also aware of this. The Resolution of the CC CPSU and USSR Council of Ministers of 4 May 1984 which I quoted above (p 244) proposed that the republics' councils of ministers and Soviets of People's Deputies at all levels 'work out and implement in 1985-95 measures to develop the material base for the labour training of schoolchildren'. The ardent executors of the authorities' designs, however, are unwilling to wait so long, whether the resources essential for the forthcoming reform exist or not.

The USSR Minister of Education Prokof'ev responded warmly to the final text of the basic trends of the school reform in Uchitel'skaia gazeta, 28 April 1984, opening his article with the remark that it was especially important that the preparation of the basic trends had been carried out 'under the direct leadership of Konstantin Ustanovich Chernenko'. As we noted above, the late Andropov had first spoken of the impending reform at the June 1983 Plenum of the CC CPSU. Until 9 February 1984 - the day when Andropov died - the Education Minister had mentioned his name, and his name alone, in all his speeches, whether it was appropriate or not. Now he did not even consider it necessary to give him a passing mention as one of the initiators of the reform. Such 'forgetfulness' and unconcealed flattery of the next 'leader' are taken for granted by teachers, who are responsible for the moral education of their pupils (and the pupils notice everything).

Another point of interest is that the 4 May 1984 Resolution of the CC CPSU and USSR Council of Ministers envisaged that the new curricula in labour instruction would be introduced in the period 1986-90 'in so far as the necessary conditions are created'. These 'necessary conditions' included, apart from the creation of the necessary resources (the most difficult one): the reduction of class size; simplification of the curricula of the general subjects; and the introduction of an extra year of schooling. Only after these goals had been accomplished did the Resolution envisage increasing the time spent on the pupils' labour instruction and productive labour. This zealous official, however, in a hurry to gratify his bosses, did not want to wait for the entire educational process to be reorganised. Even though, as he wrote, the schools would continue to use the old curricula in the forthcoming school year, he wanted to introduce from 1 September 1984 what the Resolution had envisaged as beginning only in 1986: 'The fundamental question of the reform is a decisive improvement in the labour instruction and upbringing of schoolchildren. Senior pupils are to be brought to the level of acquiring a trade.'[23] Even now it was possible to find the necessary time 'by allocating special hours outside the school timetable and by shortening somewhat the school holidays.'[24] Thus, the Minister proposed introducing labour instruction without reducing class size, without reducing the load of material in the curricula of the various subjects, without a corresponding reduction in homework and essential reading outside school, at the expense of the children's free time of which even now the really conscientious senior pupils do not have enough for reading, sport or rest. One thing can be sure: people will be found in the schools who will be willing to implement these exhortations diligently.

In the final account, the reform, which is primarily designed to help the state carry out a particular cadres policy and not to improve secondary education, depends on colossal investment of material resources and labour, the infeasibility of which for the socialist super-power had previously frustrated Khrushchev's innovations in the field of schooling. In order to demonstrate to the reader what an enormous gulf lies between the actual situation of Soviet schools today and the one envisaged by the reform, and the vast funds needed to bridge this gulf, we shall turn now to some of the most pressing problems facing the Soviet educational system today and examine them on the basis of official Soviet data.

4. PROBLEMS, PROBLEMS!

The Soviet teachers' press in the 1980s is far from inclined to be critical or to emphasise uncomfortable facts or shortcomings. For this reason the recurring reports on the difficult conditions of work in the schools and of the hardships of the rural teachers' life, which have not improved since the war in a number of areas of the country, stand out even more sharply. On the threshold of the reform, when it was being discussed, these distress signals became more frequent. There were reports about construction projects for schools and pre-school children's institutions that had remained uncompleted for years; about how high-quality repairs cannot be carried out in time; about non-functioning heating systems in urban schools and the lack of fuel in rural schools; about the difficulties which teachers have in procuring fuel and food products; about the lack of refreshment rooms and canteens in schools and pedagogical colleges.

The following excerpt describes an urban secondary school in Krasnovodsk in the Turkmenian SSR (N. Lenskaia, 'There are no minor matters', Uchitel'skaia gazeta, 13 October 1983):

> I happened to be in school No. 10 in winter on official business. The situation was not conducive to a long conversation: the thermometer showed only seven degrees. Both teachers and children are thoroughly 'insulated'. But even this does not help: several pupils are absent from every class. The mood, as they say, is definitely not a working one.
>
> 'More than ten letters have been sent now to various agencies from the administration, party and trade-union organisations of the school', recalled the deputy director, T. Iu. Brykova. 'And all of them are a cry for help. We have a sadly notorious exercise book which records the absence of teachers because of illness. There are many.

T. Khlebnikova describes in the same paper on 27 September 1983 the situation in the Moscow School of Working Youth No. 137 in an article entitled 'The lesson took place, but the conclusions?'. She notes that 'The school lacks many things. for example, a refreshment room ... Or the heating system has just broken down. The teachers and pupils freeze. They have been freezing not for three days but for three years...' If that is the situation in Moscow, then what can be expected in the provinces and the villages?

On 1 November 1983 the Official Section of Uchitel'skaia gazeta ('In the USSR Ministry of Education') reported that during the current year over half the plans for constructing pre-school institutions had not been fulfilled in the country as a whole. The situation of school construction was not much better. The plans for constructing special boarding schools for sick children had been fulfilled by not more than 15 per cent and the need for them was extremely urgent. This, for example, was the situation in Secondary School No. 27 in the Tel'man Kolkhoz in Tashkent Oblast:

> The building does not have a roof. However, half of it had existed when the school was officially opened. But in May there was a hurricane - and no roof at all was left. And the panes in many windows were blown out. Since then ... no one has done anything serious about

repairs.

The school was officially opened over a year ago, but the floors have already rotted in twenty classrooms. The rooms for the extended-day groups have become quite unserviceable: the floors are in pieces, the heating system does not work.

'I've been working in the school since April', its director, Umarkul Usmankulov, sadly relates, 'and I've wasted over half my working time on visits to various authorities. What we could do, we did ourselves. But where can we get 189 plates of slate, or glass from? And relaying the floors is a task that is beyond the teachers' powers.'

Alas, this task also proved to be beyond the powers of the kolkhoz administration. Its chairman merely spread his hands in grief:

'Where can I get slate, glass and especially scarce timber from?' 'Fifteen memoranda to all authorities and as many vague replies with resolutions' were of no help either...

The ministry's report mentioned above proves that this situation is typical. Against this background, all the talk is meaningless about the capital and material investments required to make the productive labour of schoolchildren really effective when the forthcoming reform is implemented.

An article in Uchitel'skaia gazeta, 5 August 1982, called 'And the deadlines are postponed' reported that out of eight schools under construction in Khabarovsk Krai, not one would be ready by 1 September. 'Establishments of public education are built here extremely slowly, the deadlines of operation are postponed from year to year.' Meanwhile, the situation in the krai was disastrous. Participants in a special mission to investigate new school construction projects reported on a school in the Lesnoi District of Durmin:

> Things are extremely bad here. The builders are already declaring: we won't make it by the beginning of school. This means that once again classes will have to be housed in the small, cramped rooms of the office of the cooperage factory ... new schools in Komsomolsk-on-Amur, in Birobidzhan, etc. are built in a similarly unsatisfactory way.

The town of Kushka is situated on the Afghan border. Not far away the Soviet army is introducing the Afghans to the Soviet way of life with fire and sword. But what do we see in Kushka and its environs? N. Sotnik from Ashkhabad reports in an article 'Three to a desk? ...' in Uchitel'skaia gazeta, 12 August 1982:

> The settlement Poltavka is right next to the town ... The school is small, with one storey.
>
> Last year two rooms were built on with the help of the senior pupils. They are small, meant only for 16 pupils. But there are more children in the classes. For example, this year 35 first-graders are expected. But there is room for only half of them. What can be done? Are the children to be seated in threes like last year? Even so, not all of them will fit in...
>
> The population of the settlement mainly belongs to the indigenous nationality and the instruction in the school is in Russian, in accordance with the parents' wishes. This is fine if the children have attended a preparatory group in the kindergarten. But what if they haven't?

Indeed, what happens if they haven't? The children do not know Russian and there are almost no kindergartens which teach it. The same situation, according to Sotnik exists in another settlement near Kushka, Morgunovka:

> In 1980 the foundations of the new school were laid. At that time 130 thousand rubles were allocated to its construction. But then the general contractor - the directorate of 'Murgabsel'stroi' - halted the work. No attempts are being made to renew it. And what a need there is for a school there! Since there is no instruction in the Turkmen language in Kushka, we transport the children to study in the settlement of Morgunovka at the expense of the district department of education.
>
> Or the same problem with the children from Poltavka...

This means that there is no instruction in the children's native tongue not only in remote Poltavka but also in the town of Kushka. 'In accordance with the parents' wishes' - but what choice do they have if children with a poor knowledge of Russian are unable to continue their studies and advance in life?

Two days later the same paper published an article called 'Housewarming with repairs' which described the disastrous state of school construction in Uzbekistan. New buildings are not authorised for use for years, and if they are, this is the condition in which they are opened (the article was describing Tashkent School No. 134 - in the capital of the republic!):

> It was put into operation a year ago. The first failings had already begun to occur on the second of September. The lights were switched on: the electricity had been incorrectly installed. After lessons, the teachers and pupils painted the panelling (the builders had not had time for that) and cleared away the remaining rubbish. But in December the floors collapsed, the walls cracked: the rains washed away the soil which had been poured in instead of solid concrete. The floors in the sports hall rotted within a mere six months. The building was declared a hazard.

On 17 August 1982 the paper published a short article in the section 'Alarm signal' called 'Seven years later'. This time the scene was set in Riazan' Oblast:

> Our new school - a project of the Riazan' City Repairs and Construction Trust - is not being built. Although work began on the site as early as 1975, by this August the first storey has been completed. The school is small, with only 192 places. Its estimated cost is 166 thousand rubles, but only 35 thousand have been released over the past seven years.

It should not, therefore, be thought that the Russian people gains something from the Kremlin's chauvinistic cultural and language policy towards the non-Russian nationalities. In Riazan' Oblast the situation is no better than in the districts of Kushka or Tashkent. It is no accident that all the innovations of the reform that require huge capital investments are projected for the future (the 1990s).

The reports from the various areas of the country and editorials reveal the usual trend for the USSR - to shift the cost of building rural educational establishments from the state to the kolkhozes. A report from the Moldavian SSR described how 'Schools with almost ten thousand places will be built in the republic in the present year at the expense of the kolkhozes.'[25] Reports from the Chechen-Ingush ASSR and other republics described how kindergartens were being built with the help of the resources and labour force of kolkhozes, sovkhozes and other organisations and institutions connected with agriculture. As we have already noted, this means that although the rural population pays the same taxes to the state as all other citizens, it is in effect deprived of state financing for the construction of educational institutions on which a considerable proportion of the revenue from taxes should be spent. As before, the state takes the same from the rural population as from everyone else, but deliberately gives it less in return. Various ministries which have nothing to do with education are also enlisted to build schools and kindergartens, but this does not improve matters.

In order to rule out the impression that these reports on the shortcomings of school construction refer only to particular, chance instances, I shall quote data from the Official Section of Uchitel'skaia gazeta on 17 August 1982. The highest state and trade-union instances of the educational system reported that only 43 per cent of the half-yearly limit on capital investments in school construction had been utilised in the first half of 1982, including only 41 per cent in rural areas:

> In a number of union republics the situation is considerably worse. For example, in the Tadzhik SSR the plan has been fulfilled by 29 and 26 per cent, in the Kirgiz SSR by 30 and 29 per cent, in the Turkmen SSR by 31 and 35 per cent, in the Kazakh SSR by 36 and 32 per cent, in the Moldavian SSR by 38 and 32 per cent ... capital investments for the construction of pre-school institutions were utilised by 37 per cent, and in the Kirgiz SSR by 29 per cent, in the Tadzhik SSR and Latvian SSR by 33 per cent.
>
> In the past year the organisations of the Ministries of Rural Construction, Industrial Construction, Construction and Heavy Construction realised the programme of contracted work on school construction only by 45-53 per cent of the annual capacity.
>
> There were many deficiencies in supplies on the part of the organisations of the Ministries of Energy, Oil Industries, Light Industry, Food Industries, Agriculture, Fruit and Vegetable Farming, the State

> Committee of Agricultural Machinery, the Ministry of Water Supplies and the Ministry of Communications.
>
> Work on pre-school construction projects has been fulfilled by the USSR construction ministries at a level of 38-43 per cent of the annual capacity.
>
> What on earth are the reasons for this?

However strange this may seem, no attempt was made to answer this question. The reports from the various localities, however, do attempt to provide an answer. The reason that not even the far from adequate capital investments allocated to the construction of schools and kindergartens are not utilised is primarily the lack of the necessary building materials. Quotas for these scarce materials are issued last of all to the construction projects of the educational system. There are not enough skilled construction workers, their turnover rate is ominously high even in the large cities, while in the villages and outlying areas there are simply none at all. Transport also presents difficulties. In other words, the difficulties in the construction of schools and kindergartens are merely one example of the economic difficulties constantly suffered by the entire country. There is only one kind of construction project that does not encounter these difficulties - those with military significance.

How, therefore, can the grandiose plans for school reform be realised in such conditions? At the countless political information sessions, talks and debates held in schools, Soviet schoolchildren display their civic consciousness and principles, under pressure from their educators, by abusing the American President and exposing the vices of capitalism. At the same time the situation abroad is either distorted beyond recognition or misinterpreted. Thus, a certain class teacher described the debates he conducted in his class (*Uchitel'skaia gazeta*, 30 November 1982): 'My pupils spoke with pain and sorrow about the children of their age who work sixteen hours a day for a piece of bread.' He was referring to the developed 'capitalist countries' in which the working day does not in fact exceed eight hours (and in some countries less) and child labour is as a rule a thing of the past (except when children want to earn some money in their spare time and during the holidays). Teachers use the newspapers for preparing their information sessions, aware that the pupils have to be concerned only with foreign troubles. Nonetheless, even *Uchitel'skaia gazeta*, which is extremely sparing in its criticism, reported in an article entitled 'On foot through the mist' (4 December 1982) the following scene:

> The pupils, from the fourth grade (usually 35 children) attend the Dubov Secondary School over seven kilometres away. But there is no transport to take them to school. Sometimes the children get a lift to school in passing lorries, sometimes on a tractor, but more often they walk... The pupils who study in the first shift leave home early in the morning, in autumn and winter before sunrise. But those who return after the second shift arrive home in the late evening. We are especially worried about the children now because of the rain and mud. They come home soaked to the skin. And what will happen in winter?

This is not happening in America but in a central region of Russia, in Lipetsk Oblast, and is therefore not discussed with the pupils. Meanwhile, children who walk 14 kilometres a day also have to do their homework and take part in all the school productive and other extra-curricular activities. How long is their working day?

Fifteen teachers from the village of Mal'kovo in the Tiumen District of the RSFSR wrote:

> Our village, Mal'kovo, is located a few kilometres from the central town of the oblast but the impression arises that we live in some backwoods ... sometimes there are no matches, sometimes the bread isn't delivered...
>
> It is cold in the flats, cold in the school. This year the situation reached the point where, when doctors from the Borovsk District Hospital came to give the pupils a medical check-up, they were forced to close the school. The temperature in the classrooms was between four and seven degrees![26]

This is not a sad exception. In Tuvin ASSR, it was reported, of 52 teachers in one school, only two had received their quota of firewood. 'The rest sit without fuel and outside it is already winter.'[27] On 7 December 1982 Uchitel'skaia gazeta published an open letter from its special correspondent, E. Matveeva, to the head of the All-Union Timber Industry Association, 'Dal'lesprom', N.S. Savchenko, in which she described the intolerably difficult living and working conditions of teachers in an area equal in size to the territories of several European states put together:

> Complaints about bad living conditions ... This is the main trouble of the local teachers, but not the only one. In these places, rich in forests, firewood ... has become a problem for them. Huge, gnarled, untreated logs are brought to their yards. When the inhabitants of the settlements see the lorry with this 'firewood', they determine unerringly 'A delivery for the teachers...'
>
> The situation in which teachers are not allowed to purchase goods that are in great demand, with the excuse that 'You don't belong to the timber industry enterprise' seems to me extremely humiliating ... this is a normal occurrence.
>
> Almost every timber industry enterprise has a subsidiary farm. Those who work directly in the enterprises are entitled to purchase foodstuffs there. Teachers are not ...
>
> Now, when the head of the Kharpichan Timber District of the Evoron Timber Industry Enterprise, O.I. Ianson, found out that the teachers wanted to lay in potatoes for the winter, he did not brush them aside. He even promised to help, if they and the school-children would pick the harvest in the subsidiary plot. The harvesting was done quickly and very well. But at this point Oleg Ivanovich refused outright to keep his promise.

In the summer worried letters would begin to appear in Uchitel'skaia gazeta warning that the teachers and schools were going to be without fuel. In winter the desperate cry 'It's cold!' resounded from the pages of the newspaper. Under this heading a selection of teachers', parents' and pupils' letters were published on 19 February 1983. Below are some extracts from them:

> Pupils of Kurush Secondary School No. 1 in the Khasaviurtov District in Dagestan SSR write to the editors: 'In these days the temperature in our school is such that it's better to study outside, where it's warmer. Even the teachers are dressed during lessons in warm shawls and hats - so as not to fall ill!'
>
> Pupils of grade seven 'A' of Secondary School No. 1 in the Kagan District of Bukhara Oblast write the

> same: it has been cold in the school for six years now.
>
> And here is a letter from parents in the village of Maskaika in the Chebarkul'sk District of Cheliabinsk oblast: 'This is the sixth year that it has been terribly cold in the school. There are now more children being treated for colds in the village first-aid post than old people for ailments.'

This is not only the situation in the villages. Here is what 15 teachers of Briansk Secondary School No. 49 reported in a collective letter: 'This year our school is hardly being heated because the boiler-house ... to which we are connected does not have the necessary amount of fuel.'[28] From Tiumen Oblast came the report (on 22 February 1983) that 'In the recently constructed secondary school ... the walls and ceilings leak even when there is light rain. It is very cold in the school. In the second and third terms we work with coats on. In some classrooms the temperature is between four and seven degrees.' They added that the canteen was still not functioning in the school. The report cited a multitude of such items and, in his conclusion, the correspondent wrote:

> Let us recall the lines of some more letters which simply cannot be more alarming: 'The pupils and teachers are falling sick.' 'We cannot study well, we're thinking about getting home as soon as possible.' 'They came to our village from the district [authorities]. So what happened: they glanced into the school, went to the director, ate *pel'meni*, and that was it. We're freezing in the same way as before.'

It is doubtful whether even the unceasing ideological influence on the pupils, which was declared to be one of the most important tasks of the reform, can operate well in these conditions. However, those who determine the fate of Soviet schools are apparently unable to remove this scandalous situation which is described in the press every year, so how will they carry out the planned reform?

To the average Western reader the cries of despair in the press may sound almost like a joke, as in the following example:

> What to write with?
>
> Yes, it's hard to believe, but the pupils in our school don't have anything to write with because neither pens nor refills are obtainable ... This situation does not exist only in our district but ... in the region as well. During the winter holidays we teachers didn't manage to purchase for the children pens or refills.
>
> V. Trifonova
>
> Deputy Director of the secondary school in the village of Krasnoarmeiskoe in Saratov Oblast.[29]

A correspondent described a large rural ten-year school in Uchitel'skaia gazeta, 22 March 1983:

> The school fell into a dilapidated condition long ago. There is no canteen, no refreshment room, no sports hall or playing fields. There are no technical resources. Geography is taught without maps or a globe...
>
> How are we to work? How can literature be taught without texts?! There are none in the village ...

These cries for help seem to come from another era, from the period of war Communism or the Second World War, but readers of the pedagogical press have become accustomed to them.

In recent years the problem of food has become increasingly acute for Soviet citizens, particularly for students who live away from their families and for the extremely overworked teachers who do not have the time to stand in queues. The canteen of the pedagogical college or school is therefore of vital importance. Uchitel'skaia gazeta has written many times about the lack of eating facilities for teachers. On 19 February 1983, for example, the paper's special correspondent, G. Perepelkina, reported the struggle that the director of the Perm Pedagogical College, Iu. V. Korshanov, had been waging for four years to have the canteen repaired after it had been flooded because of a faulty sewer system.

*

The situation briefly portrayed above leads to irreparable moral damage as well. The insurmountable shortages which prevent the vital needs of individuals and society from being satisfied drive even the most well-intentioned people to break the law.

Every era introduces new words into the language,

called into being by new phenomena or the re-interpretation of old phenomena. On 27 August 1983 Uchitel'skaia gazeta twice canonised the neologism 'nesun' ('carrier') which had long been current in Soviet common parlance - once in an article by a teacher, a Veteran of Labour, E. Zolotvitskii, 'Not only by the school's efforts', and for the second time in the editorial comment on this article. 'Nesun' is someone who 'carries' (neset) home from his place of work items of state property that he needs, usually because these items are unobtainable and sometimes because they are too expensive. The elderly teacher, an Exemplary Educator of the RSFSR, noted instances in which small boys took from school laboratories and workshops everything that they needed for their work at home, in which schoolboys and -girls stuffed their pockets and bags with stolen vegetables when they went to the sovkhoz with the school to pick them. It turned out that their parents had asked them to do this, only advising them to be as careful as possible not to be caught. Angry at these practices, the writer grieves:

> Alas, we teachers also sin. The chemistry, physics and literature rooms have to be equipped... This is the teacher's task, but where can he obtain plywood, plexiglass, screws, nails, paint? The school does not have these materials, and you can't buy them in the shops. He has to turn to the children, to their parents, for help. And the parents do 'help': they bring everything that is needed from the works, construction site, factory or laboratory. And now the room gleams but the heart is heavy.
>
> At lessons, Pioneer gatherings, Komsomol meetings, at parents' lecture organisations, we talk about teaching honesty, care for socialist property, and in practice we encourage the 'carriers'.

Thus ends the article by a thinking, educated, experienced man. He makes no attempt to generalise his experience, to ask himself and the reader why it is that in a mighty industrial power and in our electronic age neither the schools nor the shops have plywood, glass, screws, nails or paint, all of which abounded in the country even before the First World War. In any event, none of the most fiercely critical essays by any of the Russian realist writers at that time reported a shortage of these articles. The newspaper's comment at first almost coincides with that of the teacher:

> The parents' desire to make their home beautiful, the teacher's desire to put his room together beautifully are understandable. But at times they cannot buy elementary things in a shop - and the school cannot obtain them from the depot: laths, Whatman paper, wooden panelling, paint. And then all this is carried out through the gates of the enterprise.

This, so it would seem, should have been followed by the question why these 'most elementary things' are unobtainable, but the author is scared of this natural question and sidesteps it.

With the help of these 'carrier' parents it is possible to prepare display boards or even, if the parent is highly placed, equip a special subject room or laboratory, but these illegal means cannot be used to construct the workshops, educational-production complexes and secondary vocational-technical schools needed for implementing the reform. Where is the guarantee that the state, which does not satisfy the population's vital needs today, will allocate a sufficient quantity of funds, materials and manpower for this purpose? If the basic essentials do not exist today, where will the funds be found within the next decade for such a grandiose restructuring of the educational system? The newspaper does not explain why for 70 years there has been a shortage of the most essential and simple things because the only explanation is the irrationality of a system which cannot satisfy society's needs.

N. Morozova, a teacher in Moscow School No. 228, wrote how grateful she was to the party and government for the confidence in teachers expressed in the 'Basic trends' of the school reform (Uchitel'skaia gazeta, 31 March 1984) and, since the authors of the reform had not deemed it necessary to speak of the sins and shortcomings of the teachers, called upon them to repent of their wrongdoings on their own initiative. She did not notice, however, in what light her criticism of her colleagues portrayed the reality of developed socialism:

> ... Haven't you had the occasion to observe somebody's mother knocking at the classroom door with a bag full of foodstuffs? And the teacher coming out into the corridor right in the middle of the lesson and gratefully accepting this bag of 'shortages'? Or pieces of knitted garments lying on the teacher's desk and the teacher

> telling her colleagues: 'This is what the parents brought. Advise me which one to take.' Or the director admitting a girl from another district into the ninth grade, contrary to the rules (her mother's in charge of a shop).

Morozova did not make allowances for the fact that the terribly overworked schoolteachers and directors (whose work-load is increased even more by the reform) have no time to queue not only for 'shortages' but also for the most basic essentials. She was also not alarmed by the fact that, as she put it 'Everyone does it!', since 'That's the wisdom of Philistines. But teachers should not be "not worse than the others" but absolutely better, not "like everyone" but above everyone. We mustn't join the Philistines' roundabout: "I'll scratch your back if you'll scratch mine".' Ordinary mortals are another matter:

> There is an enormous difference of principle between the misdemeanour of a parent and of a teacher. When a parent engages in money-grubbing he does not even hide his misdemeanours behind fine-sounding phrases. On the contrary, he supports them with the philosophy of 'knowing how to live.'
>
> But how is the schoolchild to form a relationship with a money-grubbing teacher? For in this case theory and practice are quite at variance: in this case the deeds are bad but the words are good. Sometimes movingly right and good. But if you listen closely, you'll detect cynicism.

However, let us ask the writer, does not the teacher's cynicism, including her own, lie in the fact that whether the teacher grabs the bag of 'shortages' or whether he is irreproachably incorruptible, he describes Soviet life as being different from what his pupils constantly observe around them?

Even the perceptive writer Chingiz Aitmatov published an article in Literaturnaia gazeta, in 1983, in which he linked the declining authority of the teacher to the 'mercenary virus' which had spread among some teachers. Surely Aitmatov is not unaware of the general problems affecting the entire state which determine the teachers' and schools' dependence on the parents' services? Or is this another case of cynicism?

*

The reform envisages that in the years to come there will be a radical change in the material and technical resources of schools, that training brigades and workshops will be set up in base enterprises, including in the agricultural sector and that educational production complexes will be constructed, each one serving several schools. But how can these changes be introduced in the rural schools which are the most numerous today - the undersized schools. How can their work and life be rationalised?

These schools are discussed in the Soviet teachers' press mostly with reference to the staffing difficulties which they are facing, but they also have other problems which have remained unresolved for decades. For example, a teacher in an undersized primary school has to teach in the same classroom pupils of two and sometimes three or even all four grades at the same time, combining various kinds of lessons, which is difficult both for the teacher and for the children. In the undersized eight-year schools teachers have to teach several subjects and even so do not always have enough hours of teaching for a full-time teaching post. The ten-year schools, which the graduates of undersized schools attend, complain that their teachers do not have the time to fill in the gaps in the pupils' knowledge in the last two years of schooling. Even when they graduate from the central secondary schools which serve children from several villages, they are known to be of a lower standard than other school-leavers.

The situation has been deteriorating instead of improving since the 1940s. There are numerous such undersized schools, and their number is increasing because of the flight of young people from the kolkhozes and sovkhozes. On 2 June 1983 Uchitel'skaia gazeta reported that the average size of primary rural schools in Pskov Oblast was nine pupils, of eight-year schools 46 pupils, and that there were even undersized secondary schools. Some schools had only three pupils, and in others the four pupils constituted three different grades. Of the 291 rural schools in Kostroma Oblast 280 were undersized. Graduates of the Kostroma Pedagogical Institute who had done their teaching practice in such schools stated: 'We'd like either never to go back to the village or to change everything there.'[30] 'But what can be changed if every year the villages become smaller and nothing depends on the teachers?' ask the young people. Out of the 21 graduates only five expressed the very problematic intention of staying in the village beyond the three years stipulated by law.

The innumerable official publications on the school reform, as well as its basic text, avoid the painful problem of undersized schools. Its authors apparently cannot see a practicable solution to it. In the Khrushchev era, when the collapse of rural schools had not gone so far, boarding schools were seen as the solution, but this project was cancelled before it had barely begun because of its high cost. Meanwhile, another solution does exist, and one that has long existed in developed countries, where the rural population is very small because of the high productivity of its labour. This is to set up normal, large central schools to which children are brought from the whole micro-district, and from where they are taken back home after school. This would also solve the problem of the labour and vocational training of these pupils. The functioning of such schools, however, depends on a good road network and capacious, rapid transport, which is a problem not for the schools but for the entire state, and which cannot be solved by the school reform. In the USSR, roads that have purely local importance, that are not strategic or arterial, are regarded as being of secondary importance by the state, even though they are vitally necessary to the population, and frequently remain unsurfaced, i.e. impassable to motor vehicles for much of the year. Moreover, motor transport is inadequate in the periphery, for which the bad roads and lack of spare-parts depots are largely to blame. Transporting children to school remains an insoluble problem for the educational authorities.

A particularly difficult situation arises when the undersized boarding schools and schools are, in addition, a long distance not only from the centre of the country but also from the centre of their own republic or krai and located in sparsely populated areas without roads. On 10 June 1983 Izvestiia published a truly frightening article in its 'Schools' section by its special correspondent L. Kapeliushnyi, 'The fifth angle', about the Olenegorsk boarding school in the Iakutsk ASSR. Fifty girls and boys between the ages of seven and 17, pupils in grades one to ten, live in the boarding facilities. According to the documents, a total of a hundred and sixty pupils attend the settlement's school, but in reality there are only a hundred and twenty. Behind the restrained text of the article a horrifying picture is revealed which applies both to the boarding facilities and school and to the entire north of the

Iakutsk republic.

Dirt, neglect, cold and hunger reign in the boarding quarters. Pupils of all ages are chronically drunk, there is no crockery, baths, elementary conveniences. Over the ten years of its existence it has had either ten or 15 directors (they had lost count). Half of the building is used to accommodate the administrative and teaching staff. The room called the reading room is padlocked. The television is broken. 'The doors are covered with knife cuts, the walls are peeling, the furniture is mutilated.' There is no sick ward, and there are many pupils who fall sick. The correspondent continues: 'Adolescents ... escape through the windows when the educators appear, burn bedclothes, drink wine, fight, are impertinent ...' There is a permanent staff of ten for the 50 children using the boarding facilities, who do not work, but merely draw fat, 'northern' salaries. The cook often takes several days off without permission and then the children remain hungry. The residents of the settlement are profoundly indifferent to what is happening beneath their noses. The situation in the school attended by the boarding children is not much better. A commission of the district Department of Education inspected it at the end of the year. Only 34 per cent of the pupils were given a positive assessment and only seven per cent of the school-leavers coped with the physics and mathematics tests, even though the school issues school-leaving certificates to all its tenth-graders every year and all the pupils progress from grade to grade with fictitious pass marks. They are given the mark of 'two' 'conditionally', which is amended to 'three' at the end of the year. None of the graduates of the school's grades eight to ten has enough knowledge to be admitted to an institute or technicum. In most subjects the curriculum is not completed by the end of the year. Nonetheless, as they have grown unaccustomed to the life and work of their reindeer-breeding parents, almost none of the school-leavers return to their native nomad camps to take over from their parents. Indeed, they grow completely unaccustomed to their homes in general. 'They do not want to go and work in the tundra', writes the correspondent, 'the youngsters look for work in the offices and institutions of the settlement.'[31]

However, it hardly makes sense to organise schools in the nomad encampments, of which there are very few in the area: there are hardly any young people in the reindeer-breeding kolkhozes and sovkhozes and the birthrate is very low. The settlement schools take in children from these remote places, with the result that their graduates never return to the occupation of their fathers. At the same time, however, the education which they receive is very poor, and they turn into badly educated semi-ignoramuses, incapable of continuing their studies to become specialists in the fields needed in Iakutia. Thus the occupational and demographic structure of the peoples of the north is being destroyed irreparably. How can the schools cope with this situation, and how can the school reform be implemented in such regions of the USSR?

What astounded the correspondent most of all was that the administrators and teachers did not consider the situation in the boarding quarters or school to be extraordinary or disastrous. They replied to his questions cheerfully and insisted that children from undersized, tundra primary schools should in general be sent straight to a PTU and not to eight-year or ten-year schools, as they are too poorly prepared to study in such schools. 'As for the boozing', the deputy director for extra-curricular work noted optimistically, 'in the north everyone drinks and it is doubtful whether anything can be changed'.[32] The workers in the Olenegorsk boarding quarters and school did not, therefore, consider the picture of their pupils' utter degradation which had so shocked the correspondent to be in the least extraordinary, but typical of and natural for the Soviet north. Moreover, these workers had sunk so low that the conditions and results of their work did not seem to them at all offensive.

Even the meagre evidence in the press shows that the difference between the central and outlying schools remains scandalous, as in all periods of the Soviet state's existence. Nothing is being done to improve it; official documents ignore it.

There is no section in the text of the 'Basic trends' of the reform or the printed materials accompanying it that is specially devoted to undersized and remote schools, although teachers and correspondents write about their problems year after year. Several sections of the reform propose (in general terms) to pay more attention to rural schools, but do not specify what concrete form this will take.

*

Among the numerous problems with which Soviet schools are deluged, I should like to touch upon the question that is extremely important for schools everywhere in the world and that has not been solved satisfactorily anywhere: the question of the punishment and impunity of pupils. The contemporary Soviet pedagogical press and one document that has made its way outside the USSR show that this problem is extremely acute in Soviet schools. The text of the 'Basic trends' and other official publications concerning the reform not only do not solve this problem but do not even mention it. Teachers, however, were greatly hoping that the reformers would pay attention to this problem, as they are gravely disturbed by the deteriorating discipline in the schools. The problem has long since passed beyond the boundaries of the schools: difficult adolescents become law-breakers. As Minister of Education, M. Prokof'ev, wrote in a leading article, 'Decisions of the Party are the main guideline' (Narodnoe obrazovanie, no. 9, 1983): 'In the country as a whole the number of offences among schoolchildren is not declining. Most of them are connected with theft of state or private property.'

Judging from other materials in newspapers and journals and from my own experience, the diplomatic 'is not declining' means in practice that the number of offences committed by schoolchildren and young people who have recently left school is on the increase. Many teachers consider that the bad conduct of pupils in and outside school is a result of their virtual impunity. V. Kalagin, a teacher from Moscow Oblast, wrote in an article entitled 'Impunity is sham humanism':

> The rules of schools of general education and other normative documents provide for various measures of punishment: reproof, reprimand, cautioning, dismissal from class, discussion at the assembly of the section, detachment, council of the [pupils'] regiment, a dressing-down, unsatisfactory mark for conduct, explusion from the Pioneer and Komsomol organisations, expulsion from school.[33]

In his opinion, however, the trouble is that all these measures have no effect on hooligans, while more severe measures (he does not say what) are not employed. The teacher feels helpless in relation to a difficult pupil and appeals to his parents. Some teachers and administrators even demand that special sanctions be used against parents who bring up their children badly. The director of a school in

Kiev Oblast, V.I. Kovtun, wrote in Uchitel'skaia gazeta, 15 November 1983:

> The question should be raised, when summing up socialist competition, when awarding bonuses and other forms of moral and material incentive to workers in production, of being sure to take into consideration the school's opinion of how the parents raise their children.

When the draft law on work collectives was being discussed in the press, school workers demanded in their letters that even the allocation of living accommodation should be decided by enterprises and institutions on the basis of whether the school was satisfied with the way in which children were being brought up in a particular family.

One of the forms of communication between teachers and parents is the entries in the pupils' diaries (daily report books). Parents have to be constantly acquainted with what is written in their children's diaries in order to know what is happening to them at school. There is not, however, enough room in the diary for the teachers to write detailed entries. G. Bikson, a Riga teacher, wrote about this problem in Uchitel'skaia gazeta, 24 November 1983: 'What in fact is left for the teacher on its pages? A column for writing down marks, a place for signing and ... the margins. The pupils have long called them "strap" margins.' This expression sums up the whole tragedy. The teachers, feeling powerless to influence a pupil and usually not having enough time to give him serious individual attention, complain about him to his parents. The latter frequently resort to what the schools coyly term 'non-pedagogical measures of influence' - i.e. hitting the child. Hence the term used to describe the margins in the diaries. In many cases the teachers are aware or guess that the children are hit at home, and in this way resort to corporal punishment indirectly, through someone else, feeling that they are incapable of influencing them in any other way.

An article in Narodnoe obrazovanie, no. 8 (1983), 'Together with doctors', by a psychologist and senior lecturer at the Komsomol-on-Amur Pedagogical Institute, S. Shuman, described children with acquired mental abnormalities which were cured thanks to the intervention of doctors and psychologists. In five out of six cases the children were hit and intimidated at home, in one case with the full knowledge of the teacher.

But what is the solution? Many teachers consider that the real post of class teacher should be created - educators who would be entirely or almost entirely free of teaching responsibilities and would have special training and the time to give thought and attention to the conduct and moral disposition of the pupils, to study their families and help parents to raise their children without ever resorting to hitting. There was something similar in pre-Revolutionary schools: class mistresses and masters. However, this solution seems utopian for the time being, as it requires a considerable increase in expenditure on education. The clash between impunity at school and terror at home (or its combination with impunity at home as well) remains an insoluble and pernicious contradiction that is exacerbated by the day. Today the problem is solved by sending adolescents who have become criminals and who can no longer be educated at school or home to special closed school colonies or prison schools. There are grounds to assume that the situation in these schools is far from satisfactory from the pedagogical point of view, and in a number of cases disastrous. I shall give two examples.

The teacher Liudmila Magon died in the USSR in 1974 of a brain haemorrhage at the age of 43. She had been virtually exiled to work in a prison school for difficult children near Iaroslavl' for her support of Solzhenitsyn. The dissident writers Raisa Orlova and Lev Kopelev, who left the USSR, published letters which they had received from her through illegal channels in the Paris newspaper <u>Russkaia mysl'</u> ('Russian thought'), nos. 3480, 3481 and 3482 (September 1983), which constitute the unique story of the experience of a humane, thoughtful teacher in this kind of closed reformatory. The horror which she experienced, the unequal, impossible struggle for humaneness which she waged there, undoubtedly contributed to her premature death.

On 7 June 1984 <u>Uchitel'skaia gazeta</u> published an account of a <u>good</u> colony where, according to the author, N. Anisin, the adults also abuse their position. Nonetheless, the article is entitled 'To believe the reformed?', with a fat question mark, but the question that arises is whether the reformed are really reformed. The good manners of the young residents and their outwardly perfectly normal conduct struck the correspondent, but then he was shown letters from former pupils (which had evidently not been delivered to their destination) and was taken aback:

> The first letter: 'Hello, my pals Prokop, Palekha, Kiriukha, Ogloblia and Slon! I've decided to write to you about myself. Everything's fine with me. I'm drinking a lot, I've already been in the wash [sobering-up station - N.A.], but Mum arranged everything ...'
>
> The second letter: 'Zakhar, brother, don't be cross with me for not having written for a long time. Me and Chernyi went out and just didn't crawl out of the pubs for two weeks. Dear brother, come as quick as you can, there are lots of girls here, I'll get you any one you fancy ...'
>
> The third letter: 'Now on every day off we go into the country. A portable record player, two guitars and off into the woods - romance! It was Ritka's birthday on the 25th. Well, of course, we took a case of wine for twelve people ...'
>
> ... I made an enquiry about the authors of the letters. All three had been activists in the colony and had received due thanks; they had been released early on probation - the court had declared them to be reformed. But it can be assumed that all three are now once again leading a way of life conducive to crime. The whole point is that they returned to the same environment from which they had come to the colony.

There is no doubt that juvenile delinquents are created by their environment and that the destruction of their personalities frequently begins in the family because of the parents' moral degradation and alcoholism. But how can another environment be provided for them? When the young people come back from the colony nothing has changed - not the family, not the street, not the school, not the PTU - while in the colony itself the measures which are used to influence the young inmates are mostly of a purely superficial nature. This is a 'carrot and stick' policy without any serious intervention in the inner world of the children who have been crippled by their environment and life. Quick-witted hypocrites adapt themselves to it easily and profit directly from their dissembling. Anisin writes:

> When the juvenile deliquents arrive in the colony they immediately become normal children because forbidden

> behaviour is ruled out here. Moreover, they become very good, normal children because the colony's environment does not allow for laziness or disobedience.
>
> If you do not work during lessons, you are not allowed to see your relatives. If you do not overfulfil the quota in the factory workshop, you are deprived of the two-ruble coupon for sweets and gingerbread. If you deliberately make a defective product, get into a fight, fail to carry out an educator's order, you end up in the disciplinary solitary confinement cell ...
>
> ... Those who have no offences or reprimands can be released early on probation after serving a third of the sentence. This is why the children try from the very first day to show their best side ... But nonetheless, recurrence of crimes is not a rarity among those who have been in a colony.

It 'is not a rarity' because, outside the colony, there is not found the combination of punishment and incentive with many actual restrictions which exists inside the colony, while the colony apparently has no influence on the children's convictions, thoughts, feelings, principles and views. In effect, therefore, the juvenile delinquents remain inwardly unreformed. There is no profound psychological influence, and neither the author of the article nor of the editorial commentary on it suggests how such influence could be exerted. But surely this is the crux of the matter? The reform, however, is not in the least concerned with the closed reformatory-labour school colonies, as though they did not exist or as though the situation in them were perfectly satisfactory.

Turning to the PTU, we can find that the educational work in many of these institutions also leaves much to be desired. G. Ryskin, a former PTU teacher in what was considered to be one of the best PTUs in Leningrad, left the USSR and had the opportunity to speak out. Here are some of his accounts and reflections on life in the PTU which were published in the New York Novoe Russkoe slovo, 31 March 1984:

> Over the past decade the system of vocational-technical schools has been widely developed in the USSR. In Leningrad and the oblast alone there are over two hundred of them. Everybody is talking about the

> Leningrad experience today. The creation of the PTU system has led to the even greater de-intellectualisation of young people. The standard of 'universal secondary education', which in any case is extremely mediocre, has declined sharply. The causes? Lack of co-ordination of curricula, overloading of PTU pupils (along with subjects of the ordinary secondary school they study the special disciplines), the reduction of the humanities subjects to the level of secondary subjects, the lack of parental control, the barrack-like atmosphere of the hostels.
>
> At conferences of workers in the system of vocational-technical education the same refrain is heard: 'Dear comrades, we are not, after all, preparing academics.'
>
> A large proportion of young people today are being put through a system of brain-washing.
>
> I worked for two years in the Leningrad PTU No. 49. There were 900 adolescents, torn from their families, thrown into the concrete barracks of a hostel, delivered up to the command of mostly ignorant masters [teachers of technical subjects]. The 'pedagogy of the fist' flourishes. Almost all the masters use corporal punishment. But how can they control the group otherwise? A recalcitrant pupil is shut in a special room and the boy is thrown from wall to wall, stunned by iron fists.
>
> A day never passes without new crimes being announced at the parade: either someone has broken the tram cash-box or cut the head of an innocent passer-by with a bicycle chain. And even this happened: a master himself went thieving with his own pupils.
>
> There are two hundred PTU in Leningrad. And No. 49 has many times been called one of the best.

It is not surprising that Ryskin compares his former PTU to the provincial seminary (elementary church school) described over a hundred years ago by the Russian humanist writer Nikolai Pomialovskii. The comparison, moreover, is far from flattering to the PTU. It is impossible to imagine that even the most evil, cruel and ignorant teacher in a seminary of those times would accompany his pupils on a robbery.

*

The fact that all these problems were presented so

graphically in the pages of the press on the threshold of the reform or during the discussions of it shows that the teachers were naively expecting all the most pressing problems of their work and life to be solved by the forthcoming innovations. These expectations were displayed especially clearly in articles and letters devoted to the everyday professional routine of teaching and the prestige and appeal of the teaching profession. Official statements on these subjects are also very instructive, as are their interpretation in the forthcoming reform. And so, let us now consider the situation of Soviet teachers on the eve of the reform.

The August 1982 issue of Narodnoe obrazovanie was devoted to discussion of the 19th Congress of the VLKSM (All-Union Leninist Communist Youth League), which had taken place not long before. The discussions of the congress were closely linked to the decisions of the May 1982 Plenum of the CC CPSU, i.e. to the Food-Production Programme, which at that time was at the centre of all the party's and government's propaganda efforts. After this main urgent business - which could be summed up in the words 'to feed the country!' - other tasks, derived from the Food-Production Programme, were outlined at the congress: to provide rural schools with skilled staff and to 'fasten' school leavers to agriculture and also to force schools to work effectively in the national economy, especially in the agricultural sector.

The actual expression 'to fasten' (zakrepit') rural school-leavers to the kolkhozes and sovkhozes - so close to the menacing 'zakrepostit'' ('to make a serf') - constantly crops up in the reports of the congress. Behind these appeals lies a depressing picture of the lack of teachers in rural schools and, ever more frequently, also in urban schools, even in the centre of the country, and the lack of both specialists and ordinary workers in the kolkhozes. The talk about 'fastening' school-leavers to the villages turns into talk about 'fastening' teachers to rural schools and sometimes simply to schools, i.e. to urban ones as well.

A hint creeps into the report of the First Secretary of the VLKSM CC, E.N. Pastukhov, that almost military methods are being used to recruit young people into teaching. He says:

> At the urging of the 18th Congress of the VLKSM, over thirty thousand young people from among young

> workers, demobilised soldiers and school-leavers were assigned by the Komsomol to institutions of pedagogical education. Volunteers - the best young teachers - were sent to make up pedagogical landing-forces in remote rural schools of the country![34]

In the seventh decade of the existence of Soviet power, work in schools repels young people to such an extent that mobilisation campaigns are needed to send them to pedagogical institutions, while 'pedagogical landing-forces' have to be sent to remote rural schools. But do these 'landing-forces' work for long in the schools? Even graduates from pedagogical institutions frequently fail to turn up at the jobs to which they have been assigned or flee the schools before they have worked the stipulated three years. 'Over the past three years', writes the RSFSR Education Minister, G. Beselov, in Narodnoe obrazovanie, no. 12 (1982), '2,135 specialists with higher and secondary education were sent to schools in Briansk Oblast, while in the same perid 3,511 teachers left the schools of the oblast.' Which means that even those who have been working for a long time leave.

The teaching community and administration are concerned with a problem which was not specifically discussed either in the draft of the reform or in its final text: the flight of young teachers from the schools. Decisive and radical measures are needed because schoolchildren in vast areas of the country are suffering from discrimination. An article in Uchitel'skaia gazeta, 27 March 1984, 'Refrain from a false step', reported:

> The Primorskii Krai Department of Education has also become accustomed to letters, telegrammes, telephone calls, all demanding one thing: 'Send a teacher!' Parents are anxious: in a number of schools important subjects are not taught. The teachers are concerned: they have to carry an excessive teaching load. Today the krai lacks three and a half thousand qualified specialist teachers. However, it is worth mentioning another disturbing figure: according to the most modest estimates, over eight thousand qualified teachers are no longer working in schools, have left for various reasons.

But what is the position of those disciplined graduates who did turn up at the jobs to which they were assigned and are working in them?

> In Primorskii Krai six hundred teachers live in hostels, two hundred in private flats, two thousand are in need of improved living conditions. What is a place in a workers' hostel? It means three or four people living in a room for whom the evening hours after work are primarily for rest. But for the teacher this is a time of intensive work: he has to check exercise books, analyse the day that has passed, prepare for the next day. But he does not have even the tiniest corner of a table to himself. Our graduate, L. Koll', began her work in Vladivostok by checking exercise books in the boiler-room of a workers' hostel. There was simply no other place. Graduate Iu. Vol'nykh went round a dozen settlement schools in Primor'e. The only teacher of the primary grades who was a man. A man with initiative, one of those who are a find for a school ... The young specialist had only one condition - accommodation to which he could bring his aged mother. And not a single school could accept him.

In an article, 'An alienating tradition' (Uchitel'skaia gazeta, 22 March 1983) correspondent, G. Frolova, writes about the life of young teachers who have fled villages in Novosibirsk Oblast:

> 'We do voluntary Sunday work in teachers' collectives so that together they can make a stock of firewood', explains the head of the district Department of Education, 'and the village council pays the teachers money for chopping the firewood ...'
>
> You start to think, there are 15 teachers in the collective, of these one is a man ... Who is it then who makes the stock of firewood during these voluntary work sessions?
>
> A graduate who was sent to Kochnev Secondary School lived until mid-winter in the village 'hotel' where uninvited guests would constantly open the door without knocking at any time of the day or night. But she had been promised a comfortable flat which the village council had suddenly given to someone who was 'more needed' ...
>
> In the village of Krasnoiarka the sovkhoz director, Chvalinskii, permitted a limited quota of potatoes to be

> sold to young teachers in the autumn - by February it had finished - and he refused to sell them cabbages, carrots, beets ...
>
> The Workers' Committee of the sovkhoz denied the teachers the right to purchase goods and food imported [from outside the sovkhoz] 'You don't belong to us.'
>
> A teacher, Bryzgalova, in the Kupin Secondary School was turned out of her room in the hostel close to the new year ...
>
> Two university graduates were 'accommodated' in one bed in the home of an alcoholic landlady ...

N. Boev, director of the Luchegorsk Internal-External Secondary School (attended by daytime pupils but also offering external courses) in the Pozharskii District of Primorskii Krai, described the situation as follows:

> The schools are absolutely frantic through the shortage of teachers. In some periods many subjects are simply not taught at all.
>
> ... Yet, with this 'deficit' of teachers, just look how so many teachers of the most varied subjects are employed in various enterprises in only one district centre - Luchegorsk - that they could staff a secondary school with 1,500 pupils.
>
> The personnel department of the Luchegorsk Coal Section is headed by biology teacher, V.V. Gutsevich. Mathematics teacher, T.D. Prokopenkova, is among the exemplary production workers of the Primorskii GRES [State-District Electric Power-Station]. Primary grades teacher, L.N. Ivanishcheva, feels comfortable in her job as commodity researcher of the Pozharsk District Trade Administration. Chemistry teacher, N.D. Kuznetsova, the district's ichthyologist, is counting silver Siberian salmon in the River Bikin. Teachers who have left their posts can also be found in the roles of laboratory assistants in the Pozharsk Oil Mill, and petrol pump attendants in the Luchegorsk Timber Industry Enterprise.
>
> At the end of the first six months, without even having given his pupils their total marks, A.S. Pustyntsev changed his job as physical education teacher at Luchegorsk Secondary School No. 2 for the post of deputy head of the medical sobering-up

centre.[35]

The author condemns these teachers who have deserted their professional duty even though this situation exists throughout the country and, as his report shows, these people are not work-shy but are active in various sectors of the economy in the same district - even in the sobering-up centre. It would seem that the time has come to seek the reason for this spurning of teaching elsewhere than merely in the moral character of these individuals. The terrible work-load in and outside school, the low salary, difficult living conditions and, most important, the necessity to serve as the constant mouthpiece for the official lies, the outright ideologisation of the teaching and educational processes - these are the reasons for the unpopularity of the profession which are there for all to see and allusions to which sometimes even slip through into the press. However, there are also ominous signs in the press that repressive measures will soon begin to be used to fight this rapid turnover in teachers, as in the 1940s. Thus, for example, a 'group of Ukrainian miners' proposed on the pages of Pravda that it be forbidden to change one's job at all, while a 'group of Siberians' insisted that people who left their jobs should be arrested and tried after two weeks if during that time they had not found another job.

It does not occur to the powers-that-be that dictate such letters to anonymous 'workers' that repressive measures will only exacerbate the situation. Teachers are frequently quite simply physically incapable of handling their work-load. Besides teaching proper, they are responsible for political self-education, the study of all the party and government directive documents, the political and pedagogical education of parents and the general population, they have to participate actively in all political campaigns, including elections, in productive work outside school with their pupils, along with countless other obligations. The constant tests and written reports also take up their time. In January 1983 a teacher of Secondary School No. 72 in Krasnoiarsk spoke to a session of the RSFSR Supreme Soviet:

> Where on earth can the time be found to meet all the demands made on the modern teacher? This question is constantly on the pages of our press. The Ministries of Education have adopted decisions to regulate the

> teachers' working time many times. And even so teachers often do work that does not belong to them, even to the extent of distributing theatre tickets.[36]

Uchitel'skaia gazeta, which quoted this speech, added that 'Our editorial post, unfortunately, constantly corroborates the deputy's critical remarks.' The same newspaper supplied the information that the termly reports which the district Departments of Education demand from the class teacher in some cases run to around 120 questions, and once again emphasises that this is not the exception but typical. A teacher's time belongs to everybody but himself and his family. A teacher, V.V. Il'ina of Lipetsk Oblast, wrote in protest that:

> One Sunday we had a subbotnik. And afterwards the school director decided to conduct a Sunday campaign in the village. I and my husband are teachers. We have two pre-school children. We could not both take part in this activity. My husband went on the campaign. The following day the school director gave me a severe reprimand.[37]

The newspaper was indignant that one of the spouses was not released from the 'Sunday campaign', but the very fact that all the school's teachers had been deprived of their legal day off, which is needed not so much for rest as for work at home and preparing the week's lessons, did not disturb the author of the editorial comment in the least.

The insistence by the party and government that teachers and schoolchildren take a serious part in implementing the Food-Production Programme allows kolkhoz and sovkhoz leaders to treat them as if they were their own workers, and in an even more cavalier fashion. On 24 March 1983 Uchitel'skaia gazeta published an article by its correspondent in Kirov Oblast, 'They listened and decided', which described the work-load of a village teacher Liudmila Ivanovna Vazhenina. In addition to all her other duties, the teacher has been obliged to take her turn in being on duty in the kolkhoz stock-raising farm. Vazhenina reports:

> What does this duty consist of? Twice a month for twenty-four hours I have to be on the farm, tie up the cows if they break loose from the chain, clear out the

> manure and, if calving-time is approaching - receive the calf. But if I am not on duty and an accident happens, I shall have to compensate the kolkhoz for the damage.

There are three eight-hour working days in twenty-four hours. Thus the teacher was forced to work on the farm a full working week every month. The school director did not manage to rescue the teacher, and in her attempts to defend herself against the kolkhoz leaders' arbitrary decree Vazhenina went as far as the district procurator. On hearing her complaint, the guardian of the law shrugged his shoulders and said that he had 'never come across anything like it' in his experience, but that if anything happened 'you'll most likely have to compensate them'. Uchitel'skaia gazeta had to send a correspondent to raise the matter at all-union levels before the teacher could be rescued from some of these extraneous obligations. Could, however, such a situation ever arise unless physical labour, with economic results, were officially declared to be a matter for pupils and teachers? Presumably not, but the reform does not alter this state of affairs.

The paper's correspondent, L. Lazutina, published an article on 14 April 1983 entitled 'Individual cases?' which, along with other reports on the same subject, testified that the cases described were far from individual. What, then, do teachers do in their time outside lessons? 'Teachers ... are used for the population census and gathering information; they have to collect money from their pupils for various cultural outings and activities, to collect subscriptions for every possible kind of voluntary society ...' In one of the districts of Kirgizia the district leadership 'devised an urgent plan according to which teachers and senior pupils in every school would be charged with the task of producing almost a million adobe bricks!' At the same time 'The teacher is supposed to work as an errand boy or tally clerk in his free time from work. He is charged with vast reams of questionnaires. The range of those questioned: from pre-school children to pensioners.' Moreover, in a number of places:

> It is required of every teacher to patrol the streets from seven to eleven in the evening. The teachers are mainly women, many of whom are elderly. How are they to cope with the hooligans, rowdies, drunks? But

> the reply is: everybody should be a patriot of his home town!
>
> Under the same slogan teachers and pupils are mobilised to clean the streets.

This happens everywhere, but in Frunze teachers were entrusted with a particularly responsible task. They had to fill out a lengthy questionnaire on all the members of every family in their micro-district and, in addition, 'to find out from the neighbours as delicately as possible how the comrade behaves on the staircase [of the apartment block]. Is he inclined to infringements of the law? Or does he abuse alcoholic beverages?' The teachers had, therefore, to induce the city's residents 'delicately' to inform on their neighbours and then deliver these denunciations to the district executive committees which had sent them on this special mission. This fact in itself arouses not the slightest indignation in the newspaper's correspondent. In this case, too, she is only disturbed by the excessive load of out-of-school work with which the teachers are burdened.

All directives concerning education and the majority of printed material in this field emphasise that every teacher is obliged, regardless of the subject in which he specialises, to form the pupils' Marxist-Leninist ideology. Senior lecturer V. Medved'ev, head of the Ul'ianovsk problem laboratory of the Scientific Research Institute on Problems of Upbringing in the USSR Academy of Pedagogical Sciences, published a short but succinct article, 'The ideological becoming of schoolchildren' (Uchitel'skaia gazeta, 20 November 1982) in which he described the methods used in the ideological education of schoolchildren and the ideological control over them carried out in experimental classes. The article devoted much attention to effective methods of elucidating the real views of the pupils, even of those who seemed perfectly reliable and 'willingly carry out social assignments' since, the author explained, outward loyalty sometimes concealed alien views, and it was most important that even an outwardly sound pupil should not have hidden ideological vices. But this was not all. Teachers were not only to investigate their pupils' ideology but record the results of this investigation throughout all the years of schooling. Medved'ev writes: 'The teacher later uses his conclusions in the pupil's individual character reference and also when giving the socio-political testimonials to senior pupils which make up part of the

Lenin assignment.' It should be borne in mind that the institutions of higher education and technicums do not accept the documents of school-leavers who are seeking admission without the school's character reference. Ideological failings prevent a senior pupil from passing the 'Lenin assignment', which means that he will not be given the complete school-leaving certificate needed to enter an institution of higher education or technicum. The better, profounder and more moral the teacher, the less such work agrees with him since it turns his intimate, educational relations with the pupil into a source of material for the pupil's file which determines the latter's fate to a considerable degree.

On 12 November 1983 Uchitel'skaia gazeta published a despairing letter from a young teacher, Liudmila Shutkina, who had just started work. She described her monstrous work-load, in addition to the subjects which she taught, which even with the best will in the world would be impossible to carry out conscientiously, and she expressed the fear that she would soon have to leave her school. Her letter provoked a deluge of responses, selections of which were published in Uchitel'skaia gazeta from 26 November to 10 December 1983. Only a few of these tried to persuade her that she simply had to learn to manage her time rationally, which was either thoughtlessness or hypocrisy on the part of the authors of these letters, as the tasks with which teachers are loaded simply do not fit into the 24 hours at their disposal, whatever system is used. This is precisely what most of the teachers who replied to Liudmila's letter wrote. Here are extracts from a letter from a teacher, Dobrokhotova, from Belgorod Oblast:

> The author of the letter still somehow has time to 'turn round' as, judging from her letter, she isn't yet married. But what are we to do who have children? I have three. There is almost no time to give them my attention. It's even a big problem to take a child to the doctor, you can't get a medical certificate as there's no one to replace you at work. And the conflicts and arguments with my husband are only because of my work.
>
> As a matter of fact we don't have any days off. Many people say that we have a lot of holidays. Let's count. People have two days off plus [public] holidays. According to the most approximate estimate eighty odd days can be added to their holidays. However, we

> teachers are often once again with our pupils during the school and public holidays. My husband says: 'Leave the school, find another job.'
>
> For myself, I've decided the following: if the new reform does not lighten the teacher's work (in the sense of free time), I'll have to leave the school for another job, even one I don't like, just to have more time for my family.

The ideologically irreproachable and optimistic magazine Oktiabr' ('October') published a short story about schools by Veniamin Kaverin entitled 'The enigma', which was imbued with sincere alarm and did not inspire any high hopes.[38] The story is related in the first person by a geography and astronomy teacher, Galina Petrovna, a plain 40-year-old spinster who has no interests in life apart from her school. Despite her extreme conscientiousness and love of her profession and the children, she finds it extremely difficult to work: the school is permeated with lies, pupils cannot be given the marks which they genuinely merit, open lessons are performed like theatrical shows with the pupils previously coached to give the right answers. The story does not, of course, refer to the ideological lies openly, but their presence is implied between the lines. 'I do not think that the situation is the same in other towns, and I'd very much like always to tell the truth. But I don't succeed', says the narrator naively. However, this mollifying reference to 'other towns' cannot deceive the reader, for later she speaks of teachers in general and not only in her particular town:

> Teachers are not trusted. The result of this distrust is that I, for example, among people I don't know on some beach, am embarrassed to admit that I'm a teacher. There are prestigious professions: the manager of a shoe or food shop, artist, commodity researcher, garage manager. But teaching, alas, is a profession that no longer commands respect. This was not the case previously. In one old story a police officer salutes a teacher and treats him like one of his superiors. Perhaps this is because teachers used to have ranks and wear a uniform? But the point is not only distrust. There are quite a few other reasons as well: the relatively low pay, the immeasurably greater (in comparison with many other professions) amount of work, the loss of

authority over schoolchildren, of which parents are well aware.

The main reason for this loss of authority is the lies which invariably reign in the schools.

*

Such is the reality in which the reform is to be implemented. How do the official agencies react to this reality? From time to time phrases about the need to 'regulate' the teacher's time, 'rationalise' the allocation of teaching loads, 'organise methodically' the teacher's work make a fleeting appearance in official speeches, articles and Resolutions. But the authorities have never specifically discussed the need to relieve teachers of any part of their load in or outside school. We shall discuss below how the reform treats the question of pedagogical personnel. Here I shall merely note that from time to time the education authorities and even party leaders have brave words to say in their speeches and in the press about the need to improve the teachers' work and living conditions in order to prevent their flight from the schools, but such an improvement is evidently beyond the leaders' powers. Besides, they are mainly concerned not with this problem but with purely administrative measures of attracting school-leavers to teaching and 'fastening' graduates to the jobs to which they are allocated.

As in previous years, institutes announce non-competitive conditions of admission for rural school-leavers and workers in order to attract them to institutions of higher agricultural and pedagogical education. We have already noted that this simply amounts to attracting to these institutes those who are afraid of competition, that is, the weakest candidates. Nonetheless, even this measure is ineffective, as in most cases the weak students scrape through the institutes, are awarded the same degrees as everyone else and find jobs in places which they prefer and not in the outlying regions or in the villages, or in a different profession altogether. This problem is to be tackled by yet another measure which was extensively discussed in an editorial 'We shall carry out the decisions of the May (1982) plenum of the CC CPSU!' in Narodnoe obrazovanie, no. 8 (1982). This is not a new measure, but when combined with the repeated appeals in the article to keep agricultural workers and teachers in the villages, it acquires particular weight. It is proposed that institutions of higher education in the fields of pedagogy, agriculture, medicine, librarianship, culture and education and physical education admit without competition those candidates whose grants will be financed not by the state but, as the article puts it, 'by the kolkhoz, sovkhoz or other agricultural enterprise'. This measure does not only have economic significance, consisting in the fact that the kolkhozes, sovkhozes, etc. will have to pay their money for an item of expenditure which the state is obliged to finance, as in the case of the do-it-yourself repair and construction of schools. There is also a far-reaching organisational purpose here. If these enterprises spend their fairly meagre resources on stipends for higher education awarded to students from their districts, they will make certain that graduates who have studied at their expense will return to the villages and work off their debt for at least the three years stipulated. This is of great importance to the state - which, incidentally, appropriates approximately 82-3 per cent of the kolkhozes' produce - because it does not succeed in forcing young specialists to return to the villages by any other means.

'The demands of life for pedagogical cadres' - such was the title of an article by G. Veselov, the RSFSR Minister of Education, in Narodnoe obrazovanie, no. 12 (1982). In this context the 'demands of life' mean the party's and government's demands of workers in education. The minister was disturbed not only by the reluctance of school-leavers to enter institutions of higher pedagogical education but also by the drop-out rate of those admitted, which made up between three and seven per cent of the intake in the country's pedagogical institutes. Of the drop-outs 51 per cent were students in the first and second years of all faculties. Veselov reproached the professors and teachers in these institutions for failing to fill in the gaps in the former schoolchildren's knowledge in the first years. He ignored the fact, however, that the state curricula of the institutes do not provide time for this, while if only well-prepared candidates were admitted into the pedagogical institutes they would be left without any students at all. Veselov noted with satisfaction that 'During the tenth five-year plan 50 thousand rural school-leavers were admitted to pedagogical institutes of the RSFSR by non-competitive selection' and he calls for this method of selection to be extended in the eleventh five-year plan. This meant that the drop-out rate of students unable to cope with the curricula of higher education was destined to continue. The minister quite seriously attributed the shortage of teachers to the fact that their work, life and rest are poorly organised, to the 'annual non-fulfilment of the plans for school construction and housing for teachers', to the 'interruptions in the provision of teachers with food products and fuel' and to the shortcomings of 'cultural and medical facilities'. He singled out in particular 'the overloading of pedagogical cadres with extraneous tasks to the detriment of their main work'. At this point he laid the responsibility for the failure of graduates to turn up at their jobs on the professors and teachers of the pedagogical institutes. But surely the job of controlling the behaviour of adults who graduate from these institutes has little to do with the main task of their staff? Similarly, they can hardly be held responsible for their former graduates who flee the schools or for the gaps in the knowledge of the former schoolchildren who are their students or for their reluctance to enter the pedagogical institutes. Veselov also considered that the teachers of the pedagogical institutes should be responsible for recruiting students. It is clear a priori that they would be unable to carry out these extraneous tasks. True, the staff of the Krupskaia Moscow Pedagogical Institute triumphantly announced its decision to make sure that all the institute's graduates would turn up at the jobs allocated to them by the state (Uchitel'skaia gazeta, 1 March 1983), but I wonder by what means.

There is another paradox: at first, as already mentioned, the RSFSR Minister of Education called for teachers to be relieved of extraneous tasks, but later he declared that the teachers' 'participation in realising the Food-Production Programme' was the most 'effective means of forming the active personality' of the teacher. Some pedagogical institutes, he reported, had already planned such work for the years 1983-90. Teachers in pedagogical institutes and colleges, students and schoolteachers were instructed to take 'a whole number of measures aimed at raising the yield of agricultural crops and the productivity of stock-raising'.[39] This, however, is precisely the kind of 'extraneous tasks to the detriment of their main work' to which he had just objected. Such assistants will not benefit agriculture, but they will certainly ruin their immediate work.

'Candidates in short supply' was the title of an article in Uchitel'skaia gazeta, 25 August 1983, which described the shortage of secondary school graduates who desired to go to pedagogical institutes. Throughout the school year these institutes attempt to recruit future candidates:

> Today you probably will not be able to find a pedagogical institute that does not engage in the vocational guidance of schoolchildren towards the teaching profession. It is also conducted in Ioshkar-Olia. The teachers do not only visit schools in their own republic but even go as far as Bashkiria. A Faculty of the Future Teacher (FBU) has been set up for schoolchildren in the institute. The local press and radio have been enlisted to vocational guidance and students who do their teaching practice in rural schools also engage in it. An abundance of energy is expended with scant results. Evidence of this is the lack of competition to be admitted into many departments, the shortage of applicants for the physics and mathematics department. On 1 August there were 60 vacant places in this department. Prolonging the recruitment ... only barely improved matters ...

No so long ago there was still great competition for admission to the history departments, as mathematics was not required. According to the newspaper's special correspondent, Iu. Iakovlev, the pedagogical institutes:

> patch up the gaps in their intake with those who have not passed the competition for university entrance and who have not achieved the marks needed for admission to institutes in other towns. Hence the low standard of the newly admitted students for whom the entrance examinations at times become not a strict test but a mere formality.[40]

The final examinations are also a formality for most of the graduates who are admitted to institutions of higher education on a non-competitive basis. It is clear that most of the poor first-year students who have been admitted to an institute without any process of selection will not suddenly become transformed into good students.

On 15 November 1983 Uchitel'skaia gazeta published an article in the section 'The party organisation: reports and elections' with the eloquent title 'The wrong student went', describing the situation in the Sverdlovsk Pedagogical

Institute, which is fairly typical of other such institutes in the country. The paper's special correspondent, L. Dorokhova, wrote that 'recently grievances against the institute can be heard ever more frequently. The responsibility of some graduates has declined perceptibly. It is not rare for young specialists to arrive in the school without having mastered the culture of pedagogical work'. Here too a considerable number of students fail and are expelled. In the 1982/3 academic year:

> The physics department became the 'record-breaker'. Here a third of the students was lost: only 48 of the 75 admitted completed their studies. The pass rate among the physicists is also low. Moreover, this is no longer the first year...
>
> The following fact is also alarming: even such a severe punishment as expulsion from the institute does not have an educating influence on the rest - their progress does not improve ... Often 'dead souls' are expelled - students who ceased attending lectures long ago. Their expulsion is therefore not a lesson for the others ... The number of graduates ... who fail to turn up at their jobs is increasing by the year.

As in the previous decade a vicious circle is created when inferior graduates from the pedagogical institutes become poor teachers who prepare poor school-leavers who are the future candidates for admission to the same institutes on a non-competitive basis.

After the 'Basic trends' of the school reform were published, the USSR Ministry of Higher and Secondary Specialised Education ratified the rules of admission to institutions of higher education in 1984. The additions that had been introduced, as the ministry informed a TASS correspondent (Uchitel'skaia gazeta, 26 May 1984), reflected the tasks resulting from the main trends of the reform in general education and vocational schools. The authors of the Resolution assumed that the new rules would improve the level of young people admitted to institutions of higher education. In reality, however, the rules were designed to make the admission of candidates to institutions of higher education necessary to the state and in fields in which there is a shortage of skilled specialists even less dependent on their academic achievements. Instead, the data in the questionnaires which they have to fill in, the recommendations from the appropriate authorities and the non-competitive selection, which often takes place without any examinations, will acquire prime importance. The Resolution stated:

> Priority in enrolment in pedagogical institutes and the pedagogical departments or faculties of universities will now be enjoyed by persons who have been assigned to these institutions of higher education on the recommendation of the pedagogical councils of schools, secondary specialised institutions of education and vocational-technical schools, the organs of public education, labour collectives and Komsomol committees.

But this was the situation before as well! Moreover, as we showed above, even before all other subjects were pushed aside by discussion of the reform, complaints were constantly voiced in the pedagogical press that the students enrolled into institutions of higher education by non-competitive selection, on the strength of recommendations and data in their questionnaires, were incapable of work and were of a low academic standard. However, until now, even the non-competitive selection meant that the entrance examinations had been taken, even if only a mark of 'three' (often faked) had been achieved, but now the entrance examinations were to be abolished altogether for a large group of candidates:

> Preference is introduced for teachers, educators and masters of production training who have secondary pedagogical education and have teaching experience of not less than a year. On the order of the public and vocational-technical education authorities, they will be admitted to study in institutions of higher education which train teachers and masters of production training, while continuing their normal work, not according to the results of the examinations but only on the basis of a conversation.[41]

Frequently these categories of admittants, who have not studied for a long time and have completely forgotten what they learned in the institutions of secondary education and have not had to go over the forgotten material in order to prepare for the entrance examinations, inevitably become poor students or students who pass on a purely fictitious basis.

5. TEACHERS AND THE REFORM

The previous section ('Problems, Problems') outlined in general terms the position of Soviet teachers today and their attitude to their work on the eve of the reform. It would be no exaggeration to conclude that they are in a disastrous position. The public is well aware of this, which is why the prestige of the teaching profession is low and young people with general secondary and even specialised pedagogical education are not attracted to it. How do the authors of the 'Basic trends of the reform of the general education and vocational school' and the powers that be that inspire them react to this social calamity?

G. Aliev, member of the Politburo of the CC CPSU and first deputy chairman of the USSR Council of Ministers, spoke at length about the new tasks confronting teachers and teachers' collectives in his speech to the first session of the eleventh USSR Supreme Soviet to which I have already referred:

> The reform elevates the teacher's authority to new heights.
>
> At the same time, the teacher's responsibility to society for the instruction and upbringing of the rising generations grows immeasurably. Our teachers fought for the reform energetically and persistently. Now, when it is becoming a reality, we appeal to the multi-million army of workers in education: the success of the reform, comrades, depends first and foremost on you - on your energy and persistence, on your inspired service to your duty.
>
> It is impossible to raise the quality of methods of instruction and upbringing without a corresponding increase in the theoretical, professional and general cultural training of the majority of teachers. In connection with this, definite steps are envisaged, aimed at upgrading constantly and effectively the qualifications of teachers and improving the work of institutions of pedagogical education.[42]

When teachers were 'persistently fighting' for the reform,

they had mainly been concerned with bringing about an improvement in the general education secondary school, particularly in rural and remote areas, and in general education, with a drastic reduction in their actual work-load and an end to formalism and falsification in school life, and certainly not with carrying out the state's cadres policy, which was, in fact, the only goal of the reform. The implementation of this policy - the early vocational training of pupils, the organisation of their economically effective labour even during their regular schooling, enhancing the authority of the SPTU in the eyes of schoolchildren, encouraging them to leave school after the ninth grade and enter a vocational school, ensuring that most schoolchildren would eventually work (or study) in the trades which they had learnt at school, ensuring the pupils' absolute ideological conformity and military patriotism, control over their upbringing in their families and even over the families themselves, etc. - all this was laid on the shoulders of the teachers and pedagogical collectives without any reduction in their existing, already excessive work-load.

What then are the 'definite steps' designed to enable teachers to attain all the goals which the reform demands of them, mentioned by Aliev? He himself describes one of them:

> As you know, comrade deputies, in accordance with the decision of the CC CPSU and the USSR Council of Ministers of 1 September of this year, the salaries of education workers will begin to be increased by stages. For example, the average monthly salary of teachers will be increased by almost 35 per cent. Forms of moral incentive for teachers will also be improved.[43]

This is preceded by a promise to enhance the 'social prestige of education workers' and ensure a 'further improvement in their conditions of work and life'. We described above what these conditions are like today, and on the basis of this evidence from the various localities and the comments on it, we can judge what massive efforts such an improvement would require. Moreover, the speaker has nothing specific to say about the main basis for this improvement - a reduction in the teachers' actual work-load. On the contrary, even more demands are placed on the teachers while the number of their duties is increased.

On 15 May 1984 a special Resolution of the CC CPSU

and the USSR Council of Ministers 'On measures to improve the training and raise the qualifications of pedagogical cadres of the system of education and vocational-technical education and to improve their work and life' was published in the press.[44] The Resolution begins and ends with a call to subordinate all the efforts of teachers and masters of production training to the task of the effective ideological and political upbringing of pupils in schools and PTU. Most of this document is devoted to improving pedagogical cadres and giving them a new orientation (primarily production and political-ideological): teaching practice is introduced in all years of the institutions of higher pedagogical education; it is proposed to give each pedagogical institute a school as a base for carrying out research and experiments. The pedagogical institutes are required to 'bring graduates closer to the problems of production', to increase the number of teachers who graduate in production training, to introduce a new course in the 'Vocational Guidance of Schoolchildren' (as we recall, special time is to be allocated in schools for such guidance). It was decided to increase the number of students admitted to institutions of higher pedagogical education and pedagogical colleges by 1990 (even though there are not enough candidates to fill even the present admissions quota), especially in remote areas of the country, and to introduce a five-year course in pedagogical institutes instead of the present four years. It is recommended that pedagogical faculties be organised in the universities. At the same time extension-correspondence instruction is to be improved and extended (in the pedagogical institutes to about one third of the students). The duration of higher education is to be shortened for those with secondary pedagogical education. Moreover, despite the objections to the non-competitive selection of students frequently expressed in the press by teachers, it is proposed to practise extensively and even increase this 'preferential purposeful selection' on recommendations from schools, PTUs, the army, kolkhozes, sovkhozes and other institutions and organisations. The need to attract men to the pedagogical institutes is noted in particular. It is proposed to admit to the engineering-pedagogical faculties mainly graduates of SPTUs and people who have production skills and are 'inclined to pedagogical work' (although it is not clear how this can be ascertained before practical experience).

It is recommended that the institutes for the advanced

training of teachers pay special attention to problems of ideological upbringing and production training and 'render every possible assistance in the ideological-political growth' of workers of all ranks in public education. The Resolution does not make a single reference to the need to improve instruction in the main general subjects. Some paragraphs of the Resolution are devoted to the problems which the teacher faces in his everyday life. Although there is no reference to raising the salaries of teachers and workers in the Departments of Education, this is mentioned in other documents. There is a decision to raise the grant awarded to students in pedagogical institutes and faculties to the level of that usual for institutions of higher education in the field of mining, metallurgy, oil and forestry, and also to pay for teaching practice independently of the grant. The Resolution contains a multitude of general phrases about the need to show constant concern for the conditions of teachers, about the rational utilisation and allocation of teachers, about giving teachers priority in the allocation of housing and about the need to improve medical and health-resort services for teachers. But such intentions have been voiced since the early 1920s and the Resolution contains no mention of any clear deadlines, authorities responsible for these matters or specific decisions on these issues, except for a special paragraph that stipulates that sovkhozes and kolkhozes are 'permitted' (<u>but not instructed</u>) to sell teachers food products at state retail prices as part of 'the state's purchases of their produce'.

As a moral incentive to the best education workers (in schools, PTUs and pedagogical colleges), 25 Krupskaia Prizes are to be awarded annually by the USSR Ministry of Education and the State Committee on Vocational Education.

It is impossible to fit all the tasks and obligations which the initiators of the reform are loading on to the teachers into the framework of their official teaching load (grades one to four, 24 hours a week; grades five to eleven, 18 hours a week). As before, most of the teachers' time outside classes and outside school will be devoured by these activities, and this is the main burden that oppresses them today. Nor will instruction and upbringing be de-ideologised in the least, but on the contrary the ideological content will increase and will also be a burden on the teachers and turn people who are most sensitive to lies and lack of freedom away from the teaching profession.

The oft-repeated words about improving the teacher's

conditions of life and work will remain empty phrases, because a radical amelioration would require a change in the entire Soviet economic system (in the spheres of everyday services, construction, communications, agriculture, health-care, production of consumer goods and food), since there is no intention of including the army of almost three million Soviet 'educators' in the narrow elite of the nomenklatura who are supplied through special outlets, allocated housing without restrictions or delays, served by special medical institutions and health resorts, etc.

6. BRIEF CONCLUSIONS

Properly speaking, all the conclusions that can be drawn from this survey can be found in the preceding text. Here I shall pick them out and summarise them.

Most of the permanent problems of Soviet schools are connected with the general economic situation in the country: construction, repairs, the supply of schools and teachers with the bare essentials. The extremely serious problems faced by undersized and outlying schools are the direct result of the inadequate network of roads, transport and supplies. Only good country roads and specially assigned transport would enable the 'pygmy' schools, scattered throughout the dying villages, to be replaced by vigorous central schools serving a micro-district of optimal size and having boarding facilities. The fact that these problems have remained unsolved for 70 years is the result of two characteristics of the Soviet system: its low economic effectiveness and the priority it gives to solving political, security, military or potentially military problems. The school cannot do anything to change that. It should also be borne in mind when considering innovations in Soviet schools that the administration of education in the USSR is even more strictly centralised than that of the economy and suffers no less from this uncompromising centralisation. Local, specific changes and improvements are possible only in the narrowest and most mundane matters, and even then not always.

The reform, which includes creating the resources for production training in schools, doubling the number of SPTUs and modernising them, increasing the number of classes in primary and incomplete secondary schools, training special teachers-cum-production workers, a promised increase in the salaries of 'educationalists', etc. can be carried out only if the leadership decides to endow its cadres policy with the same importance as its military or security policy. But even if this happened, there is no guarantee that it could cope with this additional expenditure, and even then a large proportion of its reforming intentions would remain on paper or be faked, just as 'polytechnical training' was faked.

The problems which overwhelm the teacher immediately (apart from his difficult life) and which have been described in detail, are insoluble if the schools are not de-ideologised and teachers are not relieved of most of their extra-curricular obligations. Western teachers are completely free for all the time which is not taken up by lessons and preparation for them, except for infrequent and purely professional pedagogical councils and parents' meetings. The school holidays (summer, winter, spring), all national holidays and days off belong to him. Work with slow pupils (not necessarily carried out by the teacher of the particular class) is paid for in the same way as lessons. Teachers are not obliged to perform any social or state work apart from their professional work. The reform in store for Soviet schools gives no grounds for hoping that anything similar will come about in the USSR.

The de-ideologisation of teaching, and education in the broader sense, and the reduction of the scope of the teacher's obligations to their professional, paid teaching and educational assignments are as much beyond the control of the teachers and schools as is a transformation in the socialist economy or road construction. If we abstract ourselves from these and some other limitations of the Soviet context, the desired school reform could be conceived of approximately as the following:

(1) schooling from the age of six (despite the reservations which I expressed), since this is the norm in most developed countries and gives satisfactory results, but introduced simultaneously throughout the country and with a lighter load in the first grade and a thoroughly thought-out system of work and rest for six-year-olds;
(2) universal and compulsory incomplete secondary nine-year education;
(3) three senior grades, ten, eleven and twelve (as in most developed countries) so that children finish school at 18;

(4) introduction of the post of class leader (class educator) in grades five to twelve, relieved completely or almost completely of teaching duties;
(5) senior grades divided into speciality areas: physics and mathematics, humanities, chemistry and biology, and with technical biases;
(6) admission of approximately a quarter of those graduating from grade nine into the senior grades by competitive examination;
(7) secondary and incomplete secondary vocational-technical schools for those who are not admitted to the senior grades or do not want to be (the secondary with entrance examinations and the incomplete secondary without);
(8) secondary education in the SPTU divided into specialised areas in accordance with the 'profile' of the SPTU;
(9) evening and extension-correspondence secondary schools and external studies for those who do not have secondary education and desire to receive it, without any compulsion, on a purely voluntary basis;
(10) the possibility of studying and re-taking in an external programme of studies any subjects which a pupil did not pass in a specialised school or SPTU and which he needs for admission to the institution of higher education or technicum of his choice;
(11) admission to specialised institutions of higher education and technicums on the basis of specialised certificates;
(12) the possibility for a graduate of grade twelve who does not enter an institution of higher education or technicum to take short, vocational courses at a SPTU.

I am fully aware that my proposals are disputable and necessitate professional discussion. Moreover, I propose only those innovations which could possibly be discussed in the USSR today. Nonetheless, as I know from my experience that any school is a reflection of its times and of the regime existing in the country, I also am convinced that only the political, ideological and economic transformation of the entire Soviet system could bring about a serious, positive reform of Soviet schools.

NOTES

1. V. Golovskoi in Novoe Russkoe slovo, 7 April 1984.
2. Pravda, 12 May 1984.
3. M. Zakiev, 'Labour is joyful' in Uchitel'skaia gazeta, 1 March 1984.
4. Literaturnaia gazeta, 1 November 1984.
5. 'Basic trends of the reform of the general education and vocational school', approved by the Plenum of the CC CPSU on 10 April 1984 and by the Supreme Soviet on 12 April 1984. Published in Pravda and Izvestiia, 14 April 1984.
6. Ibid.
7. Ibid.
8. From the speech of G. Aliev at a session of the Supreme Soviet on 'Basic trends of the reform of the general education and vocational school', published in Uchitel'skaia gazeta, 13 April 1984.
9. 'The reform of general and secondary education, March 1984', Uchitel'skaia gazeta, 31 March and 3 April 1984.
10. Ibid.
11. Ibid.
12. Literaturnaia gazeta, 1 February 1984.
13. I. Malenkov, letter to the editor in Literaturnaia gazeta, 1 February 1984.
14. Uchitel'skaia gazeta, 13 April 1984.
15. 'Basic trends of the reform', see note 5 above.
16. Published in Pravda and Izvestiia, 4 May 1984.
17. Section 38 of 'Basic trends of the reform', published in Izvestiia and Pravda, 4 May 1984.
18. N. Dairi in Uchitel'skaia gazeta, 18 February 1984.
19. Section 38 of 'Basic trends of the reform', see note 17 above.
20. See note 16 above.
21. Ibid.
22. From an article by K. Subbotina in Narodnoe obrazovanie, no. 9 (1983), pp. 40-57.
23. Uchitel'skaia gazeta, 28 April 1984.
24. Ibid.
25. Ibid., 17 August 1982.
26. Ibid., 4 December 1982.
27. Ibid.
28. Ibid., 19 February 1983.
29. Ibid., 29 January 1983.
30. Ibid., 2 June 1984.

31. Izvestiia, 10 June 1983.
32. Ibid.
33. Uchitel'skaia gazeta, 12 November 1983.
34. N. Pastukhov in Narodnoe obrazovanie, no. 8 (1982).
35. Uchitel'skaia gazeta, 22 January 1983.
36. Ibid., 11 January 1983.
37. Ibid., 1 March 1983.
38. Oktiabr', no. 1 (1984), pp. 76-94.
39. Narodnoe obrazovanie, no. 12 (1982), pp. 4-12.
40. Uchitel'skaia gazeta, 25 August 1983.
41. Ibid., 26 May 1984.
42. Ibid., 13 April 1984.
43. Ibid.
44. Resolution published in Pravda and Izvestiia, 15 May 1984.

CONCLUSION

DIKTAT, CHAOS OR DEMOCRACY?

Among all the many questions which I have examined I should like in conclusion to single out one issue which seems to be of vital concern for schools in all countries of the world, including the democratic countries, and not only for schools, as this issue is part of a broader problem. I shall call this the problem of freedom and organisation, freedom and law and order.

The general tendency of the totalitarian world and its schools is to destroy freedom. The general tendency of the free world and its schools is developing into a cult of freedom capable of undermining law and order. The odds are in favour of the forces that are the least civilised and mature, in the moral sense, in favour of anarchy bordering on a-sociality. Eventually this would amount to a victory for force and ignorance.

In free schools this cult of freedom takes the form of capitulation to youthful non-conformism which does not tolerate organisational restrictions - a retreat of those called upon to teach before the onslaught of those called upon to learn. This capitulation is worrying for the teachers and dangerous for the pupils (and for all of society). All this arises from the very best of motives - respect for the pupil's individuality, for individual freedom. But in the school the confusion of respect for the individual with a retreat before the pupil's asocial behaviour in and outside the classroom makes nonsense of the entire endeavour for whose sake educators and educated, teachers and pupils, have assembled under one roof.

Organisation should not be identified with coercion, just

as disorder, which prevents any effective teaching or education from taking place, should not be identified with a victory of freedom and respect for pupils' rights. The teacher and pupil whose experience, knowledge and ethical criteria and values differ both in scope and quality, cannot function as equals with equal rights in the teaching process, just as doctor and patient cannnot have equal rights in the healing process. The disaster is that the modern democratic school views pupil and teacher as equal partners on the intellectual, moral and legal planes. The school perceives the immature being with which it has been entrusted in order that it may grow into a whole and free person, as a mature individual with rights. However, the immature intellect and morally undeveloped individual are characterised not by freedom of choice but by an unthinking semi-automatic rejection of anything that 'imposes' upon them from the outside. The task of the free school is not to capitulate to this natural, youthful nihilism but to educate the capacity for analytical thought, which includes an objective approach, logical thinking, independent conclusions and the ability to demonstrate them, and respect for the honest thought of others.

In the dictatorial school all this is possible only in those subjects which are absolutely irrelevant to the ideology, but there are no such subjects in the partocratic school. Physics, chemistry, mathematics, biology, grammar - even these come into contact with the various official philosophical conceptions which are obligatory at any particular moment. The same is, of course, true for history, literature, social science, aesthetic education and other subjects in the humanities in which even the slightest variations of interpretation are impossible.

The democratic nature of the free school consists of its right and ability to avoid this standardisation, its pluralism and its right to teach this spiritual and intellectual pluralism to its pupils. Education to a democratic (pluralistic) vision of the world includes respect for the freedom of oneself and other people, for the individual and civil rights of oneself and other people, including the rights and freedom of teachers and fellow pupils. This problem has two facets: on the one hand, the individual desires to be free; on the other hand, other individuals have the same desire, and the class as a whole or some part of it wants to carry out successfully the purpose for which it has come together - to learn. In essence this is a micro-model of social relations, and this is precisely the place where the pupil (individual) should be taught to respect the rights of other individuals and groups, and the class as a whole - to respect individuals and minorities. But: all this democratic education should take place within the bounds of non-criminal conduct and of preserving the stability of the pedagogical process. Otherwise discrimination against rightful individuals and their interests and aspirations becomes inevitable.

If the pupil is not confined by any disciplinary and legal restrictions, by any binding ethical or moral code, while the teacher is discriminated against, placed in the position of an individual who is defenceless before the crowd (or hooligan), if the teacher is not given constant support and protection by his fellow teachers and administrators, the school cannot carry out either its educational or its civic purpose. It forgets the true interests of both society and the pupil himself and betrays those children who are aware of the need to learn and want to learn. It also betrays the teacher, both as an individual who performs the most complex tasks of instruction and education, and simply as a human being by depriving him of rightful defence before the irresponsible elements of the class.

The objection might be raised that it is up to the teacher to form normal lawful relations in the classroom; but this is an empty abstraction. Many people, especially those with a delicate mental constitution, are afraid of crowds. The teaching profession is to a large extent drawn randomly from among the people, and qualities of leadership are not always compatible with the other qualities which are important for teachers (erudition, humaneness, professionalism, love of their work, etc.). Therefore, it is not enough to rely only on the knowledge and will of the teacher in the relations between teacher and class. The teacher, no less than the pupil, needs to be protected by the school's 'social contract', by the entire system and organisation of the teaching and educational procress. I am, of course, referring to teachers who satisfy all the professional requirements and need support in extreme cases and not to those who are incompetent and should simply change their profession.

In the free, democratic school the administration, teacher, parents and, to a certain extent, older pupils are free to discuss and amend the 'social contract' (the system of school rights and obligations of all participants in the educational process). It can be varied fairly widely from school to school and be revised from time to time. But the rules that are adopted and brought to the notice of all participants in the common cause should, during the time that they are in effect, be the law which can be appealed against but not ignored. Ignoring the generally accepted rules should entail punishment or special educational measures. No one should remain without rightful defence or support within the school: not the pupil, not the teacher, not the school as a teachers' organisation, and not the association of pupils. To teach the complex mechanism of democracy, which enables one's own rights to be defended without infringing the rights of others - this is the task of the school which is both free and civilised.

In no case should the school be reduced to the level of partocratic standardisation of thought and barrack-like discipline, but it must also achieve a level of regulation essential for the highly organised process of teaching and education to take place successfully and freely. The pupil must be taught that lofty human dignity assumes that lofty individual and social demands are made on the bearer of that dignity.

It is absurd to allow a twelve-year-old to participate in meetings of the pedagogical council as a member with equal rights, as was stipulated in the Soviet principles of work of schools of general education in the early 1920s; but pupils can participate in resolving many school problems on a democratic basis. As in almost all cases of democratic co-existence, the problem has to be solved specifically each time: how, to what degree, within what bounds should the pupils' self-administration, initiative and choice be included in the activity and decisions of the educational collective, the school's administration and teachers.

A reactive, unthinking, reflexive recoil from one extreme to another - from one unacceptable thesis (complete lack of freedom) to another just as unacceptable antithesis (chaos) - is more clearly contra-indicated in schools than in other social institutions. The work of the Soviet teacher is regulated in the minutest detail, enmeshed in a web of plans, reports, control measures, compulsory philosophical norms, extra-curricular duties, etc., while the Western school, in particular the Israeli one, frequently leaves the teacher without any control, any compulsory scope of activity, any standards of professional skill or improvement, etc. Having observed the latter school, which is new to me, for a number of years, I shall risk expressing the following assumptions: the teacher should be free to grow and improve his potential - to move, so to speak, upwards. He should be free to choose among various syllabuses, methods, views, that is, to move laterally. But he should not have the right and opportunity to fall below some determined standard of professionalism, conscientiousness and fulfilment of the compulsory programmes of study. In other words, a person who desires to work in a school should not be free to move downwards, below some compulsory level of commitment, assiduity and expertise.

A well-designed system of requirements which the curricula and administration should make on the teacher and a system of work control on the part of the administration and inspectors are essential here. The free school, however, in its recoil from conventionalism, standardisation and coercion, is flying to the opposite extreme: in many cases it is destroying its organisational backbone and is helpless before the natural human failings which allow pupils, teachers and administrators to exploit the school's defencelesseness.

What features of the old school seem to be continually necessary to form the new school's organisational backbone?

(1) A defined indispensable minimum of curricula, both with regard to the range of subjects studied and in the sense of the amount of information in each subject. I have emphasised the words 'indispensable minimum' because it is, of course, possible to offer more subjects in strong classes or to capable pupils, and a greater volume of information. But the minimum must be compulsory quantitatively and qualitatively. In Soviet schools, what the Ministry of Education regards as the essential range and scope of subjects is defined and fixed, along with provisions for extending the curricula (also regulated) in the specialised schools (of physics and mathematics, or with a bias to intensified study of a foreign language). It is possible to go beyond the bounds of the curricula in the optional studies, which are also provided for. In this case the material is excessively regulated, especially in the humanities, but a clear amount of compulsory knowledge is laid down.

(2) Definition of the curricula (with the possibility of extending and improving, but not narrowing and ignoring them) is especially important in the primary grades. The USSR makes a very grave pedagogical error by requiring the lowest level of education (specialised secondary) from teachers of the primary grades, which are the most

important ones, as they lay the foundations of education, and the most difficult, as this is the stage when a love of learning, an interest in learning, the ability to learn and basic ethical, disciplinary and behavioural habits have to be inculcated. Faculties for teachers of the primary grades have already appeared, but there are far too few to supply teachers for schools at that level which have the largest number of pupils. But the curriculum of the primary grades is clearly defined and was considerably enriched and broadened in the 1970s and placed on a more scientific level in the basic subjects (grammar, arithmetic, fundamentals of natural science).

(3) I also consider it a failing of the primary school curriculum that in Israel and America a child in grades four to seven is already able to choose in some cases which subjects to study and which not. There is no such choice in Soviet schools for the entire ten years, unless we include the right in Russian-language schools of the national republics to study the 'local' language or not (or the opportunity possessed by a very few children in the large cities to attend schools with a special bias - to physics and mathematics or the intensified study of a foreign language). A young person in grades nine to twelve is perfectly capable of making an intelligent choice as he already has a real notion, even if superficial, of the subjects which he is rejecting and which he prefers. In grades one to eight, schools should give the pupil a notion of what he can choose from and what to choose, i.e. give him in the main general subjects the minimum of conceptions, without which there can be no real choice but the chance whim of ignorance. In the senior grades, however, bias towards one of the main groups of subjects becomes absolutely necessary because of the excessive load placed on pupils and the ever-increasing volume of knowledge in each subject.

(4) In the classical schools (let us say until the mid-twentieth century), pupils were unconditionally subordinate to the priority of the school's teachers and administration. We have shown above how Soviet schools developed and reached the absolute priority of the state over the schools and of the schools over their pupils. Democratic schools are discarding the postulate that the teacher has disciplinary priority in the classroom. The full weight of responsibility for himself, for his future, lies on the immature, undeveloped consciousness of the pupil and the talent of the teacher. In reality this means that in the majority of

average, ordinary cases, as I have already said, the teacher who does not possess outstanding leadership qualities is unable to carry out his educational purpose. The crowd of people who know less (and are less well-behaved) holds sway over the person who knows more and is more civilised.

When the pupils' unruly behaviour and disobedience do not come up against an insuperable organisational and administrative barrier, the school once again becomes, as it were, totalitarian (like any extreme in relation to its absolute opposite). But in this case it is no longer the pupil as individual who is defenceless in the face of the cumbersome machine of all-pervasive administrative regulation and oppression (as in the Soviet, partocratic school), but the teacher as individual who stands opposed to the irreverent crowd which, like any aggressive crowd, finds its leaders. Teachers fear the 'instigators' and aggressors recognised by the class, while the school leaves the teacher to face the class alone.

As always, the optimum lies between the two extremes - the totalitarian-partocratic (etatist) and chaotic-'pedocratic' one. Schools have to be an organisation of teachers, parents and pupils and not a regiment of pedagogical servants to His Majesty the Pupil. Schools should clearly define the rights and duties of administrators, teachers, parents and pupils, within the bounds of democratic law and with consideration for the hierarchy of age, culture and education. Schools should have arbiters in this allocation of rights and duties in the form of higher institutions of public education, while the courts (or special public commissions) can intervene in extreme, extraordinary cases in conflicts between the above participants in the school organisation: administrators, teachers, parents and pupils. In any event, schools should organise themselves in such a way that the democratic rights of all their members can be realised without making chaos of the teaching and educational process. Respect for the children's freedom should be combined with the demand that we all make upon a respected person: the demand for correct behaviour. A pupil should not come and go whenever he pleases, insult his teacher and fellow pupils, be indolent, ignore the demands of his teachers and the school regulations, argue insolently and in the wrong time and place, chew gum in class, throw litter in the classroom and school grounds, be dirty, dress provocatively, that is, flout the rules of normal human society and the specific demands of school life. When a pupil is given the opportunity to overstep all these bounds, it is no longer a question of his freedom (the freedom to learn, to ask questions, to defend his opinion in a proper manner, to appeal against actions which he thinks unjust, etc.) but of a retreat before his uncivilised conduct.

Democracy in the school consists of the following:

(1) the co-existence of schools of various types and affiliations; the opportunity for parents and pupils to choose a particular type of school;
(2) the guarantee of democratic individual and civil (the latter in accordance with the hierarchy of age) rights of teachers, parents and pupils;
(3) the pluralism of gnosiological, ideological, methodological and methodological-didactic opportunities of the school;
(4) the predominance in schools of a democratic ethic which assumes not only the freedom of the individual but also non-infringement by the individual of the freedom and interests of others;
(5) the opportunity and ability to form and defend all these qualities.

A school in which the humanistic, democratic ethics - the ethics of mutual respect of rights - has been replaced by the ethics of force - uncivil behaviour, pedocratic demagogy - rapidly ceases to be a school of democracy. I use this phrase 'school of democracy' in two senses:

(1) a school which belongs to a democracy;
(2) a school which teaches democracy and its defence.

Whether the schools of the world will be able to conform to this definition will determine the future of mankind.

INDEX